"Personally riveting, academically provoking! Gunn and DeCarlo's gutsy, alluring *Bare* reveals the vulnerable and honest inner thoughts of an experienced psychotherapist. *Bare* is clinically relevant to clinicians at all levels of training and accessible to anyone curious about the therapeutic process."

Matthew Rofofsky, LCSW-R
Director of Clinical and Counseling Services, Hetrick-Martin Institute, Home of the Harvey Milk High School
Academic Advisor, Columbia School of Social Work
Private Practice, Manhattan

"In *Bare: Psychotherapy Stripped,* authors Jacqueline Simon Gunn and Carlo DeCarlo take the reader into the mind and thoughts of a therapist in session. We learn as much about the dark depths of a therapist as the patients. And the journey does get personal — like when Dr. Gunn must tell her patients of her upcoming wedding. Awkward!

"Starting with Dr. Gunn's first days at the Karen Horney Institute as an intern, up to the time she was offered a position with them and beyond, *Bare* gets into the nitty-gritty of therapy. Gunn also shares her experiences with her own therapist. From neurotic housewives to drug dealers to patients who needed to be put in jail to sex slaves to runners to all forms of people in need, *Bare* takes you on a journey of discovery. She learns, her patients learn, and we as readers learn the most. Dr. Gunn makes an excellent case on the value of listening to her patients — but more important, hearing what they have to say. Highly recommended."

D.B. Gilles
Professor and Area Head of Television, New York University, Tisch School of the Arts
Author of the nonfiction *Writer's Rehab* and *The Portable Film School,* the novels *I Hate My Book Club* and *Colder Than Death,* and the plays *The Girl Who Loved the Beatles* and *Inadmissable*

"*Bare* is unlike any other case study book I've read. It is interesting, funny and so emotionally compelling — at times, I almost forgot I was reading a book on psychology. *Bare* gives us a rare peek inside not only the mind, but the heart and motivations of a therapist during her sessions — something rarely done. It touches on themes so universal, any reader, even non-psychologists and psychotherapists, will enjoy this — and grow from it. *Bare* is certain to provide a 'good read' and is a wonderful addition to every personal library."

> Helen A. Solomon, PhD
> Professor of Clinical Practice, Fordham University
> Clinical Consultant for Sexual Assault and Violence,
> Mount Sinai Medical Center
> Private Practice, Manhattan

"When I began to read *Bare: Psychotherapy Stripped*, I did not expect to read half the book in one sitting, only to finish it in another. With great readability, *Bare* provides an interesting look at a therapist's perspective when she is treating patients — and how they have an impact on her, and cause her to think about her own reactions to things. Authors Simon-Gunn and DeCarlo create a frame in which readers journey through a therapist's world, experiencing the complexities and individualities of each patient, and how each affects the therapist, both on a professional and personal level. Whether or not you've been to a therapist, this book is utterly fascinating — a glimpse of how people process emotions and why they might do what they do. It may even help you to discover information about your own behaviors and thought patterns."

> Patricia Piroh
> Associate Director of Broadcast and Media Operations for Montclair State University.
> Co-producer, *A Ripple in the Water: Healing Through Art*

BARE

Psychotherapy Stripped

By Jacqueline Simon Gunn, PsyD and Carlo
DeCarlo

University
PROFESSORS PRESS

First Published in 2014, University Professors Press.

ISBN 13: 978-1-939686-04-6

University Professors Press
Colorado Springs, CO
www.universityprofessorspress.com

Cover Photo by Joe Gunn
Cover Design by Laura Ross

Table of Contents

Acknowledgements

Rome wasn't built in a day… nor by a single person. In creating this book, the authors collectively would like to extend their gratitude to Genna Michalkovich, Melinda Gallagher, and Dr. Brent Potter for their generous feedback on the manuscript. For their expert advice, thanks go to Louise Fury and Evelyn Storch; their counsel was greatly appreciated. And to their favorite cheerleaders, much appreciation goes to Dr. Deidre Kolarick, Alison Gaylin, Patricia Pirot, Dr. Helen Solomon, D.B. Gilles, Matthew Rofofsky, Dr. Amanda Lowe and Don Corcoran. A second thanks goes to Melinda Gallagher for contributing the foreword. And thanks especially to Joseph Gunn for his amazing graphic design and photography skills.

The authors would also like to thank everyone at University Professors Press, including Dr. Louis Hoffman, Dr. James Ungvarsky and Dr. Stephen Fehl.

Individually, Jacquie would like to thank Philip Simon, Joseph Gunn, Pamela Frank and Sharon Simon for their unwavering support and belief in her ability to chase her dream. She would also like to extend a special thanks to coauthor Carlo DeCarlo — for inspiring her creativity and giving her the confidence to push past her comfort zone.

Carlo would like to thank Elizabeth DeCarlo for her bountiful support. He'd also like to especially thank Jacqueline Simon Gunn for taking him on such an unforgettable ride in a therapist's chair.

In each therapeutic relationship, a unique world is created. Thank you to all of the patients who inspired the writing of this book and continue to generously share their lives with me; I am grateful to know each and every one of you.

In order to protect the privacy of the patients in these stories, some information has been changed. Certain demographics were altered, and in some instances, fictional elements were added to protect patient anonymity. In some anecdotes more camouflage was necessary; in these cases, patients' identities were protected by using amalgamates of more than one patient. This technique was used either by request of the patient or because the content of their story could otherwise lead to personal identification.

Foreword

Everyone has a story. And things are not always as they seem. When you are a psychotherapist, you learn this very quickly.

As for what to do with the secrets, the fantasies, the baring of souls and the ever-evolving complexity in our relationships? Well, that's not as easily learned, taught or known. A therapist must be able to trust his/her gut instinct and sit in the ambiguity of not knowing.

When I began my work as a psychotherapist, I had already been privy to many stories. I received a joint degree in human sexuality and public health, and had been working for many years to help people explore and enjoy their sexuality. Our relationship to our sexual self is fundamental to our lives. It is at the core of our nature. The erotic life of a person is their sexuality transformed by the imagination. Without it, we wouldn't exist. And yet, sex creates so much conflict for people.

Though I knew this when I began my clinical work, I never imagined some of the stories I would hear — and how many times I would be surprised to discover there was no easy way to respond. It is one thing to listen; but it is another thing to be invested, enveloped and totally immersed in the story. As a psychotherapist, you literally and figuratively become part of each person's story; and they are part of yours.

During my training at the Karen Horney Clinic, where I met Dr. Simon Gunn — or Jacquie, as she prefers to be called — I began to realize that each patient's world was like opening up a novel for the first time. Each patient has their own story, so sessions become akin to reading a few pages of a novel — you get pulled in, begin to relate to the characters and eagerly await the story's unfolding. And just like with a novel, you may imagine and anticipate certain outcomes — only to find yourself led down an unexpected path with circumstances beyond your wildest dreams.

In order to learn the art of psychotherapy, we need a theoretical basis. (Though there is an art to psychotherapy, it is still very serious work; people place their emotional well-being in our hands.) These theories of psychotherapy are helpful to the process, but they can also be limiting. Because everyone has their own story — and is uniquely living — there are so many happenings in the therapy relationship that just can't be known. So there you are, sitting with your patient, in the middle of the unexpected, unforeseen present of life — having to make decisions that no textbook could have ever prepared you for.

I think a book like "Bare" has been a long time coming. Written in a novelized format, this book offers an inimitable perspective on the practice of psychotherapy — as well as life in general. The stories are so vivid that they come alive on the pages, giving the reader the sense that they are living through it with each patient. Whether I was empathizing with Tess's loss of her sexual self, trying to figure out who was stalking Anne, or gripped by what was really going on with Tony — was he telling the truth? — I just couldn't stop reading. When I was wondering who Raul had sex with in the waiting room bathroom or if Sam was going to make it to the Olympics, I felt a personal investment.

Aside from being a good teaching book for therapists, students and patients, "Bare" also provides the same enlightenment you get from reading fiction. It tells the truth. Using patient stories, it reveals the "bare" truth about life. I found myself learning creative psychotherapeutic techniques, but also having moments of connection and reflection on a more personal level.

And just as everyone has a story, Jacquie shares some of her own. In "Bare," we come to know Jacquie the professional, but also Jacquie the human being, who struggles in her own way. I think it takes courage to bare your own soul in a profession that prides itself on neutrality. Through hearing Jacquie's personal and professional thoughts, you get a sense of the universality of the dilemmas that we all encounter as we travel along life's mysterious path.

When I read about Jacquie's recurring nightmare or her decision to squeeze her feet into the Red Stilettos, I get it. Life is challenging, and the best we can do is figure out who we are and live accordingly. It may be Jacquie's credibility as a psychologist that makes this statement ring so true when reading "Bare," or perhaps the stories in this book are so raw and truthful that you just can't ignore them.

Melinda Gallagher, MA, LMHC
Senior Psychotherapist, Seleni Institute
Senior Candidate in Psychoanalysis at the American Institute of Psychoanalysis
Author of *A Piece of Cake: Recipes for Female Sexual Pleasure*

Introduction

This may sound outlandish, but I have convinced myself I came into this world already a psychologist. At a young age, I would ask precocious questions concerning the meaning of life and human nature. I developed anxieties and worries that most young children were immune to. Acutely observant, I sponged up latent and unspoken emotions from those around me, particularly from adult exchanges. I can remember as early as grade school wanting to know the truth about the world, never satisfied with the answers I received to even the most common of questions.

"But why does she cry so much?" I asked about my newborn sister, not content knowing that hunger, a dirty diaper, sleepiness or pain might be the answer. "Is it because she's sad?"

My grandfather died when I was still a child. I absorbed the heaviness from the adults surrounding me. They were sad. I was sad. I had so many questions. And my "whys" were relentless. "Why do people we love die? Why was he going? Where was he going? Would I ever see him again? Would everyone around me die? If so, what are we all doing here, and why are we doing it if everything comes to an end? Is it all pointless? What does it all mean? Does anything mean *anything*?" I kept barraging my parents and family with nonstop inquiries. And in different forms — or the same — I am still haunted by these questions.

Years later during my freshman year at Rutgers University, my pre-calculus professor grew exasperated. "Jacqueline. This is math. There is no why. It just *is*!"

Though I possessed little tolerance for superficiality, I found myself lost in a world of school-aged kids — my peers — who demanded conformity. I struggled with these things for a long time and remained lost, uncomfortable, trying so hard to fit in. I felt estranged even in kindergarten, but I didn't really know what it meant or even how to describe it. I eventually developed a working façade to assimilate with the others. Though it helped me create quite a number of friendships and fun memories as I moved through middle school and high school, as I matured, I realized I wasn't living authentically. I entered therapy to try to re-discover myself. Remarkably, I did.

At the opening of *Bare: Psychotherapy Stripped*, I share a recurring dream I started having at 31 years old, when I began my psychology internship — the last requirement to earn my doctorate degree. This dream, as you will come to learn through the stories in *Bare*, reveals insights into my past and my present, my fears and anxieties, my aspirations and desires; with it, I have come to understand ways to help my patients. In a larger sense, we can use these learnings to discover and embrace our human potentials — while finding the self that gets lost as we each attempt to make our own way in a world that encourages conformity on a superficial level, while ignoring the genuine similarities that can bind us together on a deeper level.

In life, in entertainment, in myth, we feel drawn to archetypal personalities — to their drama, to their denial and inner conflicts, to their personal journeys, and to what makes them tick. And within each of them, we find something of ourselves; we come to learn something important about who we are and about the human experience in general.

So *Bare* is a story of life and all of its intricacies, told through real-life case studies of some of my long-term psychotherapy patients. It is the truth about what really happens in life, while providing an insider's peek into the unadulterated thoughts of a therapist in session. Through patient case studies, you will be pulled into a world, an extraordinarily raw and real world, which spans the spectrum of human nature — love and lust, fear and bravery, violence and tenderness, life and death. It is a journey that not only unmasks the psychotherapeutic encounter, but also reveals the fundamentals of the human experience.

Bare is not an ordinary psychology book. Nor is it a typical case-study book. The patients' psychotherapeutic journeys are written as stories that are weaved together in a unique way, so that the reader's experience is much like my own. The stories take place simultaneously, chronologically affording readers all the suspense and excitement that encompass my work as a clinical psychologist and my life in general.

In addition, I have chosen to bare my own life struggles and experiences as they arise and unfold during the course of the therapeutic relationship. In this way, the reader comes to learn that much of what happens in psychotherapy is akin to what humans share as basic life struggles. And through this self-reflection and exploration, I find a way to identify and empathize with each patient. As I strip away the clandestine mystique surrounding the therapy relationship, what you will see is two people sharing an incredibly authentic and profound human encounter.

Engaging in the all-too-common superficiality that distinguishes much of our social interactions — something Irvin Yalom creatively defines as "cocktail party behavior" — often left me feeling empty and bored. It makes sense that I chose a profession where I am able to maintain deeply meaningful relationships that require authentic and genuine relating; human-centered encounters that require baring truths that define the essence of our existence.

This may make me seem quite dark, but actually it is quite the contrary. Through exploration of the dark depths of both my own and my patient's psyche, I find hope and lightness, truth and meaning, strength and resiliency, humor and joy. As you read *Bare*, you will find that therapy, like life, is a process — a journey toward greater self-awareness and healing — where the "in-the-moment" experience is often as enriching as discovering one's destination.

I put a lot of thought into the particular patient stories I chose to disclose in *Bare*. I wanted to illustrate a wide range of character variability, reveal different clinical dilemmas, and demonstrate the many unique reasons people come for treatment. Each case study discloses something unique and compelling. I show how I creatively navigate the terrain of each patient's individual psychology. Throughout this book, you will really feel each patient's struggles, and be privy to the complex, mystifying process of the therapeutic relationship. Through my genuine sharing, you will also experience the thoughts and emotions — sometimes humorous, sometimes painful — I go through during the course of each therapeutic encounter.

The stories in *Bare* also tap into the quintessential human experience on a more general level. As I process my encounters with my patients and move into a self-reflective place, numerous questions arise. In this way, you as the reader will be exposed to moving processes and queries that define our basic humanity; disclosures which encourage self-awareness, even insight into one's own foibles. It offers an opportunity to glimpse the lives of other human beings and experience the patients' search for meaning, their discomfort with intimacy, awareness of individual responsibility, aloneness, death, human potential versus human limitation, and the struggle to be oneself. There is the potential for real enlightenment here as you come to relate to each patient's human dilemma, and through this process find comfort and truth.

No amount of academic training really prepares us for that all-encompassing moment when we find ourselves sitting in the therapist's chair for the first time. For most of us, it can feel exciting but also quite anxiety-provoking. It reminds me of the first time the surgical resident takes the scalpel into his own hands.

There is no explicit descriptive or didactic method that can adequately educate nor prepare a psychologist-initiate for this moment; there is no definitive formula for what it feels like to be with a patient or to perform psychotherapy. The way we actually learn turns out to be complicated, multi-faceted, and unique to each encounter. *Bare* exemplifies the therapeutic process as it is experienced step-by-step and in the moment. The way it really is — complex, intense, powerful, filled with surprises, at times heartbreaking and other times amazingly enriching and exciting. I show how rather than sitting back and distantly taking notes, I am an active participant in the process. In this way, I also experience a wide breadth of personal emotions, and I use this openness and receptivity of my own internal process to treat my patients.

Chapter 1:
The Red Stilettos

I think Dostoevsky was right, that every human being must have a point at which he stands against the culture, where he says, this is me and the damned world can go to hell.
—Rollo May

"Jacquie? Is that you?"

Oh no, please don't let it be her. The voice came from behind me.

But of course it was, the slightly nasal, overly enunciated voice always unmistakable. My body tightened. Of all the people to run into — in Bloomingdale's, no less — while looking the way I did: sweaty, smelly, and disheveled. Served me right for doing my training run, then squeezing in an errand before showering, while convincing myself I could manage to escape notice of someone I knew. The Big Apple may be big, but it is not that big.

"Jacquie? Jacquie."

Her voice doesn't sound close. Maybe if I move fast enough, I can get lost amongst the shoppers. But then I heard the distinct sound of hurried heels clacking on the tiled floor, and before I could slip into the crowd, a hand touched my shoulder.

"Jacqueline!"

I bolstered my spirits, and turned to face the inevitable. *Maybe it's time I bring this relationship to a close.*

Tess was my newest patient. I had just earned my psychologist's license a few months prior to our first meeting, and subsequently accepted a full-time staff position at the Karen Horney Clinic. I had already been employed at the clinic for two and a half years, first as an intern and then as a post-doc fellow, so when they offered me the position — nearly nine years ago now — the decision to accept it wasn't difficult. I could continue with my current patients while I received some additional supervision, all providing me with the ability to slowly transition into private practice.

A colleague who had been working with Tess for nearly two years referred her to me. Another client would pack my schedule, as I was carrying a nineteen-patient caseload at the time, so I initially felt hesitant to take on a new client. After extensive consideration, I agreed. I wholeheartedly believed I was ready to push myself professionally.

How could I have known what would happen or the effect she would have on me?

My colleague had to prematurely terminate her work with Tess because she and her husband were moving out of state. At my request, she gave me only a small amount of background information; I am not a fan of learning about a new patient second-hand. I have found it more beneficial to be exposed to patients' narrative directly from them. The referring therapist did tell me that Tess was 61 years old, suffered from chronic depression, and having an inordinately hard time with the aging process.

She added, "You'll be a good match." When I wondered why, she responded, "Tess needs a tolerant, warm and empathetic therapist. I think you'll work well together."

I was not finding that to be the case.

When Tess came in for our initial meeting, I immediately noticed her striking appearance. She was quite attractive, small framed and perfectly made up. What I found most significant was her choice of attire; dressed impeccably, she reminded me of someone clothed for a night at the theater. Though curious about the façade she put on display for the world, it was much too soon for such a personal inquiry, so I held my thoughts and associations in abeyance to be brought up later in therapy.

Within just the first moments of session, however, I managed to ostensibly muck things up. I called her Contessa. Tess does not like to be called Contessa, which I soon discovered. And her displeasure spoke to that fact through her terse reaction. "It's Tess."

Though my colleague had referred to her as Tess, I noted in her file that her given name was Contessa. Nicknames can be a highly personal experience, and I did not want to presume familiarity too soon. So I called her Contessa. But I knew better. I should have asked her outright what she preferred to be called. Just like a nickname can be personal, so too can a given name be a source of anxiety, as well as a seedbed of myriad emotional triggers.

"Tess, I'm sorry. I didn't realize you dislike Contessa."

"I hate Contessa. It's a family name. And it reminds me of someone who's ancient and stodgy." And just like that, with tightened lips appearing like she'd just sucked on a sour candy; she folded her arms in a resolute stand against distasteful nomenclature.

"Really? I think Contessa is a beautiful and rare name. It evokes such elegance."

"Nonsense." She dismissed my opinion with a wave of her hand and flutter of eyelashes. "Now, Tess. That's fun and youthful. Tess is a model's name." Her eyes twinkled when she said that, encouraging me to make the leap, to associate her with models. And honestly, though I am normally savvy enough to avoid that slippery slope, she did carry herself like one. And that is exactly where my thoughts landed. *I bet she could've been a model in her day. I wonder if she was.*

As the session moved along, Tess began describing her long history of depressive episodes, her numerous hospitalizations, and her propensity to isolate from others. I had so many questions for Tess, but I wanted to allow her the liberty to express herself without interruption during this first session. Some clinicians prefer to perform an extensive intake evaluation during the first few sessions, in order to collect adequate background information. I find this sort of structured interview interferes with the patient's process of describing personal information, so I allowed Tess to tell me her story while I listened attentively with compassion and empathy.

I learned in the first session that Tess lost both of her parents at a young age; she lost her mother first when Tess was 17, and then her father when she was 24. I felt a twinge of pain as she revealed this; it was only the first session and I already could feel the heaviness, the burden she was carrying, and I felt sad as I listened. She was also married for ten years, from 36 years old until 46 — when her husband, who was having an affair during the last year of their marriage, left her for another woman.

Now 15 years later, she still had not recovered from this. I began to notice through her narrative that she blamed herself for the numerous hardships she endured in her relationships — and this was only the beginning. Throughout our treatment together, I would hear many heart-wrenching stories from her past, as well as experience and bear witness to her suffering resulting from some serious and frightening occurrences that happened during our course of therapy.

As I listened, I also wondered about her feelings surrounding the termination with her previous therapist. I found it significant that she didn't bring this up. In my experience, premature termination most often brings up mixed emotions for our patients: abandonment, anger, betrayal, loss. *Why wasn't Tess bringing this into the room?* We were near the close of our session when I realized this — *too late to bring it up now* — so I made a mental note to inquire about this at our next session.

With only five minutes left, Tess began to inquire about me. How old was I? Was I married? (She did not see a ring and assumed that I was not.) Did I want children? When questions such as these come up at the end of a session, it is always difficult to negotiate how to respond.

Early in my training, I almost never answered patients' personal inquiries. I was trained from a classical psychoanalytic perspective. Residing under this particular model of psychotherapy, personal disclosures are looked down upon and are thought to have a negative impact on the evolving of transference — the response of the patient to the therapist, both conscious and unconscious. This level of neutrality never felt quite right to me; it truly felt inauthentic, but I was still in training and didn't have the confidence yet to feel comfortable following my intuition. My own way of working, which at times involves personal disclosures, evolved slowly over the years.

Though it was not official at the time, I considered Tess my first private practice client, so I wanted to display a sense of confidence and maturity that I believed I should possess. It was more for me than anyone else, really. I had counseled countless patients prior to Tess, so I was confident about my abilities; however, since I was not yet seasoned, I floundered when she riddled me with personal questions. Tess challenged almost every aspect of the delicate balance that I eventually learned was a key factor in using self-disclosure as a therapeutic technique. In psychotherapy, as in life, experience is often the best teacher. Well, Tess, she was akin to a full-time professor.

I felt anxious; I did not know Tess well enough yet to have a real understanding of what these questions, and my choice of whether or not to respond, meant to her. I acknowledged her inquisitiveness and replied with what I hoped embodied an empathetic tone, "We can talk about these questions at our next session." *What an unoriginal answer.* I quickly berated myself, but I really needed to understand her better before I could make a decision about how to handle these quite personal inquiries. By the time she left the session, I was exhausted. I also felt the urge to cry. I really needed to think about what was going on for me; these feelings obviously communicated something quite essential about our dyad.

I would find out soon enough.

A few nights later I had the most unnerving dream. I arrived at an important psychoanalytic conference, preparing to present on self-disclosure in the treatment setting. I walked in, my flowing mint-green dress billowing with each step. My most favorite frock. I felt confident. All eyes were on me. The dress had done its job.

And then my gaze swept across the room. The crowd milled about clad in black (mostly suits), their formal outfits a stark contrast to my lustrous gown! Sudden discomfort settled in. My skin burned from embarrassment.

I woke up drenched in sweat. Even in the dream, I remember thinking, "What a curious dream." And despite its obvious disconnect from reality, I couldn't shake the residual uneasy feeling. Quelling all the thoughts spinning around in my mind — *I know this dream, there is something so familiar about it* — I attempted to set aside my strong desire to self-analyze, and instead prepared to leave for my office with a lucid mind.

While still trying to distract myself from ruminating about the meaning of my dream, I ruffled through my closet deciding what to wear. And there it hung: my flowing mint green dress. I shuffled past it, searching for the right outfit for Tess — *For Tess? Why for Tess?* — but my eyes repeatedly returned to the green dress. *What an odd juxtaposition.* I usually wear my most professional clothes when seeing a new patient (partly to set them at ease, partly to establish professional boundaries), yet here I stand, still trying to divert my attention away from the green dress that hung in my closet before me, hindering my ability to avoid the dream and to find some "appropriate" clothes to wear. My experience that morning, after only one meeting with Tess, already began to mirror the difficult relational dynamic that would infiltrate our journey together.

Tess came to our second session flawlessly dressed and made up. Again, images of my flowing mint-green dress distracted me. However, this time I associated thoughts of the dress to the feeling I had when observing Tess's attire; she looked lovely, but over-dressed for a therapy session. This time I observed her posture and cadence as she walked in. It was incongruent with her impeccable makeup and high fashion. She walked with her head down and back slouched, a remarkable difference from her model-like stature of the previous session. I associated her demeanor with someone who was just beaten up. She slumped into the chair.

"I'm boring, right? I have nothing in my life except my dog." She frowned and averted her eyes.

"Boring?" *On the contrary, you're absolutely fascinating.* "It actually seems that you have quite a bit to talk about. Where is this feeling coming from?" It was then that she began to tell me about what I eventually dubbed "Her Fall from Glory."

Tess had been a well-recognized author and editor; she and her former husband actually met while she was working as an editor of a reputable magazine. She also published a book about her personal experience battling and overcoming breast cancer when she was 49 years old. Before her breast cancer, which eventually led to her losing her breast (she made sure to add that she had an implant), she had many friends, an exciting social life and a loving partner who stood by her through her year-and-a-half ordeal.

"I was beautiful, so beautiful; I had many men. Many." Her pain permeated every word. "Now men don't even look at me when I walk down the street." She sighed, heavy and long. "See? I have nothing."

Now this is a telling statement!

"Nothing." She repeated, overly enunciating it, drawing out, then punctuating, each syllable — each sound — with the kind of attention to detail one might find in a pillow embroidery.

My mind raced with all the different paths of inquiry she left open for me to explore, but the amount of information she generously offered so overwhelmed me that the session ended before I realized it, leaving me no opportunity to explore any of her story or encourage her to elaborate. I did want to give her something to leave with. This is vital to the therapeutic process — giving the patient a part of you by acknowledging what they have shared and offering some empathetic insight.

"You're a fascinating woman, Tess, and I have so many questions for you." I noticed her curious expression. "You've been through so many hardships."

"Interesting? Really?" Her remark took a sad turn. "But I have nothing now, Jacqueline. You're young. Don't wind up like me." *Is that a little envy in her tone? Or was it hostility? And she just glossed over my comment about her hardships?* She gathered her belongings, moving with slow sadness, and left looking even more broken-down than she did when she came in. Again, I felt like crying. And again, I forgot to ask about her experience terminating with the previous therapist.

Tess began therapy with me on a twice-weekly basis. I typically prefer to understand a patient's internal dynamics and interpersonal style before increasing the frequency beyond once per week. What one might think would be helpful for a patient —

added stability, consistency and containment — may be too much for them in the early stages of the treatment. But since Tess was seeing her previous therapist twice a week during their second year of treatment, we collaboratively decided to keep this therapeutic frame. As I thought about Tess after our second meeting, I sensed that twice-weekly sessions were ideal for her, but I did wonder if it might become a bit overwhelming for me. The content of her narrative — losing her parents at a young age, cancer, divorce — as well as the feelings being evoked while sitting with her, already felt overpowering.

During the first month of treatment with Tess, she spoke endlessly about her "Fall from Glory." I sensed that she felt shame about where she was in her life now; in order to sit with me and expose her current situation; she desperately needed and wanted me to know who she was prior to her "fall." I would later understand that this "fall" happened as a result of losing her breast, coupled with her almost complete emphasis on her outward appearance as defining her. For Tess, I came to understand relatively early in our treatment, outward appearance was all she believed she had to offer; it was who she was. This was at the core of all her issues and eventually established a quite frustrating dynamic between us.

Having conceptualized her dynamics early on, I decided that my therapeutic position should be to listen attentively to who she was prior to her breast cancer. I believed it would help her feel less shame when, in later sessions, I would be encouraging her to focus on where her life was in the present. Through this active listening, I gathered a lot of background information; although I did notice that when I tried to explore her early childhood experiences, particularly her relationships with her parents, Tess met me with harsh resistance. *Okay, so I guess this is important.* Though I made a mental note, I didn't push her; this was obviously an area of great devastation for Tess. We would get to this material at some point, but definitely not yet. She had other, more pertinent, news to share with me.

"Everyone cheats." This came out of her mouth with the nonchalance of someone placing a dinner order. She wasn't making an observation solely about the men in her life because "everyone" included Tess. During her ten-year marriage, she confessed to multiple liaisons with other men. For some reason — likely having to do with my sense that she thrived on external validation of her desirability and worthiness from men — this information didn't surprise me in the least; but it piqued my curiosity.

"Tell me more about this?" And she did. She went on to describe the many sexual partners she had through her twenties and thirties. In fact, all her friends had extra-marital affairs and, she reiterated, cheating was merely a part of marriage. I experienced a visceral reaction as she provided this information. How strange to hear those words come from this 61 year old woman sitting across from me.

I pondered why I felt strange learning about Tess's clandestine liaisons. *I don't get it. I've heard countless stories like hers, especially from all those sex workers I've counseled who have repeatedly described having sex without any emotional connection. I guess this Tess, the Tess-Post-Fall-From-Glory, is not the same woman who enjoyed those extra-marital affairs. This Tess is depressed and broken.* I found it difficult to imagine her with the sexual prowess she described, of being a woman who ostensibly detached emotion from many of her sexual experiences and enjoyed sex for the pure physical pleasure it offered. It was clear that she did; that is, before she came to see her body as deformed.

One of the men she had an affair with, Barry, was the man she eventually developed an ongoing and quite serious relationship with after her divorce. She described Barry as "the love of her life" and the man who stuck by her during her fight against her breast cancer. He eventually left her for another woman once her battle with cancer was over and she was healthy again. When Barry informed her a few months later that he was married to this other woman, Tess described feeling abandoned and devastated. This, too, added to her "Fall from Glory." Tess was 51 when this relationship ended.

"I haven't been with another man since." Tess broke eye contact with me. She focused on the floor and kept her gaze there.

Interesting. Men make up such an integral part of her life. She thrives on their attention and affections. That's a long time to keep yourself alone.

"You didn't want to pursue another relationship?"

"What's the point? What would we talk about? Anyway, what did I have to offer a man? What *do* I have to offer a man?"

"How can you say that? You're extremely interesting and have lived such an intriguing life."

She kept her focus averted. "No one wants a deformed woman. I would never feel comfortable taking my shirt off. My implant has no nipple. I used to love my body, but I no longer can even look at my own breasts in the mirror."

In that moment I actually felt an ache in my heart; this feeling stayed with me all day. I also had so many thoughts about how I might help Tess develop self-worth based on internal character traits; I also knew how difficult this was going to be. And sure enough, this disclosure marked the moment when the relational dynamics between us started to get complex.

Yet, as the day progressed, my thoughts kept returning to something Tess said. "Everyone cheats." Of course she's wrong. Everyone doesn't cheat. But many do. And it's become an almost accepted part of marriage. How long until it happens? Was it with someone we know? Do you love him/her? Can we still make this relationship work?

People barely blink an eye when they hear news of infidelity, even maintaining secret multiple indiscretions over the course of a twenty-year marriage. But mention paying for sex, even by an adult not in a relationship, and suddenly the room is aghast. How could you? It's so sordid!

And this was why Tess's comment about cheating was on my mind. Maxine was my next patient after my lunch break. Maxine and her Red Stilettos. The first time I met Maxine, she was wearing them. She was always wearing them. Now, as I hurried down the busy New York City sidewalk, the thought of Maxine and her Red Stilettos sent me on a journey back to a moment from my childhood.

The windows of the car were perspiring. I took my little finger and began to spell out my name. "J-A-C" — and then through the back part of the "C" I saw them. I am certain that my pupils dilated, pushing away the brown of my irises as curiosity arose in me, while I quickly wiped away the dampness on the window to get a better look. I sat in awe. There they were; the most amazing pair of red stilettos. The light changed at 42nd and Ninth Avenue, and my Dad drove away as I turned my head to look through the back car window. I stared as the shoes receded into a tiny red dot fading into the dark mystique of 42nd Street.

It had been years since I thought about those red stilettos — until I met with Maxine for the first time. She slinked off the elevator with her long, lean legs, and when I looked down I saw them: the red stilettos. The sight of the shoes whisked me back to that long-ago day in the backseat of my parents' car. As I reflected on this memory, I remembered that even as a young girl, not quite a teen yet, I knew the woman in the red stilettos on 42nd Street was a prostitute. It was the early 1980s when 42nd Street was home to many of them. And at twelve years old, not only did I know this, I was already fascinated.

Maxine was one of the many sex workers I treated in psychotherapy over the course of my internship, through my post-doctoral fellowship at The Karen Horney Clinic, and into my private practice. Our therapeutic journey began early in my internship year. We worked together in twice-weekly psychotherapy for a little over three years. And her story and our work together changed me. Maxine had a horrifically painful story; sometimes it was really hard to hear. But at the same time, her intelligence, self-awareness and resiliency was so moving; she afforded me insights, and revealed a sense of hopefulness that was worth every ounce of difficulty I experienced listening to her story.

Maxine took her seat in the patient chair and crossed her fishnet-covered long legs. She possessed the posture of a ballet dancer — straight, centered, erect — but her dark brown eyes revealed profound sadness.

"I need help, Dr. Simon. I'm with this guy and I... he's just horrible." She was shaking just talking about it. Patients often react strongly when they are admitting something aloud for the first time.

"What does he do, tell me?" I already had a sense of her struggle, but I wanted her to have a chance to find the words. *Let her say it. It'll help make it real for her.*

"It's terrible. Ed screams at me, beats me, pushes me around. I — I just can't take it anymore. I want to leave him. Start new. But —," her voice cracked. "But I can't. I just can't." Then she began sobbing. We sat for a few moments, letting the tears flow. I handed her a few tissues. As upsetting as it was to watch, it was a healthy beginning to her therapy, finally connecting with what had been troubling her, with what she had been compartmentalizing for 20 years.

Once she collected herself, she cleared her tears with the tissues I'd handed her, sat up straight and crossed her legs. And there they were, out loud and proud. Ready to tell their tales. The red stilettos; actually, Red Stilettos — I decided they were a proper noun deserving of capital letters. It almost seemed Maxine wouldn't have to speak one word to me about her life. Those shoes could do the talking for her.

But Maxine had a lot to say, and didn't shy away from the work ahead of her. She began to describe her past and her present: a synopsis of her life story. And it was a tough one.

Maxine was 39 years old, and she was the oldest of five, all girls. Her father physically abused her mother in front of them while Maxine and her sisters were still young. Maxine described living in fear. Finally when she was 16, she had had enough. She stood up to her father and attempted to protect her mother. As her father was punching her mother with a steel-covered ring, Maxine lunged at him, punching him over and over in the back as he hovered over her mother. He finally turned around. Maxine described feeling like "time stood still." And then...

Maxine cried as she was retelling her past, a story she said she had shared with just one previous therapist. She was so expressive; I could see the difference in her emotional states just by the changes in her eyes. While she was sharing with me, I noticed her rather intriguing, almost peculiarly discordant appearance.

Maxine exuded inner strength and elegance, but simultaneously she looked a bit raunchy. She was quite beautiful underneath the overdone makeup; her skin glowed, but she covered it. Her hair, thick and wavy, was bleached blond while her roots were nearly black. Her clothing was too tight and actually looked uncomfortable. Yes, she had a fabulous figure, but her clothes were just too small on her. She also carried a designer bag, but it was ripped, frayed, and her things were sticking out because it was not zipped up. As I observed her in the room, I already had some early, but quite viable hypotheses. Eventually it was the Red Stilettos that represented the incongruence Maxine experienced in regards to her self-image. As the treatment unfolded, it was her amazing shoes that helped us understand and reconcile her internal struggle.

Which brought us back to the present: Maxine was stuck in a tragically abusive relationship.

"Maxine, you're saying, 'I want to leave, but I can't leave?' Help me understand what this means." As I awaited her response, I noticed that her tears had washed away some of the makeup that had been covering what appeared to be a black eye. My heart sank. And Maxine folded her body in half, leaving her head between her knees and began sobbing again, this time uncontrollably. It was only our first session together and I already had a sense that Maxine had experienced a severe amount of trauma beyond what most sex workers experience to cause them to turn to their profession.

It was only toward the end of the session when Maxine finally sat up straight and explained it to me. "I can't leave because I'm a whore, and like Ed has said over and over, no one will want me! I'm used. Worn goods." Maxine was with Ed since she was nineteen years old, when he "rescued" her from her abusive father. He first encouraged Maxine to work as a prostitute, then turned around and employed her occupation to emotionally threaten and destroy her self-esteem. Within a few sessions, I completely understood Maxine's predicament; she defined herself as a worthless whore and believed that was all she would ever be. Could ever be.

Essentially, she believed the label "prostitute" pigeonholed her, put her in a file to never be re-categorized. But in only our first hour together, I already surmised that Maxine had so much more to offer. My goal became to help her see that!

It was uncanny, despite the intensity of our initial session and the tremendous amount of tears Maxine shed, she left the session looking composed and confident as she strutted out in her Red Stilettos. *This must be what it's like for her to turn her feelings on and off when she approaches a client. Put on a happy face for the world to see; take off the façade when the work is done.* I watched her walk out; I felt pretty wiped out, but I sensed her resiliency and was hopeful for her. I didn't know why at the time, but I liked her immediately.

Maxine worked on the streets. Like every profession, sex work has its own jargon. "Working on the streets" is a term that describes a person who has a pimp. And in Maxine's case, Ed was her pimp. Basically, he solicited clients from the procession of men walking by, a common occurrence on 42nd Street until the late '80s when the mayor of New York City "cleaned up" the area. And it was there that I noticed the Red Stilettos for the first time.

So much time had passed — years — since then. I wasn't that young, naïve girl, and this wasn't Maxine's first therapy session. She had made some progress since our initial meeting, becoming more confident, self-assured. She certainly possessed more self-esteem now. And as she left, I thought how truly similar Maxine's situation was on her first day in therapy to how Tess was feeling now: damaged and obsolete.

But, this was not Tess's first day in therapy, either, just her first couple days *with me.* After nearly two years with my colleague, an effectual one at that, I wondered: Had she made any real progress? Might Tess be resistant to self-improvement? Sometimes, patients just do not want to change, ironic that they seek assistance for it. This thought started my anxiety juices flowing. I strive to — need to — feel useful to my patients. I get fulfillment from helping others. So concern began to gnaw at me:

Would I be able to help Tess? More importantly, would she let me?

Chapter 2:
The Fall from Glory

Tess arrived at our next session dressed in her typical, flawless fashion. Her choice of makeup — a cream shadow with a barely discernible lilac tint — accentuated her penetrating eyes. I had been ruminating with such heartbreak about Tess's experience of herself as "deformed." I also had been pondering over my fears about taking her on as a client. *Is she going to let me in? Will she allow me to help her change?*

"Tess, you look lovely today. Your eye makeup really brings out the blue in your eyes." I tensed a bit inside following this disclosure; was it timely? And I had no sense of how she might respond. My compliment, though unexpected, was born from an intuitive sense that this was something Tess needed, and possibly would help to open the relational space between us.

"Thank you. I have been meaning to tell you that *you* need to wear more makeup. You wear practically none. You're never going to meet a man if you don't do more to enhance your appearance." *Wow, that was particularly harsh.* I had noticed Tess look me up and down in previous sessions. I had planned to query about her experience of me and my physicality — but prior to her response, I thought it to be too confrontational so early in her treatment. She continued her critique. "You also need highlights in your hair. It's too dark." She paused. Then, "You also need to change the way you dress. You just don't look put-together." *Tell me how you really feel.*

I was at a loss. I needed to respond to this quite provocative information, but what would be an appropriate reaction? I had been devalued by patients numerous times in the past, but their comments were rarely so direct — and never about my appearance. I felt angry. I felt insulted. And truth be told, I felt a little hurt. My immediate inclination was to defend myself against her attack and retaliate with my thoughts about *her* appearance. Although I found Tess quite attractive, I thought she looked too made-up. But I maintained my composure and distanced myself from my feelings enough to give an appropriate, clinically informed response. "I'm curious, Tess, why my appearance is so important to you?"

"It's important to look your best so that you can find a husband." *Interesting. I never did answer her question about if I were married or involved with a man.*

The session ended leaving me with a complex array of feelings. I was shocked by her response to me, and some residual anger still pecked at me. But then I began to wonder what the process of her comments about my appearance meant in terms of our relational dynamic, as well as her overall interpersonal style. I had to really think about this one, and I spent a good portion of my evening doing just that.

The night following this session, I had the dream again: The important psychoanalytic conference, but this time I wasn't presenting. Again, everyone was mingling about in black (mostly suits), and I noticed that the female attendees were painted with too much makeup. The orchestra was playing Franz Liszt's *Hungarian Rhapsody*. I couldn't actually hear it in the dream, but I knew they were playing it — and though it's a popular piece, it's not a favorite of mine. I find the piece to be emotionally withholding, and for some odd reason, associate it with aristocratic pretentiousness. In my usual conspicuous fashion, I entered wearing an eye-catching outfit: a bright red halter jumpsuit. The music stopped. All eyes were on me. *Gulp!*

I woke completely drenched in sweat, my shorts and tank top sticking to my clammy skin.

I got out of bed, my eyes still partially closed, and phoned my own therapist to ask for a second session for the week. The dream felt familiar; I did have a sense of what the dream meant, but I wanted to process it with the help of my own therapist, Dr. Gwen. In addition to again dredging up uncomfortable, cloistered feelings from my past, this time I knew the dream was also unconsciously communicating something unique and essential about the dyad between Tess and me. My therapist agreed to fit me in, which eased some of the anxiety I was feeling. Not only did I have to skip my daily run in order to make it to my session, but I put a rush on my entire morning; nevertheless, it was a fair trade. I made coffee, showered quickly, then stood in my bedroom staring into my closet. There was the red jumpsuit staring back at me — *Ugh, this is a waking nightmare* — mocking me, interfering with my ability to find an "appropriate" outfit for work.

Finally, I pulled out a pencil skirt and a T-shirt-like top, then threw a blazer over it. I practically sprinted to the subway. At the stairs, I was swept along with the crowd into the underground. To the turnstiles. I could hear the tell-tale rumble of the approaching train. *Made it.* Then, my card wouldn't swipe. The train pulled up. *C'mon. Swipe, darn it.* I tried again. Again. I saw the doors open and people rush the train. One more time. *Please work.* And it did. I heard the turnstile beep, pushed my way through, and made it between the doors just before they closed. *Whew!* I grabbed hold of a support bar and clung to it as the train pulled away from the station. I breathed a sigh of relief. Someone squeezed by and brushed my leg. I instinctively looked down and —

Perfect. Just perfect. I sighed, half-defeated.

The entire time I was dressing and getting my things together, my mind was on the dream and the growing connection to Tess. So naturally, I didn't notice that I slipped on two different shoes. On the ride downtown, my head reeled with thoughts about Tess, her critique of my appearance, how the dream related to this, and now the irony of my two different shoes. I chuckled — a little too loudly. The woman next to me looked my way. "Shoe calamity," I explained.

She looked down and laughed. Then she lifted her pant legs slightly to reveal two differently patterned socks. "Mercury must be in retrograde," she quipped. I didn't understand the astrological reference, but I'm guessing Mercury messes with the order of things. Well, if nothing else, this happenstance took me out of my head long enough to relax.

Once in the presence of my therapist and the safety of the therapy room, we collaboratively figured it out. I have always felt different. I grew up in a family of artists; I made a habit of dressing with creative flair. The comments I heard from Tess were not so different from comments my peers made to me in high school, even grade school — a time in most everyone's life when "fitting in" felt important. I tried numerous times to conform to what was considered an appropriate way to dress; the same way as everyone else. I always felt uncomfortable, insecure and suffocated when I dressed conventionally. I just couldn't do it; I couldn't live that way. So I maintained my more artistic ways, thus leaving myself open to scrutiny from my peers. Although I had many friends growing up, I often heard playful comments from them, such as "What's with the get-up?" or "Leave it to Wacky Jacquie."

I believe the pressures to conform to societal expectations may lead to painful alienation of one's true authentic self. Through my own journey, I learned a valuable lesson — one that now translates into my clinical work and my emphasis on fostering uniqueness as tantamount to attaining a more satisfying life. Although remaining true to oneself may cause some discomfort (at least initially), it is far less damaging then the sense of estrangement one experiences when conforming to imposed expectations and losing what is most valuable: one's own way of being in the world.

The dream reminded me of my own process of getting back my own sense of self, and it brought to mind a quote I love from Richard Bach's book *Illusions.*

> We're iron, wrapped in copper wire, and whenever we want to magnetize ourselves we can. Pour our inner voltage through the wire, we can attract whatever we want to attract. A magnet is not anxious about how it works. It is itself and by its very nature it draws some things and leaves others untouched.

It took me some time to fully integrate the meaning of this quote. Once I did, though, I was free. It became clear to me from the content of my dream that my experiences with Tess and my involvement in the psychoanalytic community were pulling me back to a time in my life prior to my recovery. I shuffled through the row of volumes on my shelves until I found the book of quotes. I grabbed it from the bookcase, then flipped through it until I found Richard Bach's quote. As I re-read it, I felt a sense of relief. His words once again validated my experience. And Tess's need to break my stride eventually led to important information about her life and struggles.

I happily discovered when I entered college — and then graduate school — that this new community accepted my unconventional ways with open arms. I actually heard many compliments on my fashion sense and overall maverick-style ways. However, even those new friends would, on occasion, offer an innocuous, though equally unsolicited critique: "Why do you wear your glasses so often? You'd be much more beautiful without them." "You'd be a real knockout if you wore more makeup." "You have a great body. You should show it off more." By the time I was thirty years old, I didn't much care what people said. I embraced my way of being and actually felt free.

The dream illustrated some of the differences I felt becoming a part of a relatively conventional psychoanalytic community. No one ever said anything at all, but when I saw my mentors dressed in a more conservative manner, I was faced with an internal neurotic dilemma based on my earlier experiences.

"You are like a breath of fresh air," Dr. Gwen shared.

"Really? Gosh, thank you." I will admit this felt great; she was giving me permission to be myself and facilitated my experience of uniqueness as a strength. We discussed how Tess's comments were triggering past issues I had struggled with. I left the session feeling confident, validated, and ready to process Tess's insults from a more objective clinical position. Still, I felt a little unnerved continuing through my morning and afternoon wearing two different shoes. My one saving grace: I wasn't seeing Tess until the following day.

When I got home that night, I couldn't pull my sneakers on fast enough. The cool breeze mixed with a temperate evening created the perfect night for a run in Central Park. My session with Dr. Gwen had diffused most of my angst surrounding the dream, but a long run would dissipate the rest. Right before I left for my run, I wrote down Bach's quote on an index card and left it on the shelf right above my computer. I thought with the dynamics between Tess and me, it might be a good idea to have a concrete reminder. As it turned out, the index card almost became a premonition.

As I took each stride, my thoughts drifted back to the similarities between Tess and Maxine, their feelings of inadequacy, how Tess's relaxed perspective on casual sex really differed by only degrees to the practice of prostitution: a fine line dividing one's personal morality question. What would Tess say about Maxine's profession? Having repeatedly cheated on her own husband and lovers, would she find Maxine's existence sordid? Or would Tess be more understanding about it? And how about Maxine? Would she compartmentalize how she spent her nights (and sometimes days) into a neatly wrapped parcel, demarcating her johns as nothing more than business — while judging Tess as a cheater and liar, breaking the trust of her beloved?

As I dwelled upon Maxine's life, I turned out of the park and headed back toward home when a gust from the Hudson reached me, a salty breeze. The sensation drudged up a memory from years past, from my days living in Miami. It made me think about Ralph and his "mothers," also sex workers.

I had not thought of Ralph in a long time. My relationship with him bordered on intense. The physical sensation I felt running with the breeze enhanced the memory, making it so vivid, I almost felt as though I was back there…

"No, get your hands off me!" The screaming was jarring.

I turned to see who was killing my buzz. Earlier that morning, I had achieved my nirvana: the perfect run along the beach on Ocean Drive in Miami Beach's famous "South Beach." The warm morning sun, tempered by the ocean breeze, cooled the sweat on my skin. I was still on that runner's high a couple hours later when I arrived at work. That was, until this young man murdered it.

The guards were literally dragging Ralph, the source of the ruckus, onto Unit 6 of the South Florida Juvenile Detention Center. Even beneath the standard-issue blue prison uniform, I could see how very thin Ralph was. The two guards were gripping him under his armpits; Ralph kept his body limp, so his legs, therefore, were dragging behind him.

Eeee---clang! I still couldn't get used to the sound as they practically threw Ralph into an open cell and slammed the bars shut. I had the sense that Ralph was a bit of a "regular" to Unit 6 by the way the guards related to him; I noticed the familiarity. *Hmm, what's his story?*

At South Florida Juvenile Detention Center, generally referred to as "Juvey," Unit 6 was where felonious inmates with behavior health issues were sent. Our job as the Unit 6 team was to evaluate each adolescent that was referred to us by the correctional officer during intake. Once the evaluative process was complete, our team would make an often difficult decision. We would either keep the adolescent on Unit 6 for therapy and advocacy, or have them placed on a regular unit.

We had a number of frightening young men in Juvey. Some, like tall, big-muscled Abdul, were true menaces. I recall seeing him one time outside of the center. I was — once again — running along the beach, feeling relaxed, strong, and peaceful, when I spied him; well, them, I should say. My heart started racing.

Abdul and his "homies," a big pack of about fifteen boys in the Crips gang, clustered across the street near The News Café. We made eye contact for a second, which prompted my fight-or-flight adrenaline to kick in, pushing me to run faster — a full-out sprint — for nearly a mile until I was far away and feeling safe. I had to pause for water sooner than I would normally stop during one of my five-mile runs when the overwhelming fright finally dissipated, leaving me panting and parched. After a few minutes, I was able to calm myself.

Abdul was one of the most fearsome adolescents I worked with at the detention center. He was in Juvey for raping a young girl as part of a gang initiation. After a full battery of forensic testing, our team concluded that Abdul was a psychopath, and at 17 years old, he had already exhibited a frighteningly complete lack of empathy. He was also open about his disturbing sadistic fantasies of hurting women. One day he created a hangman drawing, and in the lines for letters, he spelled out J-A-C-Q-U-I-E. He was horrifying.

After three months in Juvey, Abdul was released. I remember my exasperation.

"Released!?" I asked my director. He could see how shocked and angry I was. This boy should not be out on the streets.

"Yes," Dr. Jerry responded, emotionless, having seen this scenario become standard operating procedure at the correctional institution. "There wasn't enough evidence to keep him."

Great! I'm sure he's completely rehabilitated now! I withheld my sarcastic remarks, but I'm sure Dr. Jerry noticed the sentiment in my expression at his news. I had only been working at the detention center for five months, and I was already jaded by the correctional system and some of the things I witnessed while I was there. It was a month after this Abdul incident that Ralph was dragged onto the unit, just another criminal, but over time, he inspired in me a sense of hope and faith in the rehabilitative process of this detention factory.

So whereas someone like Abdul would have been placed on the regular unit had he not been released on some technicality, Ralph was special, different. Ralph, sixteen years old at the time, had been in and out of Juvey since he was ten, practically becoming the Unit 6 version of a human mascot. We all wanted to help him. In fact, conversations within our team, in our small private office away from the guards, often involved discussions about who could take him in as a foster parent.

During the two years that I worked on Unit 6, I was exposed to many atrocities; scores of disturbing events. I was privy to the behind-the-scenes unspoken despotism of the correctional system. I eventually, sadly, became somewhat inoculated to what I witnessed; it was self-protective, a mechanism necessary to engender my ability to engage fully with the adolescents I worked with. Most of them, despite the severity of their crimes, I genuinely wanted to help.

Once Ralph was settled in, Dr. Jerry asked me to work with him. And so Ralph became my patient. The following day, once Ralph was done with his classes, we met in the therapy room for the first time. He was a bit defensive in the beginning, which is most often the case with court-stipulated patients; I felt neither put off nor surprised. I did have some background information, as Ralph had a pretty thick file on Unit 6 from his past incarcerations. Dr. Jerry also provided me with some quite compelling historical information.

Prior to the session, I learned that Ralph was a 16-year-old Haitian boy. He was a member of the "Bloods," a well-known street gang famous for their violence and illegal drug involvement. Both of Ralph's parents were crack addicts who abandoned Ralph when he was 10, leaving Ralph alone in a dangerous part of Miami to fend for himself. Within a few months, Ralph met a woman who was working as a prostitute. She basically picked him up off the street and brought him to her tiny, ramshackle apartment where she lived with two other colleagues; these three remarkable women raised Ralph as their own.

Ralph began dealing crack in order to make money. He never used it. I learned from many dealers, Ralph included, that it is poor business judgment to use the drug one is dealing. He explained, one day early in our treatment: "Jacquie, I would never use crack. It's a bad drug. Besides, it's just not good business. If I used it, I would become addicted to it, consequently using up all my product. Therefore, I would have nothing left to sell." *Interesting. This is one smart kid. Extraordinarily articulate. And an impressive vocabulary for someone his age.* Later I would learn that while in Juvey, or one of the numerous halfway houses he was sent to, Ralph spent most of his free time reading. And the literature he read was usually dense philosophy, psychology or classic literature. He was an amazing boy, born into unfortunate life circumstances. I began having fantasies of saving him. I guess our whole team shared this idea.

Ralph and I worked together three times per week in individual therapy for almost a year. Of course, I did see him every day, as he was on the unit where I worked. Within about three months, we had a strong alliance, which also set Ralph apart from the many other patients I worked with in forensic settings.

It is incredibly hard to establish a working alliance with court-stipulated patients, markedly different than working with patients who come in for treatment on their own volition and are aware and willing to expose emotional dis-rest.

There was a relatively complex dual process that characterized the treatment with Ralph. On the surface, he was tough — a gang member — and often referenced himself as "owning the streets." But underneath this thinly veiled visage was a broken, depressed little boy crying out for his parents to take care of him. I understood the duality as a maladaptive, yet paradoxically, constructive way in which Ralph needed to exist in his world. To let down the facade would leave him vulnerable, likely opening himself up to eventually being killed. I was acutely aware that this loss defined him, and his participation in gang activities was his attempt to avoid such a painful all-encompassing feeling.

Despite his rough exterior, I felt the essence of his sadness. However, unlike my work outside of the forensic setting, I didn't try to break down his resistance. After a few years of working in forensics, I knew that he needed the defense to literally survive in the world he lived in. Additionally, I had come to learn that the inner city was an entirely different culture than mainstream society — and just like any other treatment, I needed to remain culturally sensitive.

By the time I arrived back at my New York apartment after my Central Park run, the memory of Ralph had taken my mind off Tess. And the workout had released the last remnants of tension from the day.

Tess arrived at our next session with a "gift" for me.

"I brought you something." Tess, grinning with pride, slapped an Avon magazine on my desk in front of me. *Seriously? Is she kidding me?* She then picked it up and flipped to the pages she had dog-eared, pointing to the products that would best suit me. I indulged her for a few moments, as I breezed through the makeup she suggested for me. In reality, I was busy trying to process what significance this relational dynamic meant, and what was being communicated more latently by her actions. I sensed her attempting to avoid the shame and concomitant envy she felt having to expose herself to her younger, successful, and confident therapist. In fact, I believed she was trying to unconsciously place me in her role and shift the dynamic of our dyad, empowering herself by occupying my role as the expert. It was far too early in our treatment to interpret her behavior; a premature interpretation would likely lead to shame and rage that she did not have the ego strength to tolerate at this time.

I closed the book, but continued holding it with both hands. "Thank you for bringing this in for me to look at. I'm wondering what you're imagining I'll do with it?" Clearly my question puzzled her, as her face contorted into various expressions of surprise.

"I want you to use it to order makeup. I circled my suggestions, colors I thought would complement you well. You're never going to meet a husband looking as you do." And there it was again. Yet, as harsh as Tess's statements were — she would continue devaluing my appearance for the first two years of our treatment together — except for that first occasion when I went home steaming, I never really felt that angry with her. Usually when I am devalued, I feel irate, insulted, and attacked, as most anyone would. Although she often inspired those feelings, the experience would dissipate quickly. This was quite significant and positively communicated something unique within our dyad. I stewed about this disparity for a long time.

Then one day it became inordinately clear. We were five weeks into our treatment together, and we still hadn't discussed Tess's feelings surrounding her termination with her former therapist. This is quite unusual; often when treatment terminates prematurely, patients have complex feelings about it, which are typically brought up intermittently throughout the early weeks of treatment with a new therapist. I had wanted to bring it up myself, but the timing never felt quite right, and the windows of opportunity were sparse.

My understanding of Tess's fixation with my appearance provided a most opportune opening. I wondered what feelings she still had about Sally, her former therapist, leaving. Did she also have analogous feelings about Sally's appearance? Parenthetically, Sally was quite unadorned; she was slightly overweight, never wore makeup, had short hair and dressed simply. Her presence was appealing as she was usually smiling, had healthy pinkish cheeks and warm brown eyes; but she was, without a doubt, less "put together" than I. Then I realized how to address both issues, to kill two birds with one stone.

"Did you bring in beauty magazines for Sally, too?" I looked on as Tess thought for a moment.

"I miss her warm smile," Tess commented. "She always seemed so cheery, but I don't think she helped me that much." *Wow, she just skirted right around that makeup question. And I'm probably going to have to address that issue about feeling like the work with Sally didn't help her. But for now...*

"Sally does have a bright disposition. But about her appearance, did you ever bring her Avon catalogs or remark on her presentation?" Tess took a much longer pause this time. *What's going through her mind? It looks like she's really thinking about the appearance thing. Oh gosh, I hope this isn't going to set her off.* Then...

"No, I didn't bring in beauty magazines for her and I never remarked on her appearance."

I have to be delicate about how I make this next remark. I don't want to come off as defensive, and I certainly don't want Tess to feel like I'm attacking her. Watch the tone, Jacquie.

"That's interesting, as Sally was even less made-up then me." *Please, please, please, don't get defensive.* I could see Tess's mind working, the wheels turning.

"I didn't think I could help Sally with her appearance. We're so different, style-wise." *Wow, thoughtful, gentle...*

"Besides, Sally's married. I wasn't worried about her having to find a husband. She already has one." *And a little motherly.*

This confirmed something else I had suspected was occurring within our dyad. As I observed Tess's appearance — which was rather different from mine — I glanced at the big chunky rings she wore every week to session. Big chunky rings are my primary and, more often than not, only accessory. As different as our outward appearances were, we did share *some* similarities. This exploration of her thoughts and images about Sally verified that Tess identified with me. As a result of this quite powerful identification, she was trying to unconsciously resolve her own "Fall from Glory" by assuring that I didn't make the same "mistakes" as she. Tess was attempting reparation of the pronounced regrets she had by making sure I didn't follow in her path.

This revelation gave me an even greater understanding of the assaults surrounding my appearance; however, it also left me feeling profound sadness. Tess, at 61 years old, believed her life was over. Tess's only solace was to believe that somehow she could help me. She unconsciously projected her own inadequacies and struggles onto me, because it was too agonizing for her at this point in treatment to take ownership over her own painful affect. I fully understood that it was still too early to interpret this dynamic, although the temptation to do so was overwhelming at times. When a patient uses a lower-level defense mechanism such as projection, one can be almost certain that the patient does not have the ego strength or internal resources to tolerate an interpretation. And with Tess, a premature interpretation of this kind could be toxic to our relationship. My role was to help build Tess's strengths, bear witness to her story, and create curiosity about what she was feeling.

Over the next few sessions, I began working diligently to help Tess recognize her unique and exceptional inner characteristics. This work could take months before we might make any headway, but I felt it important to begin building her up. Tess possessed many extraordinary traits: intelligence, curiosity, generosity, and remarkable thoughts to share. When I would explore these inner qualities with her, she would usually remark, "I have nothing to offer. If I did, I wouldn't be so alone." She would quickly shift the focus back onto me, providing beauty tips she believed would enhance my outward appearance. At times, her attacks were relentless. I felt that I was holding a metaphorical shield to fend off her assaults surrounding my appearance. For Tess, her outward appearance defined her identity formation. She could not even grasp the thought that she had other things to offer. I intuitively sensed that if I didn't give her a clinical push by encouraging exploration of the origin of her identity formation, we were going to remain stuck in this seemingly nonproductive dynamic spiral.

I was in the midst of my own quandary of how best to approach and encourage Tess to explore the underlying dynamic reasons that caused her to focus on outward appearances. I had my own hypothesis, but rather than risk a premature interpretation, I decided to take the more cautious approach of encouraging her to be curious with me. Tess bestowed upon me the most opportune opening at the start of our next session. She presented me with her book.

She placed it on my desk, explained that this was the story she had written and published about her battle with breast cancer, and asked that I read it. I already knew I would accept and read the book, but I wanted and needed to explore what she was communicating by giving me the book to read. And another important question floated around in my mind: *Why now? Is there something in the book that she wants me to know but can't bring herself to tell me?*

We collaboratively discussed what she wanted me to learn about her — what she was expressing — by inviting me to read her book. Tess shared that her book would show me how much her life had changed since her two-year battle with breast cancer.

"I used to have friends, a lover, and a life," she shared in a meek, shameful voice. This reminded me of her "Fall from Glory:" *Here it is,* I thought, *on my desk, just how it happened.* My curiosity was piqued, and I felt a slight flush of adrenaline.

Most patients initially adopt a closed-off, secretive stance when they begin therapy. And Tess followed suit, particularly regarding her childhood. So her frequent forthcoming attitude about her past sexual relationships, "Fall from Glory" stories, and brazen comments about my appearance caught me off guard — until I would remember that she had been in therapy for nearly two years. Regardless of how much or how little progress she might have made with Sally, Tess certainly had learned to readily share at least a segment of her feelings and experiences — and that was a building block to creating a therapeutic environment more conducive to personal growth.

"You have expressed quite clearly how your life has changed. What else do you imagine I will get from reading your book?"

"I want to know what you think." She thought a moment. "Sally read it." She rose in her chair, a little proud. I had the sense that the book was a concrete representation of who she was prior to her "Fall from Glory." *This book. She wants me to see the way she used to see herself, how she feels she used to be.* I surmised she did this as a reaction to reduce the shame that was beginning to arise through my current inquiries, but I didn't verbalize my theory, I just…

"Thank you so much for sharing the book with me, Tess. That was a generous gesture." I immediately put the book in my bag so I wouldn't forget it.

"You're welcome." Tess smoothed her blouse and sat a little straighter.

From the book, I gained a substantial amount of information regarding Tess's life prior to and during her battle with breast cancer. Tess had been diagnosed and treated for occult breast cancer, which is discovered and diagnosed through a biopsy of the surrounding lymph nodes. For Tess, it was the lymph nodes in her armpits that confirmed the diagnosis. Her oncologist informed Tess that with occult cancer, it is often the case that they cannot find the cancer in the breast itself; consequently, the safest and most appropriate treatment was to remove the entire breast.

Tess's panic was quite pronounced in her book; interestingly, it did not focus on the diagnosis of cancer, but rather the loss of her breast. In fact, upon receiving her diagnosis,

Tess's initial resolve was to ignore what the doctor told her and rush to the salon to have her hair done. I stopped, then re-read this part of her book several times. I struggled to reconcile my shock at Tess's initial reaction. I found it incredulous.

The content of her book focused a great deal on her incessant and relentless search to find a doctor who would treat her with chemotherapy without removing her entire breast. Tess searched all over Manhattan; she went to only the most outstanding oncologists. The end result was always the same: for Tess to have a high chance of beating this cancer, she had to have her entire breast removed. Tess eventually conceded; her breast was removed *and* she received chemotherapy. Once she was cancer-free, she wasted no time getting a breast implant. During this two-year ordeal, she had a huge support network.

As I read her narrative, I experienced such sorrow for her. Yet it felt as if I were reading a stranger's story, not Tess's. The person in her book relied on a support network, but possessed strong and unrelenting focus. Her life was full and hopeful. However, the person I was sitting with twice a week in therapy felt deadened, broken, and hopeless. After reading her book, I was certain that the loss of her breast instigated her "Fall from Glory." In Tess's mind, this change in her physical appearance left her damaged. This thought process eventually drove her to the place she now resided — one of complete isolation, misery, shame and deformity — and contaminated her with the feeling that no one could ever desire her again.

That Saturday, a torrential downpour prevented me from doing my early morning run, so I wasn't able to hit the pavement until nearly ten — which had a ripple effect on the rest of my day. It meant I'd have to take care of a few errands right after my training session. My sweaty, smelly training session. *What would Tess think about me shopping in public looking like a ragamuffin?* Picturing this got me ruminating about Tess and her feelings of shame and deformity.

Having had years of experience working with trauma patients, I knew that her profound reaction to the loss of her breast suggested a much earlier trauma. There is a notable difference between the ways two adult patients respond to a trauma, when one of those patients had also experienced an earlier trauma.

I had no doubt Tess's response was indicative of one who suffered previous trauma, someone left vulnerable and lacking the internal resources necessary to resiliently recover from her ordeal. I thought about how resistant she was to discussing her early childhood experiences; these experiences shape one's internal identity formation. Reviewing, perhaps reliving, the trauma would be painful for Tess, but if we were to continue working together — and honestly, I still teetered on the fence — we would need to explore these experiences, in order for us to really garner her strengths and develop greater internal resources.

This uncertainty about our compatibility to work together and my ability to help her stood at the fore of my thoughts when our next unexpected meeting occurred.

Feeling invigorated after my run, and equally in need of a shower, I forced myself to stop in Bloomingdale's before I returned home. I hoped it would not be too busy. I truly dislike department stores, and it did not help that I was there to purchase yet another bridal shower gift. I must have been to the bridal registry at least four times within the past year. *The saleswoman will surely recognize me*, I laughed to myself. It wasn't the easiest time as I had recently gone through a long, drawn-out breakup and wasn't really in a "bridal-ish" mood.

I opened the large doors on Lexington Avenue and forced myself through them. Dressed in my sweat-drenched Adidas sweatshirt and shorts, I weaved my way through the makeup department on my way to the escalator. A flawlessly-skinned woman sprayed me with perfume. *Really?*

That's when I heard my name called — "Jacquie? Is that you?" — and I tried to get lost in the crowd. Then, as I was passing the MAC Cosmetics counter, a hand touched my shoulder just as I heard my name spoken aloud. All the blood drained from my face as I turned, in what felt like slow motion, only to meet her eyes. *Of all the people I could possibly run into...*

And then I summarily passed out.

Well, not literally, but the thought occurred to me that I might, and that actually passing out could have been easier than having to navigate gracefully through this chance encounter with Tess. And in the makeup department of her favorite store. Oh, the irony.

"Jacquie! Hi. It's so nice to see you," Tess beamed. *Me. Grimy. In sweats. It must be REALLY nice to see me. Especially looking in dire need of a makeover. This, Tess, must be your dream come true. And cue up the heart palpitations. What a pleasure.* "Did you just come from a run? You look so pale and tired. Here, come with me." She was pulling me back toward the MAC counter.

A young woman with bright blue eye shadow turned around. "May I help you?"

"Yes, please," Tess stated, elated, as she kept her hand firmly wrapped around my sweat-covered forearm. "She needs a full makeover!" she continued. *Oh-my-gosh! What am I going to do?*

As dire as the moment seemed — the kind my friend Taylor would insist called for a "dramatic, concocted story to get your butt out of there, STAT!" — I decided to simply tell Tess the truth, the best road to take particularly since she was my patient.

"Tess, I'm in a bit of a rush," I stated as gently as I could.

"Nonsense. This will only take ten minutes. And you know that if you want to find a husband, makeup is the key ingredient. You more than anyone should know how important first impressions can be." She looked to the saleswoman for a cajoling nod of agreement. Now they were both staring at me. With Tess's grip on my forearm keeping me at bay, they awaited my permission to commence their pet project. I suddenly imagined myself leaving the store, bridal gift-less, strutting down the avenue, appearing clownish in my sweaty running gear juxtaposed by red-carpet face paint.

What a dilemma! I didn't want to injure Tess. Despite her annoying persistence, I believed her overture to be genuine. Her actions didn't feel like a boundary violation on her part, but rather her authentic belief that she could help me find a husband.

Were she successful in helping me, I am sure she believed my ultimate pairing with a mate might reduce her own feelings of regret and loss. However, clinically it was important for Tess to discuss these feelings in the session. If I participated in this outside-of-session enactment of her feelings, I would be colluding; I would be helping her avoid talking through what she was feeling. And this was not good for her therapeutically. It would be akin to putting on a Band-Aid, but leaving the cut untreated, and allowing a permanent scar to develop.

Okay, I need to get out of this situation. And I've got to use finesse. If Tess gets angry, we'll process her feelings in session.

I responded empathically, but firmly, "Tess, it's so kind of you to show concern for me, really, but I'm in a bit of a rush." I then tagged on an addendum, almost whispering to protect her confidentiality, "We can speak more about this in our next session." She let go of my arm, and I noticed a sense of defeat in her eyes. It tugged at my heart, but I knew I needed to hold steadfast to what I was stating.

"What are you here for? Maybe I can help you," she said. "I'm a great shopper." *Thank you, Tess, for not taking the hint to get lost and making a difficult situation even more difficult. Maybe I should just run out.* I had an image of myself turning around and bolting — opening the heavy front doors and sprinting up Lexington Avenue to my apartment.

I again responded honestly, knowing with near certainty that my answer was going to leave me in the bridal registry department with Tess at my side. "I'm here to purchase a gift for my friend's bridal shower."

"Oh!" Her deep blue eyes lit up and her pupils dilated, obvious signs of her genuine excitement. "Gifts are my specialty. I'm definitely coming with you. Did you have anything specific in mind?" I edged slowly to the foot of the escalator, trying to scramble together a plan of action. I had to get rid of her. I did not yet know her case well enough to develop an outing like this into a useful, impromptu session. And honestly, I didn't want her around. I just wanted to get in and get out of Bloomies. And I was beginning to feel infringed upon. Which made me feel guilty about wanting her to disappear. Which made me feel annoyed that she was making me feel guilty about wanting her to leave me alone.

Yet still, she followed.

"Your hair looks so frizzy, Jacquie," she stated with her usual edge. *Thank you so much, Tess, for your self-esteem booster. And for the record, you do realize that hair gets messy and frizzy while sweating during a run?* And then she added, "You really need a good haircut."

And just like that, my jaw clenched. But Tess was too oblivious to notice. I looked at her and nodded with a tight smile as we rode up the escalator together. Despite my anxiety, tension and overall annoyance, I did find the circumstances of our chance encounter a bit humorous. At least I did after the fact. Not so much in the moment.

While walking toward the bridal registry counter, I explained to Tess that I planned to give my friend a gift card so that she could choose whatever she wanted. It was what I usually gave at bridal showers. I could immediately see that Tess did not approve. Nor did she keep silent about her disapproval. "But there are so many fabulous things to choose from and a gift card is, well, it's downright cold. It'll be fun to pick something out."

"I'd really prefer to get the gift card, Tess."

"Oh, come on. Every girl loves shopping if you just give it a chance." She barreled ahead. "Honestly, I'm not even a big fan of gift registries. Oh, I know they're so practical and it keeps people from giving duplicate gifts. And I guess it's great for choosing the correct china, silverware and stemware patterns, but honestly, there's nothing personal about it. There's no heart. And there's especially no heart in gift cards."

Did she just call me heartless?

"That was terrible of me to say that," Tess spoke as though reading my mind. "I'm sorry. I didn't mean to suggest that about you. I just get so passionate about shopping."

I stood my ground, half-feeling like I might have to raise my voice. Finally, Tess backed off. But she was irritated; I could tell. And then, "You know, it should be you getting married. You really have to work on your appearance, Jacqueline," she stated, hitting my name with an aggravated tone.

And suddenly the other occasions from our therapy sessions came back to me. Whenever she felt cornered or annoyed or displeased, or the conversation was not going in the safe, non-threatening way she wanted, she referred to me as Jacqueline, rather than Dr. Jacquie or just plain Jacquie, and practically spit out my name with a snippy tenor.

As we walked away from the counter, she asked if I would like to have a late lunch. *Wow, she's a challenge, and a relentless one at that!* "Tess, thank you for the invitation, but it really isn't appropriate given the boundaries of the patient/therapist relationship." She nodded with understanding and gazed downward. I felt bad as I knew she was lonely and looking for a dinner companion, but I also knew that I was right. And I believed she knew it, too.

I finally was able to separate from the situation. I left Tess back by the MAC counter looking at lipsticks, and she said, "I guess I'll see you next week."

I responded with a smile. "Yes, you will." But as I opened the heavy front doors of Bloomingdale's and began walking home, I thought that maybe next week should be our last week. I was exhausted. She was exhausting.

I had experienced chance encounters with patients before, but this one was the most complicated. Usually, there's a bit of awkwardness in the exchange as we find ourselves caught off-guard in unfamiliar territory. Tess exhibited no signs of discomfort, and contrarily seemed thrilled and eager to engage with me outside of our usual professional context. I knew Tess was lonely; I also understood that there was a personal investment in guiding me toward making better decisions than she had.

But I wondered if I was the right therapist for her. Was our co-created therapeutic dyad creating an atmosphere that might disallow disclosure of underlying shame and self-hate? Or was it ideal, and I just needed to work hard to shift her place in the relational dynamics — supplanting her from a makeover/marital consultant to a patient needing help? Either way, Tess, I decided as I walked up the stairs to my apartment, presented a unique and new challenge.

I looked in the bathroom mirror while pulling the ponytail holder out of my sweaty hair. *I have beautiful hair! What does she mean frizzy!?* And then. *Oy. She's getting to you, Jacquie. She's getting to you.* Despite this absolute recognition of my countertransferential feelings, my last thought before getting in the shower was… *but I could use a bit of a trim. My ends are dry…*

And then…

Maybe I really am biting off more than I can chew. Maybe Tess will be the straw that broke the camel's back. MY back. She's relentless and definitely has little regard for boundaries; I wonder if she can even respect the therapeutic relationship. She tried bulldozing me in public today. Maybe I made a mistake taking her on as a patient. Maybe I was right. Maybe I'm not the right therapist for her. Is there something unique to our co-created dyad that's provoking her?

Tess and I never established a trial period, a time where we test the waters, see if we like working with each other. Many therapists do this. It allows the patient and therapist the opportunity to feel each other out. Sometimes a patient's ideology clashes so fiercely with the therapist that working together becomes impossible. Or a therapist may feel that a patient's issues could be better served by a colleague who specializes in that particular area. This trial period provides the patient with an expectation: "This new relationship is only temporary until we *both* feel that successful therapeutic progress can be accomplished."

I have known patients who burned through four or five therapists before finding one they liked working with; one that they felt they could relate to and truly understood them. This trial period is different for every therapist. It can be established within the first session; however, I have known therapists who will establish a trial period as long as four weeks.

I developed my own ideology surrounding this trial period from Dr. Gwen, my own therapist. She offered our initial session as a consult; a "let's see how it feels and decide if we want to work together" session. This felt right to me; I felt a collaborative decision was being made and early enough that I wouldn't be wasting time and money getting to know each other, only to have the treatment terminated a month later. As an addendum to this initial session, I do check in with all of my patients throughout the course of the therapy, to make sure they are feeling that they are getting what they need.

In Tess's case, already an "expert" patient with nearly two years under her belt, I transitioned and kept her at the twice-weekly sessions she had established with Sally. I didn't discuss any trial consult nor explain the "check-in with each other" therapeutic frame I offered to new patients in the first session. It was early in my professional development, and I made the incorrect assumption that since Sally believed Tess and I were a good match, I need not discuss the "trial consult" with her. Additionally, I usually start with once-weekly sessions, and then determine if two or even three times a week might be a better option for a particular patient. Maybe I made a mistake; maybe the twice-weekly sessions created an intensity that simply was too much, too soon.

We had been working together for almost two months. I already sensed a bond growing between us. But was it a therapeutically sound alliance? Did we have the clinical rapport required to survive the often complicated and turbulent nature characteristic of the therapeutic process? Without a firm therapeutic alliance, the relationship cannot withstand the necessary healing process.

It's only fair to her that, if I need to end this, I discuss termination soon. Before she gets too attached. I'm already cutting it closer than I'd like.

I've got a serious decision to make.

Chapter 3:
She Called Me Verna

I woke up feeling strange, foggy. As I stirred under my comforter, trying to rouse myself from bed to pour a steaming mug of the coffee, I could smell brewing from the next room — thank goodness for timed coffee machines — I did my best to sort out why I felt so peculiar. I ran through the previous day's events, slow and steady, ticking off each appointment. Then a rush of adrenalin surged through me. I leaped out of bed so quickly, I stepped on my poor cat as he impatiently waited for his breakfast. *Take a deep breath,* I told myself. *Feed Snoopy, eat breakfast, and go for a run.* I hoped this would help me deal with the complex aftermath of what happened with Anne the night before, the disaster that was now overrunning my thoughts.

I blamed myself for letting Anne leave my office the preceding evening. I knew with absolute certainty that something wasn't right. I could have prevented all the hysteria if I had just dialed emergency while she sat with me in therapy. By the time I had processed the session and decided to call 911 to pick her up at home, the damage had already been done. I had asked her before she left if she was okay to go.

She looked at me, eyes focused and earnest. "Yes, of course."

That specific phrasing should have tipped me off. She assured me she would come in for the extra session we scheduled for the following day. I convinced myself I felt appeased by this. *She'll be fine.* But as it turns out, I should not have let her leave; it was a huge error on my part.

And now Anne was in police custody, arrested.

It is always difficult to make a quick judgment call and decide if a patient needs to be hospitalized. I was reminded of one of my other patients, Jenny. Just about a year before the incident with Anne, I had made a 911 call to send the police to pick up Jenny at her apartment in Brooklyn. It was one of the most painful experiences I have had as a clinician. *Did this cause my hesitancy? Was I tentative to call because of what happened with Jenny?* I thought back to that ominous day. Jenny was going through a horrible breakup with her boyfriend, which exacerbated her already depressed mood. In the midst of this, she lost her mother.

Jenny's ability to manage these two profound losses led her to display symptoms of major depression. Her self-care declined (a significant symptom); she was agitated, unable to sleep or eat, and spent most of our twice-weekly session in absolute hysterics. She just could not stop crying or calm herself down. In addition, her best friend called me and revealed that Jenny was threatening suicide; she even had a plan — overdosing on painkillers. I tried to get Jenny to admit herself into the hospital. I even offered to go with her; she refused and continued to deny suicidality. I really didn't want to call 911 and have her taken to the hospital against her will; this decision is never easy, but I felt I had to. I thought it would stabilize her, and more importantly, save her life.

I consulted with a senior psychologist, and she agreed I had no choice; Jenny needed to be involuntarily hospitalized. I still remember the day she was taken into custody by the police and EMTs; it felt like it happened yesterday. Once the police arrived at her apartment, they called me. Jenny, who is tiny but quite a feisty woman, was screaming and hysterically crying in the background. It was obvious from her screaming that she was fighting them as they were handcuffing her. She was repeatedly and desperately asking if she could just change her clothes; they wouldn't let her. It all happened so fast. But eventually, the EMT, whom I was speaking with, dropped his phone, which indicated the true extent of the struggle that ensued between Jenny and the team that was taking her to the emergency room.

It was horrific. I knew I was doing the right thing for Jenny as a professional in charge of her care, but as a human being I felt devastated by what I heard. To hear one of my patients screaming, struggling, and being taken away against her will aroused incredibly overwhelming and heartrending emotions. It took me quite a while to recover from the emotions and memories of that day. In the end, once Jenny calmed and stabilized, she thanked me. Despite the tragic nature of the whole experience, I knew having Jenny involuntarily committed was in her best interest. However, on an emotional level, in the moment, it didn't feel that way.

The situation with Anne was quite different, but it did require the same kind of judgment call. As clinicians, we are often faced with situations that require quick assessments; consequently, we often have doubts about the conclusion. We affect patient's lives on a profound level, and the choices we make on a daily basis are often difficult and challenging. How Anne's story ends clearly reflects this scenario. But I am jumping ahead. The episode that would eventually end her treatment with me wouldn't happen for another two years.

I first started seeing Anne twice a week when she came to me following a violent and disturbing suicide attempt; this incident led to her having to drop out of college and move back to New York to live with her family. She was 28 years old when we began our treatment, and she desperately wanted to return to college. She had two more years to complete her degree in business, and she conveyed how important it was for her to move on with her life. But there was something, or more accurately, "someone" standing in her way. She shared that she was being stalked by a young man from college and this was preventing her from being able to move on.

Interesting. A stalker? Wow, this is a first for me! I was incredibly curious, but I needed to gather information concerning her suicide attempt before we began to explore anything else. I needed to assess the risk of another attempt in the present. So I opened up the therapeutic space and began inquiring about what led up to her desire to kill herself.

Anne was not a great historian. Though many patients are hesitant to share in the beginning, she was fully closed-off and provided only the most basic information. As for her overall presentation, it appeared entirely congruent with her need to cover and protect herself. I could tell she was attractive, but she did her best to conceal this. She wore layers of clothing, even during the warmer months; glasses, no makeup, and her hair up in a bun. She spoke quietly and barely opened her mouth while conversing. I suspected abuse, but said nothing. I didn't know Anne yet, and she didn't offer any information overtly that would make a line of inquiry surrounding abuse appropriate. So I waited and stayed with her where *she* was. In my clinical experience, trying to explore something so personal — essentially without the patient's "permission" — is a huge therapeutic "no-no."

I began by inquiring about the events surrounding her suicide attempt. It took at least three sessions for her to be able to articulate clearly and provide me with enough pertinent information to piece together what actually happened. It was so difficult for Anne, and I truly felt her struggle — but it was like pulling teeth to gather important information to help her.

This was the case throughout our entire therapeutic journey together. Her propensity to constantly return to her dissatisfaction and frustration with her life, and her inability to move on because of her stalker, acted as logjams in our therapeutic stream of progress. This eventually became the major focus of our treatment; it was quite a complex and enigmatic treatment, as I struggled to understand what was really happening with Anne and her stalker.

Anne's suicide attempt occurred right at the beginning of her junior year in college. She denied any history of suicidal ideation or attempts prior to this one, and denied any present ideation or intent.

"So what happened, Anne?" I tried to keep my tone gentle and genuine. She pulled the top of her hoodie over her head. Her eyes darted around the room. As I waited for her response, I felt the floor begin vibrating, like a subway train was running under the building. Except that the subway does not run under the building. Then I realized Anne was causing the vibrations, her legs bouncing and shaking so fiercely that her sneakers started to squeak. She finally looked out from under her hood. I met her gaze and put on a warm smile, hoping to ease her tension.

"I, um, guess I tried to kill myself." She looked at me. "I mean, you know, I *did* try to kill myself." I chose not to respond.

I wanted her to continue, so I stayed silent and waited. After a moment... "I stabbed myself a bunch of times in the stomach." *Wow, that's a painful and aggressive way to kill yourself. Either she had a psychotic break, was dissociative, or was violently angry; maybe a combination of the three.* She looked away from me. "But I survived." Anne said this with a matter-of-fact coolness.

What I was able to learn through Anne's narrative and the hospital records she gave me consent to retrieve was that Anne did, in fact, nearly die after repeatedly stabbing herself in the stomach. She had punctured her liver, stomach lining and nearly bled to death before her roommate came home and called 911. The hospital reports indicated that there were at least six gashes. Anne, this young woman, seemingly gentle, had been so distraught, so trapped, she felt she had no choice of action but to stab herself. Six times. Maybe more!

Anne was in the hospital for four months. The first month was to stabilize her physically. After that, they moved her to an inpatient psychiatric ward for three more months. Her diagnosis at discharge, which I learned from the hospital report, was Schizoaffective. I couldn't ignore the diagnosis, but because of my therapeutic style, I worked hard not to let this diminish my understanding of Anne as a unique human being. I preferred not to see Anne as a diagnosis. She was a person, a human being, and a struggling and conflicted one at that. This is the position from which I wanted to understand Anne.

And so I continued my exploration. I tried, with Anne's help, to figure out what led up to such a brutal act on herself. Anne — no surprise — found it difficult to talk about what happened, and it took a great deal of patience on my part to allow her the space to slowly explain what happened. She remained stiff and tentative during her disclosures. I found myself experiencing a dual thought process while sitting with Anne. I not only listened empathically and encouraged elaboration about what she thought triggered her suicide attempt, but also simultaneously felt strongly that Anne was a survivor of incest. The latter came to me as an intuitive feeling that I imagine developed from years of experience sitting with patients who were victims of sexual abuse.

Jacquie, stop! Don't go down that road yet. If this is, in fact, the case, wait for an appropriate opening to ask Anne anything about this. She hasn't mentioned abuse. Bringing it up could derail the little progress we've made and would likely damage the tenuous connection we've established.

Anne began to open up a bit more after about two months of hard work, establishing rapport and a working alliance. She revealed that she met a boy in the spring semester of her sophomore year in college. It remained unclear what the extent of their relationship was. When I would gently ask Anne for details about their relationship, she would often divert attention away from the topic by moving on to something else, usually something more concrete and easier to talk about. And often it included the frustrations surrounding being stalked. I had to honor her resistance, and recognize that Anne at this point in therapy should not be pushed nor confronted. I could sense her fragility.

Anne was protecting herself; her defenses were definitely not purposeful, they were there because Anne couldn't fully accept nor process what happened with this young man. It was too painful. I did begin to wonder, based on the content of Anne's derivatives and her associations, if there were some relationship between this young man and her stalker. Anne made it clear that some sort of romantic relationship transpired between this boy and her, and that the relationship ended when she saw him the first day of classes in the fall semester of her junior year with another girl. I was able to extrapolate from what Anne was willing to share that she confronted this male "friend" and it was he who ended their relationship. Anne felt profoundly rejected.

I started to wonder if the relationship with this boy was real or fantasized. There was just something intangible in Anne's narrative that was causing me to question the reality surrounding their relationship. I found the going tough with Anne. As professionals, clinical training teaches us that no matter how curious we, as clinicians, are about the "reality" of what a patient is presenting, we need to stay with what the patient is telling us;

this is the patient's experience, and we need to stay emotionally and empathically connected to the patient's "reality." However, we simultaneously need to recognize and process why one might be questioning the patient's narrative; the intuitive nature of what one is feeling when sitting with a particular patient is vitally important, but must remain contained.

This dilemma comes up continuously with my supervisees and in my trauma case conference. We cannot control our thoughts or our questioning of the reliability of what a particular patient is reporting, but we must suspend this self-query while in the room with the patient. So, for two years, I sat in this uncomfortable juxtaposition with Anne. When I look back on that ominous day when I let Anne leave my office, I believe I was so immersed in the struggle between what was real and what wasn't, that it grossly affected my clinical judgment. And it resulted in poor Anne being arrested.

It was clear that the rejection that Anne experienced led to her suicide attempt. She described that after he ended the relationship and made it apparent that he wanted nothing to do with Anne, she felt frantic and out of control. She ran back to her dorm room, and without any conscious thought or intent, she just started stabbing herself over and over. I felt chilled by her story, and concerned about her impulsivity in this moment. The fact that there was no reportable forethought made me quite anxious. It suggested that Anne was capable of doing something like this again — without any warning. *Not good. Soooo not good. I really need to remain vigilant of this propensity, particularly since it's incongruent with Anne's over-controlled clinical presentation.*

Anne's living arrangements fascinated me. She lived with her grandmother and uncle in a small apartment in Brooklyn. She didn't even have her own room. She slept on the pull-out couch in the living room, affording her almost no privacy. Months earlier, I wondered with Anne where her parents were and why she decided not to live with them. She tightened up whenever I tried to explore this with her. *Okay, I definitely hit on a sensitive topic. This is important.* I couldn't shake the idea that Anne was the victim of incest.

With some gentle coaxing, she eventually shared that her father was a medical doctor, and that both of her parents lived in a large house in Brooklyn with Anne's three younger siblings. Again, I gently inquired about her relationship with them and her decision not to live there. And again, Anne clammed up. I felt myself wanting to push her, or at least notice with her the obvious discomfort she displayed. My intuition was that this was not the correct direction; I needed to wait. As our sessions continued and the treatment progressed, I was eventually able to make some sense of Anne's situation.

Anne did possess many strengths and perfectly viable concrete treatment goals. She wanted to finish her college degree, eventually be gainfully employed and have her own apartment. I noticed that Anne was able to be more relaxed and open when discussing these goals, so we began to work towards them. My intended goal: to simultaneously foster her strengths while exploring her internal barricades. We were making progress, but with every few steps forward, Anne's stalker would enter the picture, always interfering, resulting in one step back. This young lady would be a tough nut to crack — absolutely no pun intended.

I had surmised for some time about an early childhood or possibly adolescent trauma in Tess's life — which, I was convinced, was the culprit that left her without the skills to emotionally recover from her breast cancer.

Though months before, I had nearly handed Tess off to another therapist after our meeting in Bloomingdale's, in the end I chose to keep her as my patient. If anything, her bossiness, her strong opinions about my appearance and singlehood might be the secret pass code to access her fears and self-assigned — and self-maligned — body image. Maybe, I decided, just maybe I would turn out to be the perfect therapist for her.

So as time passed, I opened, with anxious trepidation, the therapeutic space between us and slowly probed into Tess's early childhood experiences — most importantly, her relationship with her parents. Right off the bat, Tess displayed signs of discomfort over the emotions elicited from discussing her parental relationships.

"I can see this is really difficult for you. Do you have a sense of what you're feeling?"

"My childhood was awfully sad," she said while trying to keep her voice even and emotionless. "I don't like to think about it. It makes me feel more depressed."

I've often noticed that many patients hesitate when it comes to asking me questions about their treatment; perhaps they feel uncomfortable asking about the therapeutic process, yet it is my belief that educating a patient about what the therapist's line — my line — of inquiry means, and what techniques are being used that can relieve them of their dread of the unknown; that the road ahead doesn't have to be dark and scary, but rather light and familiar. And this brought me to the decision to share with Tess why it was important for me to understand her earlier experiences. I was sure that once she understood how early dynamics can become internalized, and how these internalizations define who one is, she would slowly, carefully, but assuredly, open up about her early life.

I was glad, and a little relieved, that I was right.

Tess's father first married her mother's sister; they had a daughter together. A horrible and tragic car accident killed her father's wife and their daughter about five years into their marriage. Tess's father was devastated; this woman was the "love of his life." Tess's mother — her father's sister-in-law at the time — consoled him; and he consoled her. Their shared miseries eventually led to a bond that turned romantic — quickly — and the two were married a year later. I sat, riveted to the chair. Tess's sadness was palpable as she divulged this incredible narrative.

"I'm so sorry, Tess. What's it like to share this with me?"

"When I was a young child, I didn't fully understand what he went through. But as I got older, I felt sad for my father whenever I thought about how he must have felt losing his wife and daughter. I mean, when it sunk in that I had a sister that I would never know because she died before I was born, and at such a young age, it made me sad, too. But, um…" Her mouth hung open for a few moments as she wrung her hands. "I, um…"

"What is it?"

"This is going to sound awful, make me seem cold, but…"

"It's okay, Tess. All feelings are valid."

"I felt bad for my father, but… well, it made me a little angry."

Wow. I think we finally might have made a breakthrough into unexplored territory. I waited for Tess to continue, but she faltered. I needed to give her a prod, but a gentle one, as I didn't want her to feel intruded upon and end this disclosure.

"How so?"

"I don't think he loved me or my mother as much as he did his first wife and their daughter." She spit this out like it tasted sour in her mouth, hurried, the words tripping to get off her tongue. I wasn't sure if it was because she felt embarrassed saying it, or if she truly was still angry with her father and detested the idea of what she revealed to me.

"What makes you think that?"

"I could just feel it, like he was holding back."

Maybe he was. Loss is devastating and some people never recover. I let her sit for a moment hoping she would continue, that she'd open this part of herself to me, speak the words and perhaps release some of her resentment.

"I think my mother sensed it, too. She was miserable and melancholy her entire life. And I felt like I could never do anything right. She often made passing, negative remarks about how I dressed and looked and how I held myself. My, ah, what's the word? My comportment." Tess took a deep breath, then pressed on. "My mother described a girl she knew from grade school. Verna. She wasn't well-liked and her family was poor, so she didn't dress nicely. Always had holes in her clothes and knotted, matted hair. When my mother didn't approve of my appearance, she would call me Verna."

"Gosh, Tess, that must have been a lot for a little girl to handle. All those feelings."

As Tess's eyes met my gaze, my heart sunk. Intuitively, I knew what was coming next, but I still wasn't prepared.

"I felt unlovable."

And there it is. "Do you still feel unlovable?"

Her voice caught. "Yes."

Well, at least I have some idea of why she's always critiquing my appearance. I made a mental note to further explore this connection, but said nothing as I didn't want to stop her mid-story and change the line of inquiry. It had taken over a year for Tess to disclose this to me, and I didn't want to break her stride.

The next part of her narrative must have been unbearable for Tess to live through because it was nearly unbearable to hear. Her mother became ill with lymphoma when Tess was just twelve years old. Tess knew something was wrong, but when she asked, her parents insisted everything was fine. She recalled intensely vivid and disturbing memories of her mother throwing up many times, frequenting doctors and eventually losing her hair. No matter how many times Tess asked, the answer was the same: "Everything is fine." It wasn't until Tess was sixteen and it was apparent that her mother wasn't going to recover from her illness that her father sat Tess down and explained the severity of her mother's illness. Tess recalled feeling enraged.

"How could they do this to me? They both lied!"

And the lie left Tess little time to spend with her mother before she passed away six months later.

I wasn't sure exactly what I was feeling in regard to what I had learned about Tess in these sessions. I thought about her a great deal in between sessions, trying desperately to find words for what *I* was feeling. I knew I felt the heaviness she was still carrying, but I also felt it stirred up my own anxiety about death, and the vulnerability we as humans live with on a daily basis. Our next session nearly broke me.

This was an intense session, so I wasn't surprised to see that Tess and I ran a few minutes beyond her time. When she left, I followed her out the door to let my next patient know that I would be with her shortly. Though her session wasn't scheduled to start for a few minutes, the restroom was calling my name. But when Tess and I left my office, my new patient wasn't waiting. *Great! Maybe I can get back before she comes in.* I ran down the hall to the restroom.

When I returned, Kristy, my new patient, still hadn't arrived. I looked at my watch to discover that it was only two minutes to the hour. Technically she wasn't late, but usually new patients make it a point to be early.

Then I heard the elevator make its telltale *ding* before its doors opened. The woman who stepped out of the elevator immediately made me think of Maxine.

We had been working hard in therapy to reorganize the way Maxine thought about herself, ostensibly creating a self-image that had nothing to do with the way she was earning money, which can be quite difficult for a sex worker to reconcile. It was slowly beginning to help, and I noticed her inner strengths rising on the horizon. We had been working together for just about a year when I had my first session with Kristy.

I had spoken on the phone with Kristy briefly when we set up our initial session time. I usually ask for a short summary of why one is seeking treatment. Kristy responded that she was a medical student, and was having a difficult time managing stress. *Hmm, well having experienced this firsthand toward the end of my doctoral program, I definitely can relate.*

So when the elevator doors opened and I saw the woman, I just knew this had to be Kristy. And a first impression popped into my head that I couldn't shake.

As I watched Kristy walk toward me, I waited outside of my office door — convinced I was having a momentary loss of sanity. She was dressed casually, in rolled-up designer jeans and a hooded sweatshirt. But when I looked down, I thought my eyes were playing tricks on me. She wore skyscraper-high Red Stilettos. I blinked a couple times, attempting to readjust my focus. I felt sure that I had imagined it, but no. There they were walking toward me. Kristy clacked down the hall toward me atop six-inch Red Stilettos. *Oh my God. 42nd Street!*

Get a grip, Jacquie. Prostitutes aren't the only people who wear red shoes. Besides, she's a medical student and she said nothing of sex work on the phone. Then again, why would she? Maybe she is a sex worker, but it has nothing to do with why she's seeking treatment. Or maybe she didn't feel comfortable discussing something illegal via telephone? Or maybe you're not thinking clearly due to sleep deprivation caused by repeatedly waking up from those green-dress dreams. My sense of humor helped. My last thought before Kristy sat down was, *"Am I being haunted by the Red Stilettos!?"*

This is what I mean by first impressions being hard to break.

Kristy sat comfortable and confidently on the couch. She exuded strength and poise, but also a degree of coldness, aloofness; I sensed it immediately. *Hmm, I don't like the way this feels. There is something... something?* And by mid-session, I realized — *she's quite detached, okay, that's not it. Then...*

I feel like at any moment she could punch me in the face. Oy, lovely! No, it's okay, Jacquie. It's just her defenses... her resistance... she's hiding something. Damn it! Pay attention to her narrative. You'll process this after session and in supervision. Right now, you are colluding. You are detaching from her. She's not really going to punch you in the face.

"I hate it!" Kristy was describing the ridiculously long hours she spent studying and doing her rotations. She was apoplectic, and as she raised her voice, I felt a bit cornered. And though her anger was poignant, it incited a degree of fear in me. After years of experience with forensic patients, this was highly unusual for me. But I knew we wouldn't get anywhere if I didn't address it. I needed to be curious about her resistance.

So, feeling a bit like my tail was between my legs, I spoke. "Kristy, you seem agitated, almost enraged. Can you tell me about this?"

She jumped up from the couch and stood up tall. I looked up at her with a knot in the pit of my stomach. *Is she going to hit me?* Then in a surprising move, she simply kicked off her Red Stilettos, plopped back into the couch with her legs folded Indian-style, and leaned back. Her mood changed; she appeared more at ease.

"My father's a doctor. I never really gave a lot of thought to what I wanted from life. I was expected to go to medical school. Always. And now that I'm nearing the finish line, I'm beginning to worry that it wasn't the right decision!" *Jackpot. Now we're getting somewhere!* Her intonation was markedly cool and strong, and her lips were clamped water-tight, but I definitely felt less aggression in the room.

With my curiosity piqued, "Expected? What did your father say?"

She paused and broke eye contact; she clearly was uncomfortable. She was fumbling with the zipper on her hooded sweatshirt. Finally, she met my eyes. She played with her sweatshirt, unzipping it halfway down her front, then zipping it close to the neck, then down again. Up. Down. Up. Down. This continued while she spoke. "Look, Dr. Simon, in my culture, no one has to say anything. It's an unspoken rule."

It was important for me to engage her about this. Get her to elaborate and delve into her feelings. "Okay, Kristy. Please tell me about the unspoken rule." She shared that in Asian culture, one is expected to become a doctor or lawyer. At the very least, something in a highly regarded profession, like biochemist. Since her family consisted of many doctors, she always knew that would be her path.

I was still unable to really feel anything from her in the room. Her narrative was cool, detached, and methodical. Although at the end of the session, I noticed just the slightest bit of sadness in her eyes. There was something Kristy wasn't ready to share. *I can't push her; it will come. Boy, is she is a tough cookie.* I was perturbed at the end of the session as I watched her quickly put her Red Stilettos back on and practically run out of my office.

To be honest, I wasn't sure I liked her.

And her shoes… I couldn't help but associate them to my memory from 42nd Street. *Damn first impressions!*

As I was walking home that evening, I began to notice Red Stilettos in store windows. In fact, there were Red Stilettos in every shoe store I passed. I was tempted to go in and try on a pair. I wanted to know what it felt like to walk in those shoes. I actually love red shoes and have had many pairs; I even own a pair of red vintage Saucony sneakers. But as a long-distance runner, I found stilettos incredibly difficult to wear. *Does this mean something? I feel like my subconscious wants me to see these shoes. Maybe it does mean something. Yeah. Right, Jacquie. Maybe you're just overthinking this. You, Jacquie? You overthink? Never!* I humored myself. I decided that I would go back another day, when I didn't have to go home to study, and try on those damned Red Stilettos!

And the mental image of those red shoes carried my thoughts back to Maxine, who was working hard in therapy to garner the strength to leave Ed. She was doing much better, but her identity as a prostitute was proving to be a great challenge for us. We began to refer to the day when she was 16 and stepped in to protect her mother as "Black Monday." This was the day that changed everything.

Maxine was punching her father in the back when he turned around and threw Maxine off of him, pushed her up against the dining room table, and violently raped her. The memory was slightly vague; which is common for many survivors of trauma, especially sexual abuse. She described a dissociative experience that is also common.

"It was like it wasn't me," Maxine said as she tried to maintain her composure. "It was like I was looking down on this other girl who looked like me, but wasn't me. And I watched as my father raped her." It took more than a year in treatment for Maxine to integrate her feelings associated with the rape. That day, while finally recounting the story, she moved from the patient chair to the couch, laid down in the fetal position, and sobbed like a baby.

It occurred to me that despite her vulnerability in that moment, or maybe because of it, I realized how truly strong this woman was. She did what she had to do to survive. And now she was doing whatever she could to thrive. The moment kept replaying in my mind as I walked down Second Avenue. And I found myself exclaiming aloud, "I bet she'd make a terrific mother." I laughed, quickly turning to see if anyone caught me talking to myself.

She probably would. I've found that many sex workers have a nurturing quality about them, a protective instinct for those weaker than they, possibly a reaction to abuse earlier in life.

That was certainly the case with the women who protected Ralph, took him in as one of their own when he was left on the street to fend for himself. They weren't perfect, but they were all he had.

Ralph. That poor kid. I really felt for him in his unfortunate circumstances.

Ralph spent many sessions describing his identification and involvement with his gang. There was an odd incongruence that occurred to me while listening to Ralph's stories; many of them involved excessive violence and blind aggression. Interestingly, I found Ralph to be quite gentle with me. Eventually I began to notice that he was also protective, like his "mothers" were of him. He didn't ever want anything to happen to me, so he often provided me with tips about areas in Miami to avoid and advised me on situations that might leave me vulnerable to danger.

In one session, I found him so angry after a court hearing, which resulted in a determination that Ralph needed to stay in Juvey longer, he remarked, "I'm going to blow this place up when I get out." *He would never do something like that. He's blowing off steam.* I nodded, prodding him to continue to articulate his anger. He continued, his tone somewhat muted now. "I plan to do it on a Sunday, because I know you never work on Sunday."

Normally, I would have to report such threats of violence, but knowing that Ralph would never follow through on such an act, reporting it would only bring undo retribution upon him by the correctional system, thus adversely affecting his therapeutic progression. For example, they might further extend his time or even put him in a reprimanding situation, further agitating his ire and regressing his progress. All for an empty threat blurted out in a heated moment. In reality, this boy wasn't really dangerous. On the contrary, I felt protected by him. He did what he had to do to survive. In a better environment, he would certainly be thriving. And if he couldn't feel safe enough to express and work through his anger in therapy without me running to tattle on him at every turn, he would never trust me enough to reveal the important things that must be expressed for therapy to be effective.

Looking back on the treatment now as a more seasoned clinician, I could have explored so much transferential material. But I never touched it; I didn't know if it would be effective and I feared Ralph would feel therapitized, which I sensed would shatter our alliance. Instead, I listened and aligned with him, affording him the luxury of simply experiencing me as a nurturing and understanding person who wanted to hear his story. Eventually, it was his journal that really helped me understand his internal experience.

Ralph's gang participation afforded him a sense of belonging. The stories of the violence that took place between the gangs frightened me; the wars on the street echoed military wars that occur on a much larger scale. So yes, the gang wars were scary, but Ralph was not at all. Though I did imagine scenes where I could see Ralph engaging in gang violence to survive on the streets, I never once felt personally threatened.

One session, with some prodding, Ralph shared a story with me. Ralph's anecdote and the concomitant journal entry description of the violence of his gang, taught me much about why Ralph became a member of such a dangerous community. In many ways, he illuminated light on experiences characteristic of a dark side of humanity and the social context from which they emerged.

The gang, I learned through Ralph's narrative, was a way for individuals to find a sense of power, self-worth and success in a society that supposedly promotes equalities, but where there is often a gross discrepancy in available means to pursue "success." His journal entry describing his decision to join the gang stated, "I had no family. My parents didn't want me. And I just wanted a family. I wanted to belong to something and be with people like me." He also shared, during session, that most of the violence that occurs within gangs is against other rival gangs. He told me, "Sometimes civilians get hurt, but usually only if they get in the way or are part of a gang initiation."

Ralph's journal revealed what he couldn't share verbally in session with me; I was never certain what he was afraid of.

Looking back, I think he felt too vulnerable opening up and exposing who he was beneath his tough exterior. He obviously wanted me to know him, because one day, about six months into our treatment, he handed me the entire journal and asked me to read it. It was one of the saddest things I have ever read.

And with that memory of my time served in south Florida, I entered my Manhattan apartment, shutting the door and leaving an emotionally exhausting day behind me.

Tess came to the next session and made it clear to me that the material we were discussing about her childhood was causing her to feel more depressed than usual. She experienced a strong sense of apathy as a result, but then she added, "I know I have to process these experiences in order to feel better."

I felt I needed to acknowledge her newfound self-awareness, if for no other reason than to encourage her to continue delving into her past and dredging up memories she'd sooner keep in the shadows. "You know what they say, Tess, a process a day keeps the shrink away." I thought the moment could use a little levity.

She smiled, but it melted away in only a moment. "I want to tell you a story, but it's going to be difficult for me to share and, quite honestly, it's something that I've tried really hard not to think about for many years." *She's wasting no time today. And I didn't even have to coax her.*

"I had just completed my bachelor's in journalism in Wisconsin, a nice long way from home. When I returned here after graduation, I found a job as fast as I could. I wasn't happy at home. This was nearly five years after my mother died, and my father's apartment in New York City seemed so empty. Plus, the way I felt about my father, I wanted to be out on my own. I still experience little pangs of guilt for leaving him." She trailed off and sat there, contemplating. I thought I'd give her a little encouragement.

"That's a normal reaction, even for twenty-somethings who have a happy home life. It's the innate urge to break free and build a life of your own."

"It wasn't that. It was… my father wasn't doing well. And in retrospect, I guess I saw the signs earlier, but…" Tess looked at me, then focused on one of my mother's watercolors I'd recently hung on the wall: the Grecian landscape. White houses as far as the eye could see, with a footbridge crossing running water in the foreground. I often lost myself in the soft pastels. "That's new. Who's the artist?"

I need to push her, keep her on track. How do I get her back on topic without making her skittish about continuing to open up? "Yes, it is. Tess. I'd be happy to tell you all about it, but why don't we discuss it later. For now, I'd like to get back to your father."

She continued looking at the painting for another moment, then turned her eyes back at me before averting them again. Then I heard it. Click-click. The flicking of her thumbnail against her middle fingernail, the telltale sign of her growing agitation I had come to know well during out first year together. Click-click. *It was too much. I pushed too hard. Good going, Jacquie.* Click-click-click.

"My father was suffering from dementia." *It worked; not too hard after all.* "As I said, he must have been showing signs for a while, but I didn't really notice with school and such. But once he was diagnosed, his condition deteriorated rapidly. So I quickly found a long-term care facility for him." She stopped again. She looked back at my mother's painting. Click-click-clickclickclickclickclick. *Oh no. Both hands now. I did push too hard. Great, you've really mucked it up, Jacquie.*

I leaned forward. "Are you okay to continue?" I probably felt equally uncomfortable throughout the session. I wondered if Tess could tell. I must have shifted my sitting position every few minutes as my own anxiety intensified.

"Yes," her voice barely audible. She couldn't even look at me. Her shame and guilt and the accompanying pain were palpable. *She needs supportive encouragement.*

I stopped fidgeting, leaned forward and pulled my chair a bit closer to her. "Tell me about it."

Tess, eyes glassy, brushed at her pants. "I, um… to this day, I haven't been able to forgive myself for not taking care of my father. Logically, I know I couldn't have done it on my own, and I probably would have had to put my career on hold. But ..." I waited, but she didn't continue. *Maybe if I say something supportive.*

"It must have been scary watching your father change. You were young and alone."

"But all the time he was sick in the nursing home, I rarely visited him. What excuse is there for that?" Her voice raised, which was unlike her. She's always so tightly wound. So in control of her emotions. And I clearly sensed anger and perhaps a little disgust in her words. *Don't let her rush this. This has been decades coming. Make sure she takes her time to examine as many emotions related to this as possible.*

"Why do you think your visits with him were so infrequent?"

"Even though he was sick, I was still angry with him for not telling me about my mother's condition, and for not being honest with me when I would ask them about it. Instead, I turned to my new career. I threw myself into my work. It was the perfect excuse not to visit my father."

"How often did you get to the care facility to see him?"

"I'd go about once every other month." Click-click-click-click. Tess found the pattern of the rug engrossing, small, shadowed mint-colored crescents tossed in a forest-green field.

Though I had so many questions, I withheld and allowed her to process at her own pace.

"I stopped going after he deteriorated to the point that he no longer knew who I was."

I wonder... "How did that feel, when your father didn't recognize you?"

"I guess it was sad. Honestly, between my resentment and the infrequent visits, by the time he was no longer the man I had known, I had already become somewhat desensitized to his dementia. And I guess my anger made it that much easier to turn off my feelings about his condition."

"So you stopped visiting him, and then what?" Click-click-cli- The flicking stopped cold.

"Then what?" Tess looked at me askew. "And then he died."

I withheld the gasp that almost exploded from me. I should have anticipated that answer, but she said it so abruptly. *Show empathy, but be strong for her.*

"My last visit with him was on a fall day. I think it was a long weekend. It might have been Columbus Day weekend. I remember the leaves clashing against the gray, overcast sky on my ride home. All the reds and yellows and oranges. I pulled over to the side of the road to take in the scenery. The air was a little crisp. And you could smell the leaves dying. You know that smell?" *I do. I like that smell.* I nodded. "That's when I decided that I wasn't going back. What was the point? He didn't know who I was anymore. His memories were mixed, unreliable. He confused stories about my mother and my aunt, his first wife. And me with the daughter who had died. Instead of feeling sorry for him, I felt sorry for me, for being cheated out of the love he withheld, out of being cheated of a mother, and now a father."

Tess choked back a tear, then sat with bated breath, her gaze lost in the Grecian landscape. She didn't continue, but I wanted her to. She needed to. My mind was scrambling, thinking of what I should say to her. I wanted to keep her in the moment, to prevent her from shutting down. I was about to say something innocuous to bridge the moment while I thought of something brilliant, when —

"The whole thing just made me more angry," Tess blurted. I couldn't tell if she was actually angry or just channeling the memory, but she continued. "So I stopped visiting. It was the following autumn, just before Halloween, when my phone rang at work. My father had died."

Listening to her narrative, I was on the verge of tears. Despite all the past feelings of anger and resentment she was bringing up, Tess showed no emotion about her father's passing. The way in which she described his death was flat — the matter-of-fact tone one might use when ordering breakfast.

"Tess, this is such a sad story. I'm so sorry. How do you feel right now?"

"I feel like I need to keep my distance from this in order to talk about it."

"Why is that?"

"I abandoned him. I feel..." Tess's voice caught. I watched her fight back tears. She took a moment to compose herself. I could almost see her turning off her emotion switch. "I feel a lot of guilt about it." She examined the rug again. "I can't talk about this anymore. Is the session almost over?"

Indeed it was. Tess left the session quietly, hunched over, private, sullen. During the session, I accepted so much of her split-off feelings, it overwhelmed me. Once she was gone, I cried.

I am quite affected by my patients, but it is uncommon for me to cry after a patient leaves a session, especially since I have heard many poignant and painful stories. I wanted to figure out what was happening in our unique dyad that made me feel so intensely sad and heartbroken. I realized after a bit of processing that I could really feel her desperation, loneliness and self-hate; three traits that now organized and defined her. I really wanted to help her, but I also recognized the difficulty I was up against. When a patient's personality and way of being-in-the-world is organized around such debilitating core issues, it is a real challenge to have them integrate a more positive persona.

With the weather cooperating, I was able to take a stroll during my lunch break to clear myself emotionally for the rest of my day. I wondered if other therapists empathize this much with their patients, take on their emotions. It could be draining, but I don't think I would have it any other way.

My first patient after lunch was Kristy. She was in her third year of medical school, having difficulty managing her time, and dealing with the incredible pressures fundamental to medical training. She was a strong and amazingly intelligent woman, but the exams, clinical rotations and the long hours were becoming a bit much for her to manage. *I get it. Jacquie, remember the existential crisis you had during that grueling third year of the doctoral program? If it weren't for Mom and a few close friends encouraging me, my time would have been so much harder. Mom kept repeating, "Jacquie, you can do this! Think of*

*it like one of your marathons — you always say the hardest part
is toward the end when you want to stop, but keep going!"*

And I did!

I wanted to understand if Kristy legitimately didn't really
want to be a medical doctor, or if, like me, she felt like giving up
because of the pressure and the sheer exhaustion of it all. I was
vigilant of my own experience, and with my therapist Gwen's
help, made sure I remained neutral and did not presuppose that
her emotional challenge was like mine. This is incredibly and
elementally important to being a successful clinician; we need to
always remember that although a narrative may seem similar to
one's own, everyone's experience is different. We need to
understand and explore each patient individually — and to really
listen to what their experience is!

So, I picked and probed, asking many questions trying to
truly understand the essence of Kristy's conflicts. When we
finally got there…

I knew it!

It was the Red Stilettos again.

After Kristy's disclosure in that last session, I noticed that
she was much more open. She had an edge, but her coolness
dissipated, and she felt much less aggressive in our sessions. I
was quite relieved. I felt the muscles in my neck and back relax. I
hadn't realized how tense I felt sitting with her. In fact, I don't
think I had felt this tense since studying and preparing for my
licensing exam. I imagine this must have been how tense she was
feeling before she felt comfortable enough to share the essence of
her conflicts.

When I was getting ready for bed that night, I replaced a
book on the shelf and saw the physiological psychology flash
cards I used to study for the licensing exam. I was feeling
nostalgic, so I picked them up and carried them to the bed. As I
flipped through them, I recalled my emotions leading up to the
test. Though I felt secure I would earn my license, I am not one to
be cocksure. What would I do with my life if I were not a
therapist? It had been my goal for as long as I could remember.

My parents supported my decision one-hundred percent. In fact, they would have supported almost any vocational choice I would have made. And that's when Kristy popped in my thoughts. *Did she ever have other aspirations? Did she squash any dreams for a life other than the one her parents had mapped out for her before they could take root, because she knew subconsciously that her parents would not support her pursuit of anything other than a doctor or lawyer? What must that feel like?*

I sighed, relieved to have the support network I grew up with. I stacked the flash cards, putting them on the nightstand next to my glasses. Only moments after turning off the lamp, the rhythm of the city's white noise sent me quickly into a slumber.

I had a dream that night: I was playing hopscotch, but the chalked-up concrete resembled the neurons in the brain, and instead of hopping in numbered boxes without touching the box lines, I was avoiding the neurons (brain cells) by landing in the synapses (gaps between the brain cells). I assumed this part had to do with my having fallen asleep after perusing the flash cards.

But the noise — *click, clack, click, clack* — was so distinct as I jumped around the synapses while reciting the neurotransmitters floating around (serotonin, depression, acetylcholine) — *click, clack, click, clack*. I looked down at my feet and there they were: the Red Stilettos. The image startled me … and I awoke with a jolt.

Once I gathered my senses and realized I was still in bed, I reached for my water bottle on the nightstand and inadvertently swiped at the flash cards — I guess I had left them sitting precariously at the edge — a player in both my waking anxiety and fitful dreams, spilling them across the floor. Of course, my cat, Snoopy, wasted no time. He picked one up and started chewing the corner.

When I brought the dream to my supervisor to explore the clinical relevance, he helped me understand that the dream didn't represent my anxiety. It represented Kristy's. I was now fully engaged with her, entering her world and unconsciously stepping into her shoes. I was empathizing. "Very good, Jacquie." His support felt encouraging.

Although I had thought the choice of my hopscotch chalking was related to my having been reviewing physiology that night, he had a different insight. My unconscious clearly was making a connection with Kristy's medical training. Of all the subjects covered in the licensing exam, my unconscious chose the subject that crossed over into medicine. And then, of course, there were the Red Stilettos.

Kristy's main difficulty wasn't entirely the pressures of medical school, it was her ambivalence about her extracurricular activity; she was indeed, as I had initially surmised, working as a high-paid escort. I became fascinated. Kristy had started off working as an exotic dancer during college to support herself and to enable her to live independently. Eventually, at the suggestion of one of the club owners, she slowly moved into escorting. Essentially, by the time she began seeing me for therapy, she had been escorting for four years, and had built a lucrative business.

But Kristy was exhausted. Balancing her medical school responsibilities and her escorting business was difficult, and she lived in constant fear. She wasn't sure what to do. Interestingly, Kristy expressed no shame or dissonance about her work as an escort. Her shame emanated from the imposition of the societal stigma surrounding prostitution, and her fear was that if her school found out, she would be thrown out and never be able to work as a doctor. This, in fact, was Kristy's real dilemma.

I found myself absorbed in thoughts surrounding the extraordinary juxtaposition between Maxine and Kristy's internal experiences, and the interesting differences they revealed to me about their identities as sex workers. I began to pull myself out of the deeply emerged clinical engagement with both of them, and began to process and conceptualize the incongruity from a more detached intellectual space. I was also integrating their independent psychological makeup with the influences that society imposes on all of us, and how these standards can have a profound and often damaging influence on one's psyche.

I was in the middle of a long run, the endorphins were kicking in and my mind was free, when the insight washed over me. *Shame!* I started running faster. Later that evening, I was able to put words to what I was thinking. I put on my red Saucony sneakers and my writing hat. Then I sat down at my desk and began typing with furious abandon.

Maxine's narrative and emotional experience revealed a story of survival. She was a victim of emotional, physical, and sexual abuse. For her, entering the world of prostitution was a way to escape and free herself of the wrath of her abusive father. Unfortunately, Maxine entered this world already broken, shame-ridden and feeling completely worthless. Her entire identity was enveloped in shame and self-hate. As a result, she stayed with Ed, continued to be emotionally abused, and fundamentally felt she deserved it. She had no education or work experience aside from her sex work; she stayed because she felt she had no other option.

Kristy's story revealed something different. Kristy decided to become an escort. She entered the profession well aware of the stigma and possible emotional ramifications of what she was doing. She was doing it for the money, and was able to separate the act of sex from her identity; she preserved her sense of self through this defense. When she described her experience, there appeared to be little emotion connected to it. She was pissed at society, not herself. Her shame, as she explained, had to do with what others would think if they found out.

My thoughts as I wrote twirled with the excitement I feel when I know I am on the brink of an amazing and life-altering revelation. And again, my thoughts conjured up an image of the Red Stilettos. This time I was on my favorite running trail, running, feeling free, and wearing the Red Stilettos. My feet hurt. *Hmm.*

Anne and I were in our sixth month of treatment together when she came into session and started discussing the different colleges she wanted to apply to. It was the spring and she wanted to make sure she got her applications in on time. I was beaming. Her only fear was that her stalker would try to enroll in the same school. *Odd.* Curious, I asked, "How might he find out where you are applying? The application process is done through the mail."

"He finds out everything. I don't know how, but he does!" For the first time, I heard strength and conviction in Anne's intonation. *Interesting.*

After this session, I became more focused on Anne's stalker. Try as I might, I couldn't stop my internal dialogue. *Is Anne "really" being stalked? I know that she really **feels** stalked and believes he knows her every move. I can't confront nor question the reality of the stalker. And people can actually be stalked.* I knew this from working with stalkers during my forensic psychology studies and externships. *But Anne's description just feels so... inflated. Something isn't right. How could he know where she was applying for school? Certainly he could find her once enrolled and attending, but before? Could he have hacked her computer, too?*

I kept this internal discourse to myself temporarily. Anne wanted to apply to colleges, which was one of her biggest treatment goals. I needed to help her garner her strengths and work toward this first. So we did just that. Anne applied to four schools in the area, so she could live with her grandmother and uncle while attending. She was also applying for financial aid. She made it inordinately clear that she wanted no help from her father. Again, I was so unbelievably curious about this. *What happened between them? Something had for certain; but what?* It just reeked of abuse; I couldn't shake the thought.

That evening I had a dream.

I was in Anne's parents' house and saw Anne sleeping in her room. She was much younger, probably about twelve years old. She looked so comfortable and was snuggling with a stuffed animal; a cute little stuffed tiger. Suddenly, her father came into her room, laid down next to her, and began cuddling with Anne. He was stroking her hair. Anne woke up startled; her eyes opened wide as her father placed his finger over her lips, indicating that Anne should be quiet. He began to stroke her genitals. Anne laid there with a look of horror on her face. He then penetrated her. I woke up shaking; sweat was pouring off me. Oh my gosh! It was Anne's father who abused her! I felt sure of it.

It was 4:00 a.m. when I awoke from this dream. I got out of bed and poured myself a glass of water. I found solace in my comfy chair, hoping to shake off the edginess, and thought about what this dream might mean. It is relatively rare that I have such a vivid dream about a patient. It clearly indicated the extent to which thoughts of Anne being abused were stalking me. I wanted to see it as a premonition, but I knew that really was not the case. The dream expressed my own images of what I thought happened, which clearly was important. However, Anne still provided no concrete evidence, and at this point in her treatment, no opening for exploration.

I brought my dream into my own therapy to process. The end result after fifty minutes of obsessing over the dream, and my concurrent thoughts that Anne was the victim of incest, was that unless she provided an invitation for exploration, there was not much I could do. I had to try my hardest to withhold these images and thoughts, and wait for an appropriate opportunity for constructive exploration with Anne. *Ugh, not easy!*

Outside of our sessions, I was working hard to pull together all the questions I had surrounding the relationship between Anne's suicide attempt, her stalker and her family dynamics. It was all associated; I felt that strongly. *But how exactly?* Something remarkable would happen over the summer that would provide an opportune opening.

Chapter 4:
Whore Feet

After more than six months with Anne, I felt like I was only just making headway with our relationship, slowly but surely earning her trust and getting her to open up more. To my relief, she also seemed to be making progress. During our sessions, we were working together to help Anne achieve her treatment goals. Anne did get into three of the four schools she applied to. We were processing which program would be the best fit for her. She decided on New York University. An excellent decision, I thought, though an expensive one. Anne seemed happy. When I noticed this with her, she shared that she felt a sense of accomplishment for the first time since her suicide attempt. *Finally.*

Anne came into session one sticky, hazy, hot and humid (the three unforgiving Hs that New Yorkers don't like to hear) afternoon, and shared that she was invited to Miami to visit her maternal aunt and cousins for a week before the start of the academic year. She was filled with indecision.

"Sounds like a nice invitation. What's causing your hesitancy?"

Anne shared that her two female cousins were younger than she, and had already finished college. "I feel kind of ashamed that I'm not where they are in my life." She diverted her eyes. "Plus, Maria, one of my cousins, is engaged, too. I'm so far behind. I feel like a loser."

We spent a few sessions exploring the shame Anne felt; shame is the most painful affective experience. I wanted to help Anne feel empowered by her hard work in therapy, and her recent acceptance to one of the most prestigious schools in the country. I noticed that Anne often devalued herself. Despite her obvious strengths, she seemed to feel she always fell short in comparison to her cousins and siblings. I pointed this out to her, and she agreed. We decided collaboratively that the trip to Miami could be therapeutic; possibly affording Anne the experience of sharing her new accomplishment with her extended family. Anne left for Miami a few weeks later. Something quite unpredictable happened in Miami, remarkably opening up the therapeutic space for exploration of deeper issues.

I had been working with Arthur for about nine months in twice-weekly therapy. Arty, as he liked to be called, was flagrantly paranoid and legally blind. I learned from his case manager at the blind school that he was never able to maintain a therapeutic relationship for more than three months as a result of his paranoia. So, at nine months, I thought we at least had a stronger alliance than he had with previous therapists. I was determined to help him, but he was quite a handful.

The main theme of Arty's treatment surrounded his extreme rage toward his family. He endlessly shared how they forced him on countless occasions to have electric shock therapy for his "psychiatric issues." He obsessively spoke of this in every session; no matter how much I tried to open up the therapeutic space, to explore deeper issues, he clung steadfast to this experience. Often when I tried to gather more information about the electric shock therapy and/or what "psychiatric issues" his family was referring to, he would become rageful toward me. He experienced any deviation from these thoughts as an empathetic failure. So, I stayed with him where he was, and tried a Kohutian Self-Psychology approach; I sat and continued over and over to empathize with his experience.

Arty also refused medication. I wasn't even sure an anti-psychotic would help his paranoia. It was my sense that this symptom was more representative of his pervasive way of being-in-the-world. It has been my experience that when a patient presents with a symptom that is more associated with his/her overall character style, they are more resistant to psychopharmacological treatment. Arty refused, he felt that my attempt to refer him for a medication consult was because I didn't believe his story. Eventually after a few failed efforts, I stopped trying. My hope was that if I could maintain my empathetic position with him, he would feel heard and his paranoia would lessen.

It was another one of those Three-H days again. New York is very much a walking city; we walk everywhere, so deciding what to wear in order not to be saturated with sweat once one gets to work is always a challenge. With the unbearable 90-degree heat, I decided to wear open-strapped shoes, and a flowing sleeveless, blue-and-yellow-print dress that I had purchased for twenty dollars from a street vendor. I bought the dress particularly for days like this.

Tess was my first patient that morning. It was relatively early in our therapeutic journey, so when she came in and saw me with wet hair and no makeup, she sat down and immediately reacted to my appearance.

"You don't look good today, Jacqueline. You're never going to find a husband unless you look more polished," she stated with conviction. *Oh, no. It's going to be one of those days. I can just feel it.* Tess spent most of the session with her endless beauty tips. When the weather gets hot, I start waking earlier to run before the sun really starts blasting its heat. That's how I started this day: tired and dehydrated. But I was really exhausted after Tess's session; having to contain my own feelings of anger resulting from her attacks depleted me. I had no time for one of my thirty-minute power naps; Arty was coming in for his session right after Tess.

I went into the bathroom and threw water on my face; I literally downed a Gatorade in record time. I felt a bit better. I went to get Arty for our session. He came in and sat in the patient chair. He was silent for a moment or two, which was unusual. He repeatedly clenched his jaw, and his nose exhales were so explosive they reminded me of a bull snorting. I became anxious. *What's going on with him today? His rage is palpable!* I had just finished my thought when Arty began verbally attacking me. He was so furious, and his speech was so accelerated, that I was having serious difficulty comprehending what he was saying. I recognized how angry he was with me. I shared that I really wanted to understand what he was saying. This calmed him down only a bit, just enough that his speech was finally comprehendible.

"You know I have a foot fetish!"

What? He had completely thrown me off guard. "Arty, I know you're upset, but honestly, this is the first time you shared this with me."

"Lies! You did too know."

Okay, just appease him, Jacquie, and get him to calm down. "Okay, Arty, I truly am sorry that I forgot. Please help me understand what has you so upset." *I would never have worn these shoes had I been privy to his being erotically aroused by women's feet!*

"Look at those sandals you're flaunting. You're intentionally trying to turn me on, exposing your toe-polished whore-feet!"

Toe-polished WHORE FEET!? Really? My body tensed as I desperately maintained a modicum of control.

"Arty, I'm sorry my shoes have upset you so much."

"Then you shouldn't have worn those foot thongs." *I was starting to get pissed. Before I could stop myself...*

"It's just so hot today." *Use a soothing voice, Jacquie, and don't worry about your body language. He can't see— huh?* "Wait. How can you possibly know I'm wearing sandals? Did you ask someone about my footwear?" I tried to make eye contact with him, but quickly caught myself, as it was a pointless endeavor considering his blindness. Arty's rage continued, however.

"Why would I ask anyone about the shoes you're wearing?"

"You admittedly have a foot fetish."

"So now you think I try to get turned on before I come into session? That I want to fantasize about you in here?" Reasoning with him only worsened his ranting, which continued like this for at least another ten minutes as I tried relentlessly to contain him.

From what I could piece together from his ranting, though Arty was legally blind, he still had sight in the lower quadrant of both his eyes. So the only thing he could see *was* feet. *Convenient for a foot fetishist.* He never told me about his limited sight, and I didn't know that I should have asked. All in all, this turned into an unbelievable moment in my growth as a clinician.

As much as I tried to contain Arty and empathize with what was happening between us in the moment, I was entirely unsuccessful. He got up, with twenty minutes still left of the session hour, and stormed out. But as he was leaving, he spit out, "I am never coming back and I'm reporting you to the Department of Disabilities for your inappropriate dress code!"

This was not a good day; I felt like a complete failure. I knew rationally that Arty was paranoid and had tremendous difficulty forming an alliance, two gigantic therapeutic hurdles. However, emotionally I still felt that there was something I might have done differently that would have created a better outcome. This powerful and dramatic premature termination really affected my day. I just wanted to go home, put the air conditioning on, and lay in bed. Obviously, I had other patients and couldn't do this. The fantasy was soothing, though.

I did call the blind school that had referred Arty to me. I had a signed release to speak with them. I explained what happened and provided two referrals, both male therapists. I wondered if — hoped — he might work better with a male counterpart. The woman I spoke with graciously accepted the referrals. I imagined she could hear the disappointment and shame in my voice, as she reassured me that Arty was "treatment resistant," and that I definitely did all that I could. I never heard from Arty again, but his final session stayed with me for many weeks until finally, through my own therapy, I was able to let it go. But there's one thing that still gnaws at my curiosity to this day. Did Arty have the foot fetish before he became blind, or did the "peda-proclivities" evolve from spending his days walking around only being able to see feet?

My next appointment was a student clinician that I was supervising. Just as I was about to go to the waiting room to get her, my phone rang. It was an unfamiliar number; I almost didn't pick up, and then I realized it was a 305 area code — Miami. I still have friends in the city from my three years' living there, but their names and numbers were in my phone, so the caller ID would have pulled up the name. Unless it was an emergency and they were calling from another number. *Should I answer it?* And then it clicked.

It must be Anne.

I was simultaneously surprised and pleased that she called me. Anne was so constricted; it was hard to gauge how connected she felt to me. This phone call implied that Anne was indeed engaged in her treatment, was beginning to trust me, and had successfully formed a therapeutic alliance. It was good timing on Anne's part, as it lifted some of the doubt in my abilities that I had placed on myself as a result of Arty's angry departure. So the fact that she called spoke volumes. Our actual conversation, on the other hand, went something like this.

"Dr. Jacquie? Hi."

"Um, Anne?"

"Of course."

"*Of course?*" *Really?* "How is your vacation going?"

"Nice. The weather's been nice. Hot. Sunny. And my cousins are fine. We're having a nice time together." *Miami's always hot and sunny. She wouldn't have called me to report that. Something's bothering her.*

"Are you okay? Is everything all right?"

"Of course."

Again with "of course." If I didn't know better, I'd say she sounds almost giddy. Maybe if I prod her a little. "If this isn't urgent, Anne, would it be okay if I called you back? I was about to start a session."

"I'll be quick. I just wanted to let you know that I met a guy here in Miami." She sounded excited, agitated, joyous, dubious. I don't know. Honestly, she was usually morose and blunted, so I found it difficult to discern this new emotion over the phone. "And, um, something happened."

Something happened? What? What happened? Is this good? Is this bad? Oy! I'm too tired for this. Keep it cool and calm, Jacquie. "What happened, Anne? Are you sure you're all right? Did something happen to the man you met?"

"He's fine, he's fine. Something happened… um, between us." *Could she be any more coy and evasive?* "I don't want to get too into the details over the phone because I think my stalker has the phone tapped."

"My phone? You don't have to worry, Anne. I promise my phone isn't tapped."

"No, my aunt's phone." *Okay. How would this stalker tap her aunt's phone in Miami?* "I'll tell you all about the guy next week. I just wanted to confirm our appointment for Monday. A lot's happened down here, so I just wanted to make sure we're still on." *Wow. Something REALLY must have happened if Anne is feeling this forthcoming, well, forthcoming for her.*

"Yes, Anne. Our appointment is still scheduled. I'll see you then."

My wheels were spinning, and my immediate associations when we hung up were thoughts of Arty. Not ideas about his abrupt termination, but rather thoughts about his symptom formation. Something connected in my subconscious, it poked at my mind, but I couldn't put my finger on it. I knew I would figure it out when I had more time to process it, but for the next five hours I had to be present to my students and patients.

When the curtain finally fell on my workday, I walked to my apartment — dripping with sweat from the oppressive heat — arrived home, peeled off my clothes, put on my bathing suit, and made a bee-line for the pool.

Later, I plopped on the couch to relax and enjoy my after-workout buzz. I turned on the TV. Before the picture came into focus, I could hear Glenn Close and Jeff Bridges talking. I knew it had to be *Jagged Edge*, one of my favorite movies. It was the scene before Glenn's character finds the typewriter with the dysfunctional letter, which prompts her to realize that Jeff's character had been lying to her about not killing his wife. He created a reality that Glenn's character bought hook, line, and sinker. That is when, without any conscious forethought, I made my own connection.

The entire time I treated Arty, I questioned the objective reality of his having electric shock therapy. It felt similar and was remarkably analogous to Anne's stalker. Either could be true, but I had the sense in both circumstances that though it was their reality, it did not really happen. In both situations, I sat with them in the reality they created, but they consciously and unconsciously questioned the purpose and truth of their stories.

I had to dig into my cognitive tool box; there was no other way for me to sufficiently and succinctly comprehend and encapsulate what made me question Anne's story. The shared component between Arty and Anne's stories was that they organized themselves around rigid, fixed, and unrelenting thoughts about one particular circumstance. The rigidity suggested that they were commonly struggling with a "non-bizarre delusion." Unlike other psychotic delusions, the essential feature of a "non-bizarre delusion" is that it "could" be true. In Anne's case, it was perfectly viable that she was being stalked; it happens and is a frightening experience.

Despite the possibility that one could be stalked, two fundamental features of Anne's story didn't feel right. The first, as aforementioned, was the fixed and rigid quality of her narrative. The second was the pervasiveness of her story. Her stalker came up in almost every session and entirely infiltrated and affected her whole life. The former explained why she could not tolerate any questions that suggested I didn't believe she indeed had a stalker. The latter spoke to Anne's inability to function to her full capacity as a result of being stalked; her stalker was everywhere and knew everything. Anyone employing rational reasoning would find this highly unlikely.

As I reflected on this new information, I discerned that despite her diagnosis of Schizoaffective Disorder, she really didn't have any other psychotic features. Her affect was notably flat and restricted: a possible psychotic symptom. But having treated psychosis throughout my doctoral training, Anne just didn't present nor feel as though she had a full-blown psychotic disorder. I went back and forth with this for the remainder of the evening until I fell asleep. When I awoke, my brain fresh and rested, I came to an intriguing and likely accurate hypothesis.

I thought back to Anne's description of the events leading up to her suicide attempt. Anne had no suicide attempts prior to this one, nor after. She denied even having suicidal ideation, and I believed her. She also only began being stalked after her suicide attempt when she moved back to Brooklyn. The incident was directly and unmistakably related to feeling rejected by the young man she was "involved with."

How "involved" were they? Did they "really" have a relationship as Anne alluded to? Anne, without a doubt, believed they did! I'm not so sure. Yes, her affect is restricted; this could be the reason I am questioning the validity of Anne's having an intimate relationship with him. However, over the course of the year, while treating Anne, I sensed they weren't involved on a romantic level. *But did they have a sexual encounter or relationship? I really don't think so! But... could this young man be Anne's stalker?*

Jacquie, you need to be honest. Acknowledging, at least to yourself, that Anne's stalker may not be "real" doesn't mean you are not validating or aligning with her. And besides, her stalker does exist in her mind. He is a concretization of Anne's inability to let go of feeling rejected! I felt excited; the pieces of the puzzle all began to fit and remarkably felt correct.

Anne was unable to process her feelings of rejection, and as a result of this, she could not let go of him. Her unconscious psychological and emotional resolve was to externalize her feelings, creating a concrete image of him and feeling he was following her everywhere! For Anne, her concretization of internal images of him made him quite "real." She couldn't move on because she had not processed her feelings. Though he was holding her back from moving on with her life, it was just an internal image, not an external, concrete one.

I felt a huge sigh of relief. I hadn't realized how much my confusion surrounding Anne's circumstances and internal world were affecting me. This conceptualization provided me the opportunity to understand Anne on a deeper level, and ultimately afforded me a more informed way to treat her. When she came in on Monday after her Miami vacation, I became privy to another rather compelling piece of Anne's story.

Kristy was crying. Nearly a year into our treatment, this was the first time she was brought to tears while describing her conflicts. Her words echoed my thoughts. As her long, perfectly straight black hair draped over her shoulders, she blurted out, "I am so angry!" — punctuating each word with precise enunciation. "I'm not doing anything wrong in my mind. I feel so trapped by societal norms. I'm simply trying to be self-sufficient while I'm in medical school. I'm not hurting anyone."

I pursed my lips and nodded. "Yes, Kristy, I know." And then she cried even harder; heaving sobs for almost five minutes.

At this point, Kristy was already in her residency. She was growing increasingly terrified she'd be recognized by her escort persona while working as a resident at one of the largest hospitals in Manhattan. Her fear escalated when she realized that the more patients she worked with, the more likely she would be "found out." Through our therapeutic journey, she decided that she did indeed want to complete her medical training. In the end, Kristy ended her libertine side job, giving up her $1,000-an-hour escort service. Yet the choice wasn't easy.

"I'm so upset, but I can't risk being found out," she shared, tears in her eyes.

"Your frustration is understandable. It's unfair. And I'm so sorry for your struggles. I know this decision has been extremely difficult for you."

Kristy crossed her arms. "I know this is the right thing. But it doesn't mean I have to like it."

I smirked. "Honestly, Kristy, I'm not sure I like it, either." She smiled, almost relieved when I said it, like she wasn't sure if I had been judging her this whole time we'd been in treatment together. "Now that you've put this part of yourself in your past, how do you feel?" She thought for a moment.

"Kind of sad. It was good money. And the financial freedom was liberating. I mean, it paid for medical school. I'll graduate without any debt." *Wish I coulda said the same thing.*

I laughed. "I'm sure med students across the country are crying in envy of you. Or would be if they knew."

"But I feel a different kind of freedom, too. A kind of liberating relief."

"From what?"

"Always looking over my shoulder at the hospital. Fearful I'd be found out and judged. I'll be free from that now." And she did appear lighter, like she had shrugged off 50-pound shoulder pads.

A few weeks later, Kristy came in and shared that she felt she was ready to terminate the treatment.

"Thank you, Jacquie. You've helped me so much, more than you'll ever know, but I feel that I've reached my goals in here."

I had to admit, I had sensed this coming recently. Unlike many patients I work with now in long-term therapy, Kristy wasn't looking for intense depth-oriented treatment. She came in with a specific problem, and this problem had achieved resolution. And I agreed with her assessment.

"I'm proud of you, Kristy. I know this journey hasn't been easy."

She nodded. When she was getting ready to leave, I reminded her that she could always call me to come back if she needed to. Kristy thanked me — and then she was gone.

I felt the usual twinge in my stomach when I recognize that I might never see a patient again, particularly one with whom I had formed a connection. I always — and unavoidably — feel a sense of loss.

And although I felt sad to say my goodbyes to Kristy, this fulfilling moment ended my week on a high note. I wrapped up things in my office, then headed home for a fun-filled weekend with friends. Monday would arrive soon enough, and along with it, Anne's latest development.

The day quickly developed into another scorcher. I love the summer months, but when there is no respite in between these 90-degree days in New York, the weather becomes exhausting. The Monday morning air felt thick. Tess was my first appointment on Monday. After her assaults about my appearance the previous week, I found myself angst-ridden when deciding what to wear; while applying eyeliner, I stopped to reflect on my actions. I chuckled. *Wow, Jacquie, Tess is really getting to you; you never wear eyeliner on hot days.*

I stood in the bathroom staring at myself in the mirror for a moment or two, engrossed in an inner neurotic dialogue. I couldn't decide whether I should continue primping in order to save myself from Tess's exhausting assaults or not. Finally, I stopped with the eyeliner, threw on a little lip-gloss, fed my cat, and headed out to walk to my office in the heat. I decided that putting the eyeliner on, both to indulge Tess and attempt to ward off her insults, was colluding with her. I needed to sit with her envy-driven anger and continue to process it with her; I needed to use this relational process to explore her inner experience of herself.

Ironically, Tess withheld any aggressive comments that morning. Although I knew this wasn't a permanent cease-fire on her part, I felt relieved that day; it was just too hot. Anne was my second appointment and I had fifteen minutes between their sessions. I saw Anne in the waiting room as I passed through to use the restroom. She wore her usual layers of clothing, the idea of a hoodie on this day practically brought sweat to my brow. I was suddenly struck by the intriguing juxtaposition of her and Tess.

Tess came to session immaculately dressed, with a full face of makeup and her hair perfectly done. Heat or no heat, she refused to let weather dictate her appearance. Anne, on the other hand, came in with her usual layers, also disregarding the heat wave. They were diametrically opposed to one another, yet the overarching theme felt the same. They both allowed their inner conflict to manifest in the way they comported themselves in their physical bodies. It was as if the outside world and environment didn't exist.

What an interesting and profound existential insight. I almost did the same that morning as I was pre-reflectively putting extra makeup on. *It wasn't really for Tess, it was to reduce the impact of her assaults; her attacks stirred up my own issues.* I sat and relished in this moment of self-revelation. I was nostalgically reminiscing about my days of rigorously studying existentialism. *As unique as we all are, we all share the fundamental and self-evident experience of being human. Okay, Jacquie, cool it; it's time for Anne's session.*

I noticed immediately as Anne came in that her skin was tanned and glowing. She was all covered up as usual, but her face looked different. She looked beautiful and radiant. I couldn't stop myself, "You look great, Anne," I shared. She softly and genuinely thanked me. I was filled with curiosity and couldn't wait to hear about what happened in Miami. Anne was a bit hesitant at first; I waited patiently for her to start. When she finally began her story, I learned that the young man Anne met in Miami was her cousin's boyfriend's friend.

I sensed an openness that I had never felt with Anne before; she was still constricted, but there was definitely a notable difference. She was also more forthcoming with her disclosures in session. As she shared her story about the young man in Miami, I felt freer to inquire about her intimate relationships in general. Until this session, I sensed that Anne was protecting herself from specific questions regarding her relationships. I honored her non-verbal communication these many months, waiting with a gigantic question mark for an opening. Finally, after just over a year, she offered one.

Anne had been in Miami for ten days. She met Juan on the third day of her trip. They shared an immediate attraction for and connection with one another. She spent most of her trip with him, seeing the sights, sunning on the beach, enjoying the vibrant nightlife.

She looked at the floor for a few moments; we sat in silence. That's when I felt it. Her signature legs shaking, fiercely tapping out an emotional Morse code message: "This isn't easy for me to share." Instinctively, I knew she was about to disclose information involving her sexual being. *Give her space. If you push or ask questions, she'll close up.* I waited. The humming of the air conditioning made the silence even more pronounced. It acted as melodic backup for the percussive tapping of her heels on the floor, as her legs pumped up and down like pistons.

And suddenly the music stopped. I glanced at her just as she looked up at me.

"I had sex with Juan." I barely managed to keep my jaw from dropping open. *Anne may be tight-lipped, but when this girl dishes, she really dishes.*

And she stopped as quickly as she began. Her head drooped and she went silent. She was like a toy. Turn her on. Turn her off. Except she was the one who controlled the switch.

I waited a few minutes, but didn't want to wait too long and let this newfound energy dissipate. *I better say something.*

"Anne. How did it feel to share that with me?"

She looked up, but didn't quite look me in the eyes. "I feel okay, but I'm uncomfortable with what happened." *Hmmm, was there more?*

"What do you mean when you say 'what happened?'" I used my encouraging voice to nudge her to elaborate.

"The sex. I had sex with him."

I nodded, prompting her to continued.

"I never did that before." Her pause turned into a period.

"Have sex with someone you just met?"

"No. Have sex." Then she looked me directly in the eyes. "I never had sex before."

Okay, well that answers one of my questions: she didn't have sex with her stalker. Which now leads me straight back to the possibility that she's been the victim of incest, just like I first surmised. Was it her father? Her uncle? I couldn't shake the thought. *Stay focused, Jacquie.* I needed to stay with Anne in the moment and not be distracted by my thoughts; she was vulnerable.

"Anne, how did you feel about losing your virginity?"

Anne shrugged.

"Anne, I feel like it's important that I ask this. Was the sex consensual?"

"Of course!" *Again with the "of course."*

And that was about all I was going to get Anne to reveal in the session. But as the weeks went on, we spent quite a few sessions exploring her experience with Juan and feelings about her having lost her virginity. Anne enjoyed her time with Juan, and interestingly had no expectation of a relationship. She liked him and wanted, finally, at 29 years old, to know how it felt to have sex. She appeared undeniably detached from the whole experience. When I probed her, searching for answers about her lack of expectations and her notable disengagement from what often is quite a powerful experience, she explained that her stalker knew and she had to remain detached to protect herself from him.

Having conceptualized what Anne's stalker represented, I now understood her disconnect as an unconscious protective mechanism. In other words, in order to admit to feelings for Juan, she would have to "let go" of her stalker. And at this time, she could not do this. She did reassure me that she had no regrets about having been with Juan. She often said, regarding her stalker, "I am angry with *him* for interfering with my ability to have a relationship with a man. I wanted so desperately to confront her about her "stalker," but knowing how fixed and rigid a delusion can be, I was sure she would experience any queries as an empathic failure. I continued to join her in her experience of him as "real."

Soon after, autumn arrived — and with it, Anne began her academic studies at New York University. She thoroughly enjoyed her return to school. She seemed relatively happy and performed quite well academically. She also decided to join a gym and began working out about four times a week. Her progress pleased me — and her. She was beginning to establish a more positive self-image as a result of being able to move toward her goal of finishing her degree. However, whenever she experienced even a minor setback, she went back to ideas about her "stalker," and blamed him for setting her back. *At some point I am going to have to address this. I don't believe it's going to go away on its own.*

As our journey together continued, now nearly 18 months into her therapy, Anne began discussing feeling frustrated with her living arrangements. She had almost no privacy, and she started to recognize that it was interfering with her studies. Basically, other than the library at school, she had no private place to do her schoolwork. I saw this as an opening. Anne was offering me the opportunity, only now at a year and a half into our treatment, to explore her family dynamics. And I was more than ready to share in this exploration with her. *Just don't lead her into any discussion about the possible incest at this point. It's only an intuitively-based hypothesis.* I needed to be careful.

I finally felt comfortable asking Anne how she wound up living with her grandmother and uncle instead of her parents. I knew she had her own room growing up in her parents' home; and this room was still available to her.

"I'm curious what stops you from living with your parents? Wouldn't your own room be preferable to sleeping on a couch in the living room?" I kept my voice gentle. But still, she tightened up, became silent. Then her legs started shaking. I hadn't seen this since her return from Miami. But despite her nervousness, I could see she was giving serious thought to my question.

"I just... can't," was her first response. Silence.

"Can't?" I asked, tilting my head and leaning forward, suggesting both verbally and non-verbally that I was curious.

"It's- it's- my father," she stuttered. She was so anxious; it was palpable. Her piston legs were pumping 1,200 horsepower. I also knew she wanted to tell me, but was scared.

"This seems difficult to talk about, Anne. Take your time, I'm not going anywhere." Silence. Suddenly, I felt gloom rise up from her and permeate the room.

"Look." Anne pointed to the window. Snow flurried past the window, a few flakes lighted upon the pane. Once again Anne had diverted our attention, proving how difficult this discussion was for her. "Snow falling looks so beautiful."

"Yes, it really does."

"But sometimes, doesn't it seem sad?" *That was uncharacteristic. And touching.*

Again, she became still, the leg-shaking ceased. This time the silence lasted more than five minutes; I was timing it like contractions, hoping to birth this impending disclosure during this session. The second hands ticked away on my wall clock, when —

"I never had privacy growing up in my parents' house." Her intonation was flat and matter-of-fact. *What kid does? Give me more, Anne.*

But I guess she didn't get my psychic request because she corked up for several more minutes while gazing at the snow. I waited, saying nothing. With only ten minutes left of the session, she finally blurted out, "My father used to come in my room at night and touch me." *Finally! I knew it!* I could see how painful it had been for her to not be able to get the words out, to express herself. But I hadn't noticed how tense I was about it until I felt my muscles relax following her disclosure.

When I explored as gently as I could for more information about the abuse, it was clear that Anne couldn't discuss it further. It was just too painful. So I examined her resistance, hoping that would make her feel safe enough to describe the events in more detail.

"Anne, I'm so sorry this happened to you, and it's normal not to want to talk about the details," I made sure to validate her experience. "I sense you had wanted to tell me about it for some time. Can you tell me more about wanting to disclose this information to me?"

"I wanted you to know, but I just can't talk about it yet."

"Yet?" I asked, tilting my head.

"At some point, I guess I have to, but I'm not ready." Basically, she was kindly asking me to back off. I heeded her wish. In retrospect, maybe her breakdown wouldn't have happened if I had handled this differently.

Chapter 5:
Too Close for Comfort

I was rushing to my office after an intense therapy session. It is often difficult to stop ruminating about what I had discussed and learned about myself in my own therapy. This session was particularly difficult; I discussed my uncanny ability to choose the wrong men to get involved with. I left the session with some great insight — my propensity to choose emotionally unavailable men was a result of my own fear of being fully intimate with a man. *Okay, well at least now I'm fully conscious of what keeps going wrong. I really need to remain cognizant of this inclination while dating.* I felt hopeful for the first time since the breakup of my most recent long-term relationship.

I jumped on an uptown subway and headed to my office. Earbuds securely in ears, I flipped through my iPod to find some Simon and Garfunkel to ease my mind. Once off the subway, I thought about a new patient who was coming in that day. When Tony called to set up an appointment, he spoke with a heavy Brooklyn accent, which made me chuckle a little. *And people say I have a heavy accent.* Tony was coming in for what he described as mild depression and "some other stuff that I would rather speak to you in person about." I had no idea what I was getting myself into when I took Tony on as a patient.

Tony walked into my office, and I had an immediate visceral reaction to his appearance. I always find it interesting to compare what I imagine a patient will look like to what they actually look like. Most times my images are rather analogous, but with Tony this was not the case. *Hmm, this lack of congruence may mean something.* I was remarkably curious.

I imagined Tony wearing a white "wife-beater" (a tank top T-shirt), blue jeans and Timberland work boots. He'd gel his hair up, kind of spiky, and his skin would be tanned, accentuating his bulging muscles, possibly grown with steroids. When Tony walked into session, I quickly saw that I couldn't have been more off-base. In front of me stood a tall, thin, broad-shouldered man decked out in a suit and tie. In only a few moments with him, I recognized that my reaction was not to his actual physicality per se, but rather to the way he carried himself. He comported himself with a notable stiffness. I couldn't put my finger on it yet, but there was something to his mannerisms that had an unnatural, almost creepy quality. Instead of moving smoothly with the almost involuntary quality and natural flow that most people do, Tony seemed to be performing his movements for me, each shift and stir executed with well-rehearsed choreography. It was chilling.

Holding my initial and profound observations in abeyance, Tony began to tell me his reasons for wanting to begin treatment. He described consistent bouts of dysphoric mood throughout his life. Now, at thirty-five years old, he recognized that his life was not the way he wanted it; this resulted in an exacerbation of his already depressed mood. *Interesting, he doesn't look — or feel — depressed.* Usually when a patient describes a depressed mood as a legitimate presenting complaint, I can feel the gloominess in the room, and see it in their eyes.

There was an incredible lack of congruence between Tony's reported internal experience, and the way it felt to sit with him. This is always vitally important clinical information. Furthermore, it dramatically impacts the ability to empathize with the patient's experience. Not a good feeling for a therapist. I knew then, as early as our first session, that whatever Tony was seeking treatment for was far more complicated than what he was presenting.

As I listened attentively to Tony's words, I struggled to avoid the constant distraction by my intuitive sense that he was profoundly disturbed. In my experience, it is often clinical intuition that provides the most valuable information about a patient. This is particularly relevant with a patient who presents as Tony did. The lack of congruence in his clinical presentation was communicating something more significant than his narrative. However, I needed to listen to his narrative and form an alliance in order to figure out what exactly was happening with Tony internally.

I attempted, with some success, to stay with him, contain my confusion, and gather some background information in our early sessions. I started by inquiring about his lack of contentment with where he was in his life.

"I'm 35 and I still live with my parents in the house I grew up in." He didn't look at me when he said this.

"I can tell this bothers you." When he glanced back at me, I gave him a supportive smile.

"It's not like I feel like a loser, 'cause, you know, I got a job and all and don't take no money from my folks, but I do feel a lil' ashamed about it."

"How do your parents feel about you still living with them?"

"Well, they're ol' school. You know, from It'ly." *It'ly. Wow. That really is some accent.* "They like that I'm still there. My mom loves taking care of me." *It's nice that a family's supportive, but I wonder how far this support goes.*

"How does she take care of you?"

"You know, mom stuff. Cookin'. Ironin'. Laundry."

"Do you get along with your parents?"

"Yeah, sure. I love 'em. But, to be honest, the situation isn't good for the ladies, if you get my drift." And then he winked at me, which I found quite unsettling, but also compelling. And it drove my already curious state through the roof. *Ok, I'm being drawn into something here. But what is it exactly? I need to figure out what's happening for me, and definitely not lose my objectivity.*

So I proceeded cautiously. "Not good for the ladies? Can you tell me more about this?"

Tony dragged his feet in unveiling his circumstances for me, so when he told me about his "lady" situation, it was already our third session of what would develop into an extremely difficult and tragic three-year, twice-weekly treatment. Tony's response to my question greatly assisted in gaining some understanding of pertinent underlying issues.

"I like me some sex with the ladies." He smiled wide at the funny way he put it.

"Many?" I asked, knowing I needed more information to really understand what Tony was communicating.

"Mucho many," he stated, raising his brows. "I like the chase. I get off on it. But then once I get with a woman a few times, I kinda lose interest."

Hmm, interesting. That's when I also began to sense seductiveness in the way he was relating to me.

In between our sessions, I thought about the complex array of feelings I was experiencing while sitting with Tony. I still could not entirely grasp, nor put in words, what was occurring relationally. I continued to explore his relationships with women; once I had a better understanding of this, I would be able to sort through my own feelings. So we continued.

"Tony, tell me about these women you've been with."

"I'll be honest, doc. I been with so many women, I can't even remember how many. At least a hund'erd, but pro'bly even more." He said this like he was bragging, but also with a certain nonchalance, like it was the norm for everyone. And there was also an underlying aggression and lascivious tone in his voice and demeanor. It wasn't ever-present, but when it did pop up, like now, I found it difficult to stay in the moment with him while simultaneously containing the discomfort I experienced sitting with him.

Tony described never being able to stay with any one woman. His longest relationship was four months, and during that time, he was having liaisons with two other women simultaneously. When I asked what had worked in the four-month relationship to keep it going as long as it did, particularly since he had "other options at his disposal," as he put it, he replied, "Nothing."

"Nothing was working in the relationship? Why did you stay with her?"

"'Cause I thought I should try set'lin' down. You know? I'm gettin' to that age. And I figured she didn't bug me or nothin', at least not that much, so why not make it work. But— "

"So what made you finally end it?"

"Oh, I didn't. She did. She found out about the other women." Tony wore a devilish, self-satisfied smile when he said that. To make matters more complicated for me, he then said, "I don't understand why I lose interest so quickly or why I can't remain monogamous." No surprise his sentiment didn't match his tone; on the contrary, it lacked any genuine curiosity. *What a nightmare. This man is every woman's worst fear!! Stay objective, Jacquie. It's going to be important with this patient to stay objective.*

"I'm curious, Tony. Do you see your relationships with women as a problem or are you satisfied with this lifestyle?"

"I dunno." *Ok, at least he has awareness of some discomfort.*

Or does he? I'll admit, I felt manipulated by Tony and was beginning to question his authenticity. Just as his body movements felt stiff and contrived, so did his narrative. *Not good. Why is Tony really coming to therapy?* This question haunted me for several weeks. Until eventually I was able to establish some viable hypotheses.

While Tony had planted himself firmly in his parent's house, having made no attempt to move on to a place of his own, Anne — who could use the financial support — refused to return to her family home. And, after what I had previously learned about her father's sexual advances, I couldn't blame her.

I always find it fascinating how different people respond in completely different ways to what appears to be similar life circumstances. Both Anne and Tony experienced boundary betrayals and lived in homes where they were afforded no privacy. Anne really wanted to separate and create an independent life for herself; she was making moves toward this goal. Tony was quite comfortable with his current circumstances, and almost seemed to get aroused by how easily his privacy could be violated. Neither were uncommon reactions to the experience of boundary betrayals, but each communicated something unique in their attempts to resolve or overcome their respective situations. This is part of what makes the work so intoxicating.

And the communications from each of them continued to become increasingly captivating.

We spent the next few months focusing on Anne's strengths. It is important to strike a balance, particularly with a vulnerable patient, between peeling away the layers of her symptoms, while simultaneously building up and accessing her strengths. Anne had made tremendous progress since she started treatment. I believed, based on my years of experience, that she was on the road to a real recovery. The one symptom that I wasn't sure would go away was her fixed ideas about her stalker. I was hopeful, but I also had to be realistic. In order for her to become aware and acknowledge her stalker as an internal image and process, there had a number of psychological hurdles she would need to clear.

First, she had to become curious about "him" and what he might represent. At nearly two years in treatment, any time I tried to create curiosity about "him," she would shut down, and share that she didn't feel I believed her. So, I couldn't even move her thoughts toward perceiving "him" in any other way; for her, probing was an empathic failure. Until she was able to tolerate these inquiries, there was little chance that she could integrate her externalized feelings of rejection. I had to be with her in her reality surrounding her "stalker." So, for the time being I focused on the other areas of her life and treatment where she was really doing better.

Or so I thought.

Anne was really excelling in her academics. I was so pleased for her; she seemed to feel more control and power over her life as a result of her success. She even explored the possibility of applying for additional student loans to pay her way into a small apartment of her own. Also, the increased connection and intimacy between us was undeniable. She was still constricted, but much less so. All were remarkable accomplishments. Then something happened that completely caught me off-guard.

Anne was doing really well. She had even initiated her search for a studio apartment. Unfortunately, her father was against Anne living on her own. Despite all her accomplishments over the past few years, her father felt that she was placing herself at risk for another suicide attempt if she was living unsupervised. This really set Anne back. We had not spoken about her father since that snowy winter day when she disclosed that he sexually abused her. She, understandably, became upset, particularly since her sister, who was three years younger, had her own apartment. Anne described feeling completely undermined. Obsessive thoughts about her stalker became her primary focus in the few sessions following her father's emotionally damaging comments. *Not good.*

I grew concerned about Anne. I understood the return of her ruminations about her stalker to be a concrete representation of the profound rejection she felt as a result of her father's lack of support. I imagined that Anne's sensitivity to rejection and her inability to process feelings surrounding it likely began way before college. I started to understand it through Anne's narrative as beginning with the difference in the way her father treated her as opposed to her siblings — including the abuse she suffered.

After Anne left, my thoughts settled on the relationship between her and her father and the long-term damage his actions had wreaked on Anne. I can't imagine what my life would have been like if my father had done such a thing to me. Growing up, my father treated me with respect, providing a secure home where I felt safe and loved.

And did Anne's mother know about this? Were her father's actions well-hidden? Did Anne stifle her feelings and reactions from her mother? Or did her mother notice the small things? Her husband's fleeting lascivious peek at her daughter's growing bosom. The precautionary glance of a young girl at the dinner table who wanted to put distance between her and her father. My mother, though gentle and kind, was a thoughtful, formidable woman, and I like to think that had my father done anything to me like Anne's father did to her, my mother would have recognized the signs immediately and taken him down swiftly.

Further, I do believe that some people possess an innate nurturing ability, something that cannot be taught. The mother on the playground who all the neighborhood kids flock to when they need comforting. The doctor who doesn't need to be taught bedside manners. The three women who took in Ralph off the street to give him whatever home they could, and share with this young boy what little these prostitutes had.

They weren't perfect, but they did their best to keep him safe. Still, they couldn't keep Ralph locked in the apartment. And as he grew older, there was no escaping his environment. The dangerous streets of Miami did what dangerous streets all over the world do to adolescents: it gnawed at Ralph until its gangs, its rituals, its way of life infiltrated his very existence. Yet, despite what he had done to survive, I was convinced that his nature could ultimately prevail. And I hoped the same would be true for Anne.

"I killed that boy," Ralph stated after five minutes of silence in the room.

"How do you feel about it?"

"I feel nothing." *Yeah, right! That may be what your mouth says, but your eyes are telling me a different story.* I could sense his deep regret, guilt, and sadness — but I knew better than to push him to reveal more. He would have shut down. A few days later, when he offered me the opportunity to read his journal, I believe it was his way of showing me how he really felt about the incident; but in that moment I simply asked him to continue his story.

"What boy? Who did you kill, Ralph? Tell me about the incident."

First he fumbled with his words, something I rarely saw him do; then he stopped. As he collected his thoughts, I noticed a detachment wash over him, which is when he continued without emotion. He went on to relay a chilling story. As he got deeper into the narrative, I began to unconsciously detach Ralph from the story. I didn't want to see him as a killer. Regardless, I felt it; my neck and back tightened up and a knot materialized in my stomach as I listened without interrupting.

Ralph was out one night "patrolling" the streets with three of his gang brothers. As they turned into an alley, they stumbled upon the girlfriend of one of their fellow Bloods kissing a Crips member, a no-no within the gang subculture.

"You never, ever mess with another bro's lady. And if you do and you're a Crips? Forget it. We have laws. This is one of the worst you can break." Ralph stated this with a straightforward tone that seemed to explain away any impending justice that might be incurred upon the lawbreaker. "So we snuck up on them. We grabbed the Crips, threw him to the ground. Then we started to beat the fuck outta him. He was fighting back, but was bleeding all over; I don't know where from. There was tons of blood. He pulled a knife, so I jumped up and slammed down on his face. He wasn't looking good. We beat it outta there. Just left him in the alley. And he died."

I felt numb, an unusual state for me. My hypothesis was that I, through projective identification, was feeling Ralph's defensive numbness. Simultaneously, I detached in order not to experience Ralph as a perpetrator, maintaining my empathic responses to Ralph as the victim. It was confusing in the moment, but I understand it now.

Two days later, Ralph gave me his journal. Prior to this, he had shared journal entries with me, specifically selected ones. But on this day, following the violent story he shared, a narrative that essentially was akin to an excerpt from a horror movie, he handed me his entire journal.

"Here, Ms. Jacquie. I want you to read this, but give it back before you leave today."

"Of course, Ralph. Is there something in particular you'd like me to pay close attention to? Maybe to cover in our next session?" He shook his head so fiercely, I thought his eyebrows would fly off.

"I don't want to talk about what's in there. Ever. I just want you to read it." I nodded and promised to give it back and not bring it up.

The journal was almost entirely filled with Ralph's stories. The pages were ruffled, revealing the amount of thought and time he spent with this book. It embodied a concretization of Ralph's inner world — his thoughts, feelings, and most painfully, his desperate wish to have a real family. The journal was his way to compartmentalize his horrific life, a way to maintain his humanity should he ever make it out of this city. I found myself identifying with Ralph's story: loss.

In understanding Ralph's psychology, I noticed a bit of a paradigm shift. I was thinking about Ralph psychologically, but also found myself relying on a social context model, affording me a broader spectrum of understanding. I needed to recognize the impact societal factors had on Ralph's psychology. It helped me distance myself a bit from what I heard, then read. The quite paradoxical horror running simultaneously with the profound empathy and sadness was difficult to process. I needed to contain and hold both images and feelings constant. I found it tough, but somehow, even without much clinical experience, I was able to do it.

One afternoon, nearly into my third year of therapy with Maxine, she came into session with a swollen eye and declared, "I left him! I didn't think I could do it, but I did!"

My heart fluttered. Despite the unavoidable bulging eye, Maxine looked happy and the tension in her face was relaxed. Maxine had been raped over and over by her father; she was then physically and emotionally abused by Ed. He also forced her into the world of prostitution, pawning her body out like a toy, and then controlled most of her income. She felt damaged and worthless.

Leaving Ed helped Maxine gain a sense of power and control over her own life; she was finally able to use her strengths to change her life. It was quite an intense session as I observed and felt Maxine's transformation. She turned back as she placed her hand on the doorknob of my office, at the end of the session and said, "Thank you, Doc J," which is what she preferred to call me, like an over-the-counter home remedy. "I couldn't have done this without you." I smiled and nodded. *Yes! Finally! Here is the Maxine I felt as early as our first session!* Had the moment been captured on film, I am sure the photograph would have shown me physically glowing with pride.

I remembered back to an earlier session when Maxine revealed to me that she had had to terminate a pregnancy. She was crying hysterically when she shared.

"It, it… " She looked down, trying to catch her breath between sobs, "It was my father's baby." I felt sick for her when she shared this. *Another despicable father. He should've been castrated along with Anne's.*

I maintained my outward composure, looked her straight in the eye, and simply said, "I am so, so sorry Maxine." Sometimes that's all that needs to be said. No "How does it make you feel to share that information?" or some such therapeutic question, but a simple empathetic recognition of her experience and sitting with the patient as they let loose the sadness that had been bottled up for so long. And that's what I did. We sat together as she cried.

This day, when Maxine came in and shared that she left Ed, I was proud, but I also admired Maxine's resiliency. There are many people who would have given up. But not Maxine — she knew she could change her life and leave her past behind her. Indeed, she was one remarkable woman! She came to therapy, she put in the work to change her situation, made efforts to resolve her issues and feelings about her past.

I wasn't seeing the same commitment from Tony. And perhaps that should have been a clue to the deadly situation he would bring about.

After a short time treating Tony, I concluded that gathering some additional family history might be helpful in establishing a foundation from which to work. So I changed my line of inquiry and began exploring historical information. One theme that remained a constant throughout our sessions was my feeling that Tony was inordinately manipulative. As a result, I could never be fully certain that he was telling me the truth. On the other hand, he came to every session and was never late, so I knew he was struggling with something. It was my job to figure out what it was. And he most certainly did not make it easy.

Tony did provide me with a sufficient amount of family history. He was raised by both of his parents. He had three older sisters, all of whom were married. He described his family as close. *Interesting.*

"Close?" I sat back ready to take in some information I had a feeling it might be more reliable than his relationship stories. He described family dinners, holidays, and vacations growing up. He maintained that he was always closest with his mother. Being the only boy in an Italian-American family afforded him a special status, particularly with his mother. My curiosity was stimulated. I felt as if my ears literally perked up. I knew I was getting somewhere.

We continued to discuss what turned out to be a rather complex relationship with his mother. Tony explained that his father was moderately detached. This resulted in his mother often placing him in the role that should have been occupied by his father.

"Can you tell me more about this? I really want to understand your experience." I started to recognize some damaging boundary betrayals initiated by his mother that suggestively left Tony confused at an earlier age. The betrayals were still occurring in the present. It was clear from Tony's description that he hadn't recognized his mother's behavior as a betrayal. In fact, he indulged her and colluded with her in the betrayals. *Finally, we're getting somewhere.*

I wanted to further explore the dynamics between them as I began to understand these betrayals as fundamental to his personality organization. This was important clinical material. It also helped me understand some of what was happening with Tony in his present sexual relations with women. I knew that I had to tread slowly and cautiously.

Betrayals are subtle boundary violations that are often undetectable to the person being abused. They are insidious and frequently barely discernible to the person because they don't involve overt inappropriate sexual behaviors, such as in the case of molestation. However, these types of betrayals can be just as damaging, and in some situations, even more harmful than overt sexual abuse. Patients are often confused by them, insofar as there is a lack of certainty surrounding the events, and they often don't identify them as wrong. The break in trust and the violations that have happened often reveal themselves in the way the person relates intimately as an adult.

Another important observation was the absence of Tony's father in his narrative. He described his father as detached. When I probed for a little more information surrounding their relationship, Tony offered almost none. He did describe watching sports on television with his father, but aside from that, his father's presence was practically non-existent in Tony's world. This is a common theme for many patients who are the victims of covert sexual abuse. The enmeshed parents — the solicitor of the betrayals — typically are the ones that enter the session. The more disconnected parent remains separate from his/her inner chaos, and therefore the experience remains much more inaccessible.

Since Tony only divulged small amounts of information regarding his father, I knew from experience that his feelings about their relationship were deeply buried and that Tony probably didn't have words to describe feelings associated with him. Sometimes it took a few years for a patient to even become curious about his/her feelings associated with the parent that remained absent. Interestingly, the absent parent plays an equally important role in the betrayals; by not being present, they "allow" the abuse to happen. *You will definitely have to wait to confront this one. It will take Tony a long time to access these feelings. I will listen for any possible openings, but based on my experience, this won't be for at least two years.*

Tony's narrative provided some excellent examples of his toxic relationship with his mother. He described an incident where he had a woman staying the night, which was a relatively common occurrence. His mother knew Tony was having a "sleep-over" guest. Instead of respecting Tony's privacy, she would open the door, without knocking first, and say, "Tony, it's time for breakfast; Momma's making pancakes." I felt a knot in my stomach upon hearing this.

"Oh my gosh. How awkward. Did she do it again after that?"

"Again?" He nearly chuckled. "Yes, she did it again. One time, me and the girl were both buck naked, no sheets covering us." *Wow. He likes it, which is incredibly disturbing. Tread lightly, Jacquie, he is so enmeshed with his mother. You know from experience that you can't address this directly. Just create curiosity.*

"So… after that time, why didn't you put a lock on your door?"

"My mom wouldn't like that. It's her house and she feels like she should have complete access to it." *It's not like you're a teenager. And "access to it?" Gross!*

After our session, while walking home, I was reminded of a situation during my post-doctoral fellowship training when a patient terminated treatment with me. Mary came into therapy because of excessive anxiety and compulsive behaviors that began immediately after finding out her husband was having an affair. Her story was quite intriguing. She divorced her first husband, who sounded like an emotionally stable and wealthy lawyer, to be with a Swiss photographer. Three months later, Mary and Jon were married. Mary could not leave New York because she had a nine-year-old daughter from her first marriage. Jon refused to live in New York because he preferred Switzerland. They visited each other quite frequently, but essentially it was a long-distance marriage.

Jon lived like a vagabond; he had no home of his own, no address; and at 50 years old, he simply would stay with friends, bouncing around from house to house. Mary and he primarily communicated via email. However, there were days and sometimes even weeks when Mary wouldn't get an email from him and she would have no idea where or how to find him. This left her in a state of panic. Although I knew she was replaying historical issues by choosing a non-committal drifter for a husband, I maintained my neutrality because she had so much difficulty talking about anything other than her obsessions about Jon.

Jon eventually disclosed to Mary during his latest visit to New York that he had a three-month affair with a woman from Austria. Jon maintained that he had ended the relationship because of Mary, but made it amply clear that he was still friends with the Austrian woman. Mary begged him to end the friendship, but Jon would not concede. This left Mary in a constant state of panic, unable to control ruminations about Jon's whereabouts, and fundamentally feeling abandoned.

During our year-long treatment together, I worked hard to help Mary with her symptoms and tried to create some curiosity within her about her attachment to Jon. Our sessions were almost exclusively filled with her ambivalence about ending the marriage. It was unbearable to listen to her stories about Jon; I found myself itching to tell her to leave him. I recognized and understood that the intensity of my own desire to assert my feelings was a result of her pushing, via projective identification, to do so. Essentially, I was being drawn into an enactment: She wanted me to tell her to leave because she couldn't fully admit to herself that it was the best thing for her own sanity. He was driving her "crazy."

I held off. I knew better than to respond with direct advice in this circumstance. Mary was engaged and identified with him. So purporting an opinion would be antithetic to my role as her clinician — which was to help her speak these words on her own. Unfortunately, as the treatment progressed and my inquiries changed, Mary began to sense that I thought she should leave. I never said it directly; I tried hard to remain neutral in the sessions. But, I sensed that Mary recognized my position as a result of our dialogue.

Two days after what would become our final session, Mary called to terminate treatment. I tried to have her come in for one final session, indicating that I thought it was important to process what was going on for her. She refused. I could hear her anger, although she did not admit her feelings to me. After reviewing the last few sessions with my supervisor, I surmised that Mary left treatment because she couldn't leave Jon; through my interactions with her in the final sessions leading up to termination, Mary realized that I did believe she should leave him. She couldn't bear the thought that I might convince her to do it, so she terminated.

My supervisor taught me that despite the obvious abuse my patient was exposed to, one must be careful about what is said in therapy under these circumstances. In instances like this one, the patient is often identified with the person causing them pain. As a result, one must be careful not to point out the obvious, but rather guide the patient toward their own understanding and hope they make the decision that is in their best interest.

Having made this mistake with Mary, I realized the fragile position I was in with Tony. During our first year of treatment, I listened to his stories surrounding the serious boundary violations he experienced with the associated difficulties he had with women. Tony was unable to make the connection between the two, and because of the profound enmeshment with his mother, I sensed that it was too soon to intervene. So I listened. Another compelling betrayal that was a constant in Tony's home was that both his mother and he often walked around naked; it started when Tony was a young child, but continued to the present day. At 36 years old.

Every time he brought this up, I felt disgusted, but Tony seemed aroused. I sensed that Tony was stimulated by these exchanges with his mother, but simultaneously, unconsciously repulsed, as well. He needed to keep his disgust hidden from his conscious awareness; becoming aware of the toxicity of these betrayals would force him to separate from his "mommy." This was something he just could not do. As a result, I was holding and experiencing his repulsion for him; and he quite maladaptively continued to express his confusion in his relationships with women.

I was also beginning to wonder how these dynamics were playing out in our relationship. Tony was quite seductive, but also manipulative and aggressive. His subtle attempts to arouse me or seduce me were mixed with potent aggression. It was spine-chilling, disturbing, and alarming; but it did give me insight into how he likely interacted with other women. It enabled me to generate hypotheses, and facilitated my ability to begin to conceptualize Tony's inner world.

I wanted to explore our relationship and the thoughts and emotions that Tony was having. I was so unbelievably curious to hear what his experience was like to sit with a woman — me — where there were clear boundaries; I imagined that he felt quite powerless and even emasculated. And as I suspected, his unsuccessful attempts to seduce me left him frustrated and rageful. Exploring these dynamics was key to Tony's treatment; but it was too soon and I knew it.

Classical psychoanalytic and developmental theories hold that every therapeutic issue can be traced back to one's relationship with one's parents. I don't agree with any absolutes, as everyone is different, but through my clinical work, I do believe there is credence to these assumptions. It was certainly fundamental in understanding Tony, Anne, Maxine, and many of Tess's issues. In understanding Ralph's psychological development, I believe it was his surrogate mothers that saved him.

A striking feature that fit well with my way of thinking was how much these three amazing women helped Ralph. I noticed that when reading his entries describing these women, I was getting irritated, pissed with society. *Here are these three incredible women, who of their own volition took in a young, homeless, sad boy and raised him as if he were their own child. So what if they were prostitutes? Who cares what their occupation is? They are remarkably caring women; women that mainstream society would see as vagrants, tramps, or just garbage simply because of their occupation!*

I was fuming the more I thought about it. I nearly felt steam spewing from my ears. When I feel strongly about something, I become passionate. And regarding this, I was overflowing with passion. *Why do we live in a world that is so constricted that one can be judged based on something one does for a living? And this happens without informing ones' ideas and/or judgments through understanding the totality of a person. It makes me sick!* Look at Kristy. A doctor *and* a prostitute, albeit a high-class escort. Was Kristy a better person because she was a doctor? I didn't believe so.

On the surface, Tony's family was the icon of the American nuclear family — two loving parents, financial comfort, a stay-at-home mom, siblings he was close with, and he even had a dog and a backyard. It all fit with the societal image of the "perfect" family. Yet, beneath the façade, Tony was repeatedly exposed to extreme dysfunction and abuse. And

Tony's relationships, his understanding of boundaries, his identity, basically his entire life revealed the damaging consequences.

Ralph's mothers and the structure of the family he was being raised in, on the surface, ostensibly, represented the opposite. And yet, Ralph was taught to be a survivor, to have integrity, basic care for others, and I truly believe he internalized the love he was given by these women. Despite Ralph's tough exterior, there was a boy inside who someday would evolve into a man — a man who had the strength to pursue his goals and live his life with honor.

A later incident would show evidence that my images of Ralph and his future were likely correct…

I was still seething.

I went outside to calm myself down. The Atlantic breeze was strong that day, enough to carry the salty sub-tropical air miles inland. I searched for a private spot to sit, but the courtyard was teeming with counselors and maintenance workers. I wanted to read the rest of Ralph's journal, but was having difficulty concentrating because my anger made me feel constricted sitting in my office. Finding no respite from my emotions outside, I returned to the cooler interior of the detention center, and wandered around its dark confines until I found a spot where the hot Miami sun illuminated a quiet corner. There I sat for a spell until I regained my composure. I went back into the therapy office and continued reading while the kids were in their classes. It was always quiet on the unit during class time. I continued reading. By the end, I was in tears.

Ralph's journal chronicled fictional tales; though written in the third person, it was obvious that they were all, in fact, his story. The narrative was about a young boy abandoned by his family and left to survive on the streets alone. He was then offered a home by a young female woman whom he met on the street one day when he was selling crack. She took him in and he lived with her and her two female roommates. He expressed love and gratitude toward them, but the boy in the story spent many nights crying, imagining what his life would be like if he had "real parents" who loved him and took care of him.

Although there were variations to his stories about what it would feel like to be raised by his parents, the theme was always the same. He wanted to be loved and taken care of. He wanted to not feel abandoned. He wanted to go to school and learn with other kids, instead of dropping out and having to commit felonies just to survive. He wanted to erase the images of the several people he killed just to remain a respected member of his gang. Two sentences that Ralph wrote stuck with me: "He just wants a normal life. He doesn't want to feel pangs of loss, every minute, every day."

I was in the bathroom crying by the end. Later that day when I went to Ralph's cell to return his book, I desperately wanted to reach out to him; I wanted to hug him and tell him how sad I felt for him. But I felt his guardedness; his non-verbal communication that, despite the fact that he exposed himself to me, informed me that he couldn't let me see him break down. I respected what he wanted.

"Here you go, Ralph." I stood in front of the cell that the guard had opened for me. "Thank you so much for sharing this with me." Our eyes met. He nodded as he got up from his bed to retrieve the book in my hand. Sadness was wearing lines in this young man's face. He took the book from me, then he closed the cell bars, sliding them with a clang.

"I'll see you tomorrow, Ms. Jacquie," and that was that. He turned his back on me as he returned to his bed, his shoulders slouched.

Later on my walk home after my session with Maxine, I found myself gazing into the shoe store staring at the Red Stilettos. My visceral sensation reminded me of my childhood memory when I first observed and was fascinated by the woman on 42nd Street with the Red Stilettos. I was in a momentary trance.

I went inside and tried them on, imagining myself stepping into the shoes of the many sex workers I have counseled. I slipped into the shoes to see how they felt, and it was just as I suspected...

I walked out of the shoe store with a pair of black platforms. I berated myself: *So you, Jacquie, elegance with an edge; risky and rebellious, but thinly veiled by a bit of conformity.* I was a block away from the store when I turned around, stormed back in, and bought the damned Red Stilettos.

It was my way of sharing with Maxine, Kristy, and the many other women in the sex industry I have treated. Buying those shoes, I felt I was joining those women in solidarity, standing up for them, and stomping on a societal conviction that I didn't agree with and, through my patients' narratives, found to be incredibly sexist and damaging for women!

My thoughts ran to mainstream culture, one that I, too, was a part of. Well... sort of. I felt my stride become faster; I was pissed! *How is it that something like prostitution comes with a label? How can society designate and ultimately define a person simply as what they do? It is so damaging to define a person as something without understanding the context from which it arises. Maxine, Kristy, Ralph's "mothers"... are living, breathing people. So, the President that sends innocent men in the military to kill other people is supported, but a woman (or man) who is struggling to exist in the same world, making an effort to overcome basic human conflicts, is judged using an entirely differently set of criteria — based solely on choice of occupation. Ugh!!! I wish I could change peoples' attitudes. Well, one thing's for sure — I'll never be elected for office. Huh, so there!*

Then again, don't we, as individuals, identify ourselves as what we do? How many people rate their success in life by the popularity of what they do for a living? Happiness in one's own existence is often contingent upon pride in their job. When they suffer shame, dissatisfaction, etc., in their career, existential crises often follow.

I restarted my walk home. Maxine's session had drained me in a good crossing-the-marathon-finish-line-in-record-time kind of way. Once home, I changed into my staple tank top and cutoff sweatpants, slipped on the Red Stilettos, and sprawled out on my bed staring at the vibrant color on my feet; I was lost in thought. About Maxine. About Kristy. And about the ways their shoes looked dissimilar, each independently communicating something unique to their inner experience.

I turned onto my stomach and bent back my knees, kicking my new Red Stilettos in the air. As I entertained myself, like a giddy child playacting, I began mulling over the details of their shoes and the tales they could tell as they stepped across the New York pavement. *The Real Story of the Red Stilettos. What yarns those shoes could spin.* I was starting to feel better. I was having fun. *Maybe everyone could learn something by slipping their feet into a pair of Red Stilettos.*

Maxine's Red Stilettos were patent leather. There were some scuff marks, as is relatively unavoidable with patent leather shoes. Sure they were worn, but they were tough, too; much like Maxine's strengths and her physical and emotional scars. Maxine, like many of my patients, often took her shoes off during session. Interestingly, the inside of Maxine's shoes also revealed insight into her internal world; they were softly padded, but the interior was ripped apart: Maxine's gentle, sensitive nature that slowly and insidiously was broken. She was tough on the outside, but actually quite tender on the inside, as I learned about her over our three years together.

A few months after Maxine stopped working as a prostitute, she began studying for her GED. She planned to finish her high school equivalency, and then apply for a bachelor's degree in sociology. She came to session with a new pair of heels; beautiful deep blue velvet.

"Now those are a pair of shoes." And apparently Maxine thought so, too, as she brimmed with self-satisfaction at my compliment.

"They're a gift to myself. A sort of congrats to me for making changes in my life. I wanted a new pair of shoes." She admired them again, then looked up, her eyes huge, open, and clear. "It was time."

My throat caught. I knew what she meant. "I like your choice, Maxine." I smiled.

Kristy, the med student, strutted around in Red Stilettos made of soft suede, classy, with a slight platform in front. She was tiny, but in those stilettos she stood tall. They eventually became weathered as she sometimes wore them to sessions even with some snow on the ground. Despite the stains, they still appeared sophisticated and tasteful. One session, Kristy strutted in wearing her stilettos following a rather major snowstorm.

"Wow, you're brave venturing out in those shoes with all that ice and snow on the ground. I probably would have fallen on my backside."

"I don't let the weather stop me from wearing what I want." *Yep, that's just what I expected her to say.*

I was still on the bed kicking my legs back and forth, swinging those stilettos like a little girl in dress-up mode; I laughed to myself, *I'm in the wrong shoes.* I was recalling, processing and trying to grasp the essence of what I felt when I first put those damned Red Stilettos on just an hour ago; I bought velvet ones.

They felt daring, sexy and freeing, but they were also incredibly uncomfortable; they felt just as I imagined they would. My last thought before I had to take them off — my feet were throbbing inside of them — was that though defying convention could feel incredibly freeing, bold, and courageous, it could be highly uncomfortable, physically and emotionally. And maybe next time I'll choose something a bit more subtle to express my lack of conventionality.

I took the shoes off and put on my orange low-rise bell-bottoms. With my cropped tank top, my lower stomach was exposed revealing my small, black and usually inconspicuous tattoo: EROS. I smiled as I placed the Red Stilettos on my shoe rack. I thought about returning them, my feet were begging me to, but those red shoes had quickly become a physical representation of my defiant side. And every once in a while, I slip those heels on to take my rebel side out for a walk, my feet be damned.

Chapter 6:
The Siren's Call

Tess. Dear, dear Tess.

She had spent so many years believing she wasn't worth the attention she could receive from the opposite sex, it was hard work shoring up a positive foundation for her self-esteem. So the next two years of our treatment together focused on garnering her obvious strengths, but while I was attempting to help her acknowledge and integrate these strengths into her life, Tess worked at undermining much of what I was trying to help her with. And her reason was always the same: "I'm too old."

Concomitantly during these two years, she never missed a chance to verbally criticize my appearance; it happened almost every session. Whenever I probed for further elaboration of what was happening between us, her answer was the same, "You will never meet a husband looking as you do." I would have liked to imagine that she was genuinely concerned, but there was always an underlying hostility in her tone.

It was in the midst of this challenging work when something powerful happened; this event significantly altered the relational dynamics between us. Tess had been hospitalized for "manic episodes" twice before we started working together. During our three years of sessions, I had never witnessed Tess manifesting anything even close to mania. I am also always skeptical of a bipolar diagnosis, as I believe many people diagnosed with bipolar actually have an agitative depression.

Tess's sixty-fifth birthday was just six weeks away when I started to notice a significant change in her clinical presentation. She was racing during sessions — speaking quickly and excitedly. She was phoning me in between sessions, which was a rarity. Tess was also shopping every day; she would bring in high end, expensive clothing — items she could not afford — to show me during our sessions. She also was speaking endlessly about her impending birthday, a milestone date she felt was a concrete representation that she was "old," and she even repeated on numerous occasions, "See? My life is over. No man will want me now!"

We spoke collaboratively about the aging process and I tried to help her rationalize the truth: Sixty-five was not old, and people meet and marry at all different ages. I believe this was an error in my clinical judgment, and a sign that I felt she was going to spiral into a full-blow manic episode. Aging for Tess had implications far surpassing meeting a man; aging ostensibly was equivalent to annihilation. She had long ago surpassed the age her mother was when she died. And now she was only slightly younger than her father was when dementia took over his life. The threat of death hung over her each day, which I'm sure contributed to her attitude about growing old.

No reality testing efforts were going to work for her at this point in her treatment. Her ideas about aging and the associated losses were fundamental to her self-organization. Additionally, she had no one to spend her birthday with. Tess, who up until this point always respected the therapeutic boundaries, began to ask *me* to have dinner with her on her birthday.

I knew having dinner with Tess on her birthday was inappropriate (*or was it?*), but her palpable anxiety and ominous feeling about that day left me rationalizing reasons why it might be the precise thing to do clinically, based on her circumstances. Simultaneous to my own internal quandary, Tess's manic symptoms began to get much worse. The most momentous of these symptoms was her worsening reality testing — including spending beyond her means — which increased as her birthday drew closer. Cash-poor, she splurged on a $500 timepiece courtesy of MasterCard. She selected a gold Bulova wristwatch with a brown leather strap. Though it was gorgeous and she got it discount, she still could not afford it. Then, in her last session prior to my "betrayal of her," she graced my threshold sporting a $1,000 fur vest. The choice of fashion surprised me almost as much as how much she spent on it. The vest did not seem Tess's style; it was as though she were trying on someone else's life, which made sense considering her birthday acted as a reminder of her unavoidable aging.

I began to receive frantic messages from her cousin Marc informing me about her obvious deterioration and exacerbation of symptoms; from his longtime perspective, Tess had become a danger to herself. I tried endlessly to call her, but couldn't reach her by phone. I was quite concerned. After calling her one last time and not reaching her, my choice seemed clear. I decided that the safest thing to do was call 911, have the police pick her up, and bring her to the psychiatric emergency room. I actually loathe requesting to have a patient picked up before talking with them; in this situation, I had no choice.

But the moment I hung up the phone, my mind began racing. *Did I allow her cousin's concerns to adversely affect my judgment? Should I have held off? Tried calling one more time? Maybe I should have gone to her apartment myself. What if she's fine and her cousin prompted me to overreact? This call could possibly rupture our therapeutic alliance.* I was drowning in self-doubt in the hour-and-a-half that I was waiting for a phone call from the E.R. I hoped I had made the right decision. The wait was almost too much to bear.

Not too long prior to this event, I experienced a similar situation with Anne that now pushed my self-doubt to the limits.

Anne came into session looking entirely different. Her beautiful, thick wavy hair that was always tied back in a ballet dancer's bun was flowing freely. She didn't have her glasses on, and she was dressed in a form-fitting T-shirt and tight jeans. It was jarring, really; it must have shown on my face, but I was sure Anne didn't notice, she barely acknowledged me as she stormed in and sat in the patient chair. I had never realized how beautiful Anne was; I found her attractive, but without her layers and pulled-back hair, she was a knockout.

Thrown off by her change in appearance, thoughts raced through my head about what she was communicating through this obvious transformation of her physical body. I was just about to notice this with her when she suddenly began to go off; she was yelling quite loudly at the ceiling. *Oh my gosh! I don't think I've ever seen her teeth before! What's come over her?* I definitely never heard her raise her voice this loudly before this day, curses spewing from her mouth. The content of her tirade confirmed my hypothesis about her stalker. She was screaming at her stalker and ranting about how he wouldn't let her go, nor move on with her life.

Wow, her "stalker" is her father AND the young man in college. I now had a complete understanding about what led to the development of a concretization of Anne's internal world. The incest held her back from being able to establish an intimate relationship with a man; this is often a common feature of survivors of sexual abuse. Then, when Anne was in college and tried to establish some intimacy with an appropriate peer, she couldn't and/or the young man of interest wouldn't. This stirred up historical issues of abuse and rejection, leaving Anne feeling powerless and helpless.

Anne was unable to discuss, process or resolve what happened with her father or the young man in college; hence, the power of her unconscious created a way for her to compartmentalize and avoid dealing with her feelings. The external image of a stalker was the end result, and a representation of years of unprocessed and profound powerlessness. And now, with her father's untimely and insensitive remarks diminishing Anne's accomplishments and dreams for a better life, she was unraveling.

I asked Anne while she was in the midst of her one-sided dialogue with her stalker where he was. She pointed to the ceiling. She looked at me and responded, "He's there, right there!" as she pointed to the ceiling. She continued her diatribe. Her basic theme was attacking him for not letting her move on with her life and pleading with him to, "Leave me alone!" I sat with her and listened to her attack her stalker. I was concerned about her safety, remembering that her previous suicide attempt was pre-reflective, dissociative and impulsive. However, I knew Anne was not entirely dissociated because in between her tirades, she would look down from the ceiling, make perfect eye-contact with me, and apologize for yelling and cursing.

It was a few minutes before the end of our session. I mentioned the time to Anne, asking her if she was okay to leave and if she could come in again tomorrow. Anne said she was fine; she seemed so lucid and calm when speaking to me. She did agree to schedule an appointment for the following day. While going over my appointments and finding a mutually good time for us to meet, my mind was racing through a complex discourse.

Is Anne at risk for hurting herself? She responded that she wasn't feeling suicidal when I asked her, and I actually believed her. I want her to feel safe enough to attack and yell to and/or about her stalker in session. If I suggest going to the hospital, I take away any feeling of safety in the room for her to express her feelings, and it took so long for us to get to this point. Is this a turning point or is it a sign of deterioration in functioning? The latter would suggest hospitalization; the former would make it entirely contraindicated. What do I do?

Anne most assuredly seemed to be in control when we were scheduling our appointment for the following day.

"Anne, are you sure you're okay? Do you feel fine to leave?"

"Really, I'm fine."

"This was an extremely emotionally releasing session. If you'd like to sit in the waiting room for a while to collect yourself, please do. I'd be right through that door for you."

"Thank you so much, Dr. Simon, but I'll be fine."

"Okay, then. Have a good day. You have my number should you need me."

"No worries."

" I'll see you tomorrow then?"

"Of course." *Of course. Famous last words.* As it would turn out, they *were* the last words we spoke in treatment. Anne left, gently closing the door behind her. It was the last time I would see her.

I had an hour before my next appointment, which was rather unusual, and part of the reason I was urging her to stay if she needed to. I knew I'd be free to help. But with Anne gone, I sprawled out across my couch, exhausted from the session.

Despite the vegging out my mind was screaming for, I felt compelled to really think through what had just happened. But...

I dozed off. When I awoke, I was panicked. My first thought was that I made a mistake. *You shouldn't have let her leave, Jacquie. The remarkable change in her appearance and presentation suggested that something serious was happening. Damn! I hope I'm wrong. But I don't think I am. I just wasn't able to make a quick enough assessment given the intensity and complexity of what was happening in the session. What have I done? I'd better call her.* I felt nauseous and light-headed when I got up to phone Anne. There was no answer. *Someone always answers when I call Anne. Her grandmother never leaves the house!* I went into the bathroom and threw up.

I had a student clinician, Sarah Jane, waiting for our supervision, so I had to focus. I tried to soothe myself. *I'll call again after Sarah Jane's appointment.* I managed to stay focused and supervise my student. Although, while we were in our supervisory meeting, I noticed a call coming in, it was an unfamiliar number; I was relieved to hear the beep from my phone indicating that there was a message.

As soon as my student left, I checked my voicemail. *Oh no!*

It was the police.

Anne had been arrested. I called back immediately; what happened was astonishing. After Anne left our session, she went to her apartment building, broke into the apartment one floor above hers, and completed ransacked the place. A neighbor heard her, called the police; they came and subsequently arrested her. When describing the events, she told the police that the apartment she raided belonged to her stalker.

Fortunately, they realized she had some psychological problems. They asked if she had a therapist, and Anne willingly gave them my phone number. I was seriously floored, but also somewhat relieved. I was informed that there would not be charges pressed due to her "condition." Anne was going to be evaluated by their psychiatrist and referred for inpatient hospitalization. Anne wanted to speak with me, but the police wouldn't allow her to. I was informed that I would be contacted by the hospital once she was admitted.

This is what plagued my thoughts following Marc's call about Tess and my subsequent inability to reach her.

After the police picked up Tess and had her brought to the emergency room, the waiting felt interminable. Finally, I spoke with the resident from the psychiatric E.R. I was relieved to learn that I had, in fact, made the right decision. As it turned out, by the time the police arrived at Tess's apartment, she was hallucinating. But now I was faced with another quandary.

My decision on whether to visit a patient while hospitalized is always processed cautiously and thoroughly; I always consider the unique dyad, where we are in our therapy, the circumstances surrounding the hospitalization, and the best interest of the patient. Upon reflection, I decided to visit Tess; I felt seeing me might ground her. I also thought it was relatively likely that she wouldn't have anyone else visiting.

Once my last session ended, I packed up my things quickly and headed straight for the E.R., where Tess was still waiting to be admitted. I was a bit anxious as I walked over. When the police picked up Tess to bring her on the unexpected trip to the hospital, it was quite likely she went against her will. Based on my previous experiences with patients, I knew there was a substantial and understandable possibility that she would be enraged. As I was escorted by security to the psychiatric E.R., *Please don't give me a hard time, Tess. I'm already dying over this.*

Tess was in the first of about ten small rooms; her door was ajar, and I slowly peeked into the room. She caught my face in the narrow door opening, so I pushed myself all the way in. Contrary to Tess's usual bitter edginess, she gave me a big smile and stated, "Were you on a date? You look beautiful. Is this how you look when you're not at work?" I sensed that Tess was disoriented, although, I must admit, I did find her softer, complimentary style of relating toward me relieving. I had come straight from my office and looked the same as I always did when we met for sessions. *What's going on with her? I have never seen such a shift in one's personality.*

As I sat with her in this cramped, bare, and rather depressing room, I did not immediately notice how disoriented she was. "Tess, you had me so worried. I knew you were home, but when I called several times, you didn't answer. I was afraid something terrible had happened."

"Oh, Jacquie, you silly. I couldn't answer the phone. I didn't want to tie up the line."

"Why is that?"

" I was expecting a call from Bill Murray to schedule our 'Lost in Translation' date."

Wow, she was really out of it. Still is out of it.

Tess was confabulating — she pointed to the blue on her blanket and spoke about how clear and blue the sky looked and how much sun she saw. It felt eerie; almost spine-chilling to see her so disoriented. She also mentioned a few times during the visit that we were in a subway car together.

And that Woody Allen was coming to visit her.

I made no attempt to confront her disorientation or reality testing; I was there as a visitor, and sensed that she would not be able to process or respond to my usual inquiries. *This is so upsetting; I feel utterly helpless.* I stayed about 30 minutes; Tess graciously thanked me for my visit; she looked up as I was leaving and again remarked with an admiration that I had never received from her: "You are beautiful."

I left the hospital and walked home. I was unsettled by my experience with her; it felt surreal, like I was on the set of a Lifetime movie. The resident I spoke with said that they were admitting her; she was having a psychotic episode and she needed to be stabilized. They had all of my contact information and would keep me abreast of her progress. Despite knowing she was in good hands, I was distressed by our visit. I couldn't see her the next day because the visiting hours would end before my last patient; *I'll visit again the day after tomorrow; hopefully she'll be stabilized by then.*

The following day I did receive a message from the inpatient unit. Tess was doing a bit better; they were going to change her medication and thought she would be discharged within a week. I felt soothed by the message. Unfortunately, my relief was short lived. It was later that same day that I began to receive harsh, angry messages from Tess. *I guess she's feeling better now.* Once she was stabilized and her thoughts were lucid, she realized what happened; wow, she *was* livid about me calling 911. She wanted me to contact the resident and insist that she be released. "How could you do this to me?" she yelled. I let her know what had happened and why she needed to be there. She didn't care what I thought; she wanted to go home!

As planned, Tess was released at the end of the week; a resident called to inform me that she was being discharged and the recommendation was to return to our twice-weekly outpatient sessions. After a few days went by and I hadn't heard from her, I called Tess to schedule an appointment. Considering her curt tone, it didn't surprise me when she outright refused to come in. Despite my persistence, we had reached a stalemate. *I know I need to give her some space. I'll wait a few days and see if I hear from her. If I don't, I think I should call again.* These types of situations are always difficult; the way one proceeds must always be based on the unique dyad — this is important when considering an intervention with an angry patient who doesn't want to see you.

After all the years I had been treating Tess, I felt my decision to call her back was the right one. My palms were sweating, and I was experiencing mild heart palpitations when I called her back three days later. I tried to humor myself in order to squelch my anxiety. *I think I need a Valium in order to make it through this phone call.* I skipped the Valium, dialed, and waited, bracing myself for the worst. I listened without defending myself as Tess shared her outrage with me. Quite honestly, as unsettling as her newfound temper was, I felt almost relieved for her that she was able to let loose from her normally reserved ways. She did agree to come in the following day.

It was difficult at first to listen to her ire-filled recount of what happened. Finally after about four sessions, she "forgave" me. Once her fury had subsided and she realized that I hadn't betrayed her, the clinical material that began to emerge dramatically shifted our relationship for the better; it actually deepened our rapport. In spite of Tess's gross disorientation while in the E.R., she did remember my visit. She also remarkably recalled her vision of us in a subway car, and was able to recognize that she was disoriented and we actually were in her hospital room.

My curiosity piqued, I wanted to discuss her comments surrounding my appearance; I thought it was vital clinical material. Yet, I sensed it would be a more effective exchange if she brought it up; I waited to see if she would. During the second session following Tess's hospitalization, she did indulge me. She remarked, "You looked beautiful when you came to visit me. Do you always look like that when you go out?"

Now what do I do? Do I disclose the truth — that I visited her after work, and was dressed and made-up the same as I always am? Do I just explore her images of me and the way she perceived me without such a disclosure? Come on, Jacquie, think fast! All clinicians experience moments where the course of inquiry diverges into equally solid, yet dissimilar enough paths that the outcome could be different based on the choice of intervention.

I decided on exploring her images of me, at least to start with. "How did I look different?"

"You were glowing. In fact, you look beautiful today, too." Her voice raised, almost giddy. *Hmm, interesting, I'm glad I decided not to disclose the reality of my appearance to her.* Something shifted for her as a result of my visit, and the way she perceived my appearance as different clearly indicated this shift. It communicated something about the new way she was experiencing me and our relationship.

In the moment, I hypothesized that my visit showed Tess how I really cared about her well-being, and as a result she was beginning to internalize some of the positive aspects of our therapeutic relationship. She could finally experience me as a whole person; this indicated the start of her ability to let go of her sole emphasis on my physical appearance, and to experience some of my internal qualities. This is not dissimilar to the way a man in a romantic relationship may find that as his affection grows for his "plain-Jane" mate, he begins to regard a change in her appearance from modest to beautiful.

However, there was a coincidental occurrence that I could not ignore as an additional possibility. Just three weeks prior to Tess's hospitalization, I began dating a man I really liked. Tess was not privy to this information, but I had to consider the potentiality that she could sense this on some intuitive level. Even more likely: *I probably AM glowing!*

Yes, I had met someone new, someone different than the men I usually dated. And after treating Tony for six months and hearing his "war stories" on dating women, my faith in love — or even simply meeting a decent man — had begun to falter, so meeting this new man couldn't have come at a more opportune time in my life. He was sexy (okay, he did have that in common with my former flames), honest, interesting, ambitious, and, most importantly, definitely emotionally available. We immediately connected, and I sensed with astute intuition that this was going to go somewhere. My belief was well-warranted, as this man eventually asked me to take his hand in marriage.

Things with Anne, however, did not turn out as rosy as they did with Tess. A few days after her hospitalization, I heard from both the hospital and Anne. Prior to these phone calls, I spent my therapy hours and private time completely berating myself. *Jacquie, after all of your training and clinical experience how could you make such a dramatic error?* Finally, my therapist helped me recognize, once again, that I was not omnipotent, but human; in being human, one is allowed to make mistakes.

"Jacquie, you constantly strive to be perfect. Striving for perfection is admirable, but if you expect to *be* perfect, you'll always fall short," Gwen reminded me. She was right, of course. *Of course. Anne's famous last words.*

Anne stayed in the hospital for three weeks, and then was referred for intensive five-day-per-week outpatient day treatment. She asked me in our last phone conversation if she could continue seeing me while in the day treatment. I explained to her that her insurance wouldn't cover both treatments, and also that it is usually not good practice to be in treatment with two different therapists.

I did tell her how much I enjoyed working with her and that despite what had happened, I had no doubt once she was feeling better she would be able to finally attain her life goals. And I truly believed that. She thanked me over and over. When we hung up, I felt a real sense of loss. When I took Anne on as a patient, I wanted to help her, see her case through to the end. And, honestly, my curiosity was aroused, but unfulfilled. My time with Anne ended incomplete. And neither my curiosity nor my need to wrap up her case in a neat bow would likely ever be satisfied. But rationally, I knew that for Anne's best interest, she was exactly where she needed to be.

I'm not sure if I'll ever see Anne again. But I've spent many hours reviewing her case in my mind. Ultimately, I believe my earlier thoughts were slightly off-target. Anne's "stalker" (the stalker in her mind) was never her college boyfriend, Danny, but rather only her father. The stalker seemed to make appearances and be in the forefront of her thoughts when her father's real presence increased. Ever-present in her mind, her stalker-father prevented her from desiring sex with Danny. Because she never had sex with him, he possibly didn't want to continue their relationship when she returned to school for the beginning of her junior year.

That was when her stalker-father started appearing, following her around, haunting her. He hung over her head like a dark cloud, omnipresent, which was why she yelled at the ceiling and swore he was living above her in the apartment she eventually ripped apart. And how he always knew where she was and what she was doing and what schools she later applied to. And why it manifested into a crazed episode when she returned from the vacation in which she lost her virginity. In reality, the boyfriend may have ended their relationship because she wouldn't have sex with him; but in her mind, she may well have created the delusion that her stalker knew about her losing her virginity in Miami and thought she was a dirty slut because of it.

In the end, my hypothesis could be far off the mark, but since I'll probably never know the truth, believing this possibility gives me some closure on her case.

Between Tess's sessions, I ruminated long over the "boyfriend-disclosure do-I-don't I" dilemma. I did not want to share that I was in a relationship that had the potential to become serious. Through my internal processing of how to grasp the essence of what this shift meant, I decided I would investigate this at our next session.

"Tess, I'm curious about something: Do you have any thoughts about why you have decided that I look beautiful now?"

"I was always taught not to question a compliment, Jacqueline. Just take it with grace." She smirked. I held a blank stare, awaiting a proper answer. "I don't know. You just do."

"I find it perplexing that you spent the first three-plus years of our therapy critiquing my appearance. But now you are referring to me as 'beautiful.' Any thoughts on what this might mean?"

Tess touched her hair, replacing the fictitious errant strand back to its invisible rightful spot. "When I noticed that you weren't taking my beauty and makeup tips, well, I felt a little rejected." She looked at me, perhaps to make sure I was fine with this confession. "When I was younger, I was so beautiful and all the people in my life asked me for suggestions about how to look more beautiful. You, however, never took any of my advice. I think it's because I'm old. I'm not beautiful anymore."

What do I do with this information? I don't want to invalidate her experience; this is how she feels, but it isn't reality-based. She is still quite beautiful; should I share this with her? Ugh. What to do, what to do?

"Interesting, Tess," I remarked, "I have often complimented your appearance, so what would make you think that I don't find you attractive or your suggestions valuable?"

"Well, you don't take my advice, so I assumed that you didn't like it," she retorted. I really needed to explore if she was beginning to internalize the therapeutic relationship; this was a major goal for a successful treatment for Tess. I was pushing a bit, but I sensed it was the correct intervention. After going back and forth with a similar dialogue and getting nowhere, I decided to take a major therapeutic risk: personal disclosure and interpretation. *Deep breath, Jacquie.*

"Tess, that's not the case at all. I find your advice helpful and valuable, particularly coming from someone who I find to be attractive both inside and out."

"So then why haven't I ever seen you use my makeup tips?"

"Who's to say that I haven't tried them?" This snapped her to attention. "To be honest, Tess, my decision not to use your makeup tips has nothing to do with how I perceive your appearance, but rather how I perceive my own. I feel quite comfortable with the way I look, and don't really feel I needed to change to please someone else. That's not to say I may not use your tips for a special occasion where I need to look extra glamorous, like for a wedding. Maybe I will, maybe I won't. But on a daily basis, I'm happy with how I look." I felt it was important to include that last bit to show that there was value in her advice.

"I'm sorry, Jacquie. That never occurred to me."

"You don't need to apologize to me. That's why you come here: to learn about yourself and explore not only your past, but also your current place in this world." And that's what we did. We delved into her mother's outlook on beauty, and the issues she imposed on young Tess that would overshadow her life. We learned that Tess's criticalness of herself — and of me — were direct results of the harsh statements her mother shared, as well as the almost exclusive emphasis on her looks that her mother dumped on her. After a good portion of the session had passed, I felt this new breakthrough had prepared Tess for a new perspective.

"In order to feel more at ease with your age and your looks, really think about what I've been saying. Experience who I am, someone less focused on outer beauty and more attuned to her inner strengths and attractive qualities."

There was silence; I could sense Tess mulling over what I just said. *Deep breath, again, Jacquie — you have a good rapport with Tess — whatever her response is, you'll be able to work through it.* Finally, after what seemed like an hour had passed...

"This is what they mean when they say, 'Feeling comfortable in your own skin.'"

This is amazing!! Wow, I cannot believe this worked. What a breakthrough!! Moments like this, when a patient develops strength and gains insight, are priceless. Even Tess's enthusiasm seemed uncontainable. "I never thought of this before. It's all true! What do we do now to help me feel better? I'd like to start writing again."

"I'm thrilled to see you so ambitious and engaged. Your first step will be to acknowledge your inner strengths. And before you can dispute that you have any, let me assure you, you possess many."

"I can't think of one."

"Seriously, Tess? Let's start with intelligence. Creativity. The will of a survivor. Once you acknowledge your strengths, you'll need to internalize them, own them, if you will." As a result of this process, she would develop confidence and the ability to pursue some of the goals she had before her "Fall from Glory."

We worked hard together throughout the next six months of treatment to help Tess identify and integrate her inner strengths and qualities. She began to write again, something she had great difficulty accomplishing since her "Fall from Glory." She surprised me by even going on a few dates. Of course, she experienced times she would regress; she would question herself, making self-deprecating statements, usually surrounding her age.

Fortunately, Tess now possessed a resiliency that she hadn't before, one that enabled her to quickly recover and continue on a forward path. She practically stopped her assaults of my appearance and instead actually began to express an admiration of me. However, she still seemed fixated on two pieces of advice: I needed to wear blush and I needed to find a husband. She adamantly expressed the importance of her advice intermittently during our sessions. I knew Tess's tips originated from a place of love and true concern, and not criticism, so I felt addressing them might be counterproductive. The advice seemed almost motherly.

We were in the midst of our fourth year of treatment. Tess exhibited remarkable personal growth. One afternoon, however, she arrived at our session trembling, anxious. A harrowing string of events were about to unfold, events that changed Tess, me, and our relational dynamics permanently.

Chapter 7:
Catch-22

After a year in treatment, I still sensed that Tony was not relating in a genuine and trusting manner. When he did "expose" himself in treatment, it had an erotic and seductive quality. Even his absentminded mannerisms possessed a seductive quality. He had this one habit that began appearing around his tenth or eleventh month of treatment, perhaps because he began feeling comfortable in session. It usually occurred when he was deep in thought and perhaps not consciously aware he was dropping his façade. While in reflection and focused on a spot on the wall or floor, he would softly trace his middle finger across his bottom lip, though honestly, I could not tell if he was caressing his lip with this finger or caressing his finger with his lip, as his head would arc back and forth in incremental degrees. Then there were times I knew he was aroused in session. Those were daunting.

Jacquie, you have to wait. Continue establishing a rapport. But can he? Is he going to be able to establish a therapeutic alliance without exploring the relational dynamics? I had to give it a little more time.

We continued to process Tony's relationships with women; his stories were disturbing, compelling, and filled with conflict. I also knew he was communicating his sexual prowess by sharing these stories; it was the only way he could tolerate the boundaries of our relationship. So I listened. About six months later, I gained some insight serendipitously that shifted the entire therapeutic relationship, providing the opening I was patiently waiting for.

At Tony's lead, we continued. His interactions with women followed a relatively predictable dynamic. Upon meeting a new woman, he would suavely "charm" her; he honestly knew all the right things to say. It was unnerving. He would ask them out; expensive dinners were his typical first date. He described, with pride, his ability to allure them with his "magnetism," which often left them "like putty in his hands"; most often this resulted in the woman initiating sex the same night. I tried to remain neutral; but I was convinced that he could see from my body language and facial expression that these disclosures had an effect on me. *He wants and needs me to be affected. Well, he achieved this goal.*

So after being in treatment twice a week for over a year, I again asked Tony if he found his liaisons satisfying or if he experienced them as problematic.

"Ehh." He shrugged his shoulders. *Not too enthusiastic for such a prolific womanizer.* I looked at him with raised eyebrows, urging him to continue. "Sure, I get off on seducing women. I will admit, though, that in the end, once I lose interest," and he said this without his usual preparedness, "I feel kinda lonely and empty." *Wow. Finally, a little progress. How do I handle this? Well, whatever you say, don't mention his mother.*

"What do you want to do about it?"

"I'd like to understand why I can't stay in a relationship." *For the first time, I think he's actually being genuinely curious.* I understood Tony's ambivalent feelings as having to do with the pronounced enmeshment with his mother; committing to a female counterpart essentially required leaving his mother. It was still too soon for an interpretation, so I sat with him in his confusion and attempted to address the issue by exploring his feelings about these women.

Though still stiff and relatively flat, Tony finally opened himself up to some exploration.

"What is it like when you lose interest?"

"I don't know, exactly, I just start to feel really turned off and sometimes even repulsed by them." *So interesting; he experiences the repulsion once the possibility of emotional intimacy is available with a woman. The disgust is actually a displacement of the feelings he has toward his mother.* I realized at this point that my only way to foster further exploration was use our therapeutic relationship as an opening. *But... yuck!*

This was going to take some time.

That afternoon, Tess entered my office physically shaking, fret with anxiety. Immediately noticing her unease, I rose and helped her into her chair. *Oh no, what happened now.* Now angst-ridden myself, I waited for her to start. She had just come from her routine, six-month follow-up with her oncologist. He informed her that her body scan showed a small mass on the top of her lung.

Her voice trembled. "He thinks it's cancer. That's the end, isn't it. I'm going to die."

"Tess, they haven't even done a biopsy yet, have they? Take a deep breath, then let it out slowly." After calming her, we spent most of the session discussing her fears and frustration. As I surmised, Tess still had to go for more tests in order for the doctor to make a conclusive diagnosis.

I actually felt drained when she left that afternoon. I felt the fear Tess was experiencing about all the numerous possibilities that lie ahead for her. In addition, this unfortunate news elicited in me something so profoundly personal and life-altering that I wasn't sure how, or if, I would be able to contain her fears — or my own.

That night, I repeatedly adjusted the covers and fluffed my pillow. I turned on my side, then my back. I tried my stomach, then my back again. Tess's situation had dredged up my own recent painful experience. And that caused my mind to race. *This is why all therapists need to be in therapy. Oh right, I have therapy in the morning. Thank goodness.* The thought of seeing Dr. Gwen and getting all this off my chest calmed me; I finally fell asleep.

The next morning, I went out for a run, showered, dressed, then headed to the door to make my 9 a.m. therapy appointment. I reached down to retrieve my briefcase, and as I stood up, I came face-to-face with the last painting my mother gave me. I felt the familiar burn in my eyes, but I ignored it and got out my keys to lock the door behind me.

By the time I stepped on the pavement, I was crying uncontrollably. I felt tired, broken-down and lost. I tried calling a friend, but the call went directly to voicemail. I didn't leave a message because I didn't want her to hear my cracking voice and get upset herself. I just continued walking to my therapist's office on this rather gray December day, weeping the entire way.

I entered Dr. Gwen's office crying; it actually took me a few minutes to compose myself enough to speak.

It had been only two months since I had lost my mother to pancreatic cancer. By the time she was diagnosed, we had but one month with her before she passed away. I had spent the majority of my sessions with Dr. Gwen trying to process this most horrific loss. It all happened so fast. Watching my beloved mother deteriorate so rapidly was the most absolutely painful experience I have ever endured. Even as I processed it with my therapist, there was still a part of me that was in denial that she was gone; on this particular day, I was overcome with the magnitude of the emptiness, confusion, and helplessness of my loss. I felt broken.

I shared the details of Tess's news with my therapist and attempted, albeit with much difficulty, to describe how her possible diagnosis felt so frightening. Although Tess was my patient, I was experiencing the same helplessness I felt when my mother was originally diagnosed.

"How am I going to help Tess? How can I contain her feelings and bear witness to her story while I am still ensconced in my own grieving process?"

Dr. Gwen handed me another tissue. "Jacquie, it's still soon after your mother's passing. And from what you've told me, she was as much a friend to you as a mother. So yes, you're still grieving, particularly because her death is fresh in your mind. I think you mentioned while she was sick about discussing her own fears on death and dying."

I nodded. My mother and I had shared a close relationship. No topic was taboo with us, so when she got sick, we were able to talk openly and honestly about the cancer, dying, and her fears about getting sicker.

"Consider this, Jacquie. Because the experience is so recent in your memory, think about the perspective you have that you can share with Tess. To help her through this rough time. You understand some of her fears and the possibilities that lie ahead."

Dr. Gwen was right, of course. Though my grieving wouldn't end that day, she helped me realize that, with strength, my unique perspective and empathy could help Tess. I left feeling a bit better; talking about my feelings helped me to feel calmer and more in control, but I still had an overriding pain deep in the pit of my stomach.

Tess went for a CAT scan the following week. We spent the next three sessions exploring her fears surrounding the impending results of the test. The waiting also exacerbated her depressive thoughts. As she reflected upon her life, she used her sessions wondering what she even had to live for. It was nearly unbearable to listen to, and it continued to bring up excruciating thoughts about my mother.

Unlike Tess, my mother wanted to live; in no way was she ready to die, but her Stage 4 pancreatic cancer had other plans, leaving her with little strength to fight the disease and little hope that she could be cured. I knew that regardless of Tess's diagnosis, she had a much better prognosis. The doctor had even informed her that if it was cancer, it was in an early stage and most likely treatable.

Two hours following our Monday appointment, Tess called in hysterics; the CAT scan came back positive for lung cancer. I listened to her dread and horror with as much openness as I could muster, all while intrusive images of what my mother must have felt once they informed her of her terminal illness continued to plague me. I scheduled an extra appointment with Tess for the following day. I hung up the phone; I was deeply distressed. Thankfully, because Raul cancelled — incredibly uncharacteristic of him — I had 30 minutes before my next patient. I laid down on the couch in my office to rest my brain and try to relax before I needed to be emotionally available for my next patient.

Working as a clinician is intensely enriching and satisfying, but it often leaves one vulnerable to having to make quick decisions; sometimes this part of the work can be disarming. I was rather unprepared for the question that Tess brought into our session when we met the following day.

While running the next morning, I trotted by a man who resembled Tony, which brought thoughts of him intruding upon the usual zone of relaxation that running provides for me. I tried to imagine and figure out what these women found so appealing about him. Objectively speaking, Tony was attractive; he was tall, long and lean, though muscular, with big green eyes, and a charming crooked smile. However, his way of relating was unsettling and did detract from his overall attractiveness. But that wouldn't be apparent until a woman spent a significant amount of time with him. In the beginning, when he felt more in control, I'm sure he was all charm. The debonair, suave and mysterious lure hanging off a hook in a sea of women, just waiting to snag the catch of the day.

With these thoughts still in mind, once we were in session later that morning, I decided to cautiously address Tony's experience of being in the therapy room with me. But something far more significant, disturbing and revealing overshadowed my plan. As is often the case working as a psychologist, it is impossible to predict when something astonishing will throw a wrench in the works. Next thing you know, you are entrenched in a clinical dilemma. This one was almost unbelievable.

I had been working with Raul, the patient who had cancelled the previous day, twice a week for nearly three years. His presenting problem was issues surrounding his sexual orientation. At 22 years old, and after silently struggling for years with his identification as a gay man, he decided to enter treatment. Raul was Puerto Rican-American; his parents moved to New York from Puerto Rico just after Raul was born. Raul described being aware that he was attracted to boys as early as eight years old. He had a difficult childhood. His father was racist, sexist, and made his antipathy toward homosexuality inordinately clear.

His father's position toward gay people left Raul feeling alone, immensely ashamed, and hopelessly trying to "change" his sexual orientation. In high school, Raul described dating women; he enjoyed their company, but felt nothing erotic toward them. He even had sex with one young girl who he left pining over him and broken-hearted because he couldn't follow through with the relationship. He described vivid fantasies about some of the boys on his soccer team. He would masturbate at home, after soccer practice, over thoughts about having sex with one particular boy he was attracted to.

Unfortunately, as a result of his father's apparent detestation toward gay people, Raul suffered in shame; he did not share his sexual preference with anyone until he entered therapy. During our first session, Raul came out to me. He had been holding his thoughts and feelings in for so long, it felt like he was throwing up words through the entire first session. He described a sense of relief when I asked him how it felt to share this intimate information with me.

Our therapy over the next few years primarily had two general themes. The first was his struggle to accept himself as a gay man, regardless of his father's attitude toward homosexuality. After nearly three years of working together, Raul was still hesitant to share his sexual orientation with his family; he was terrified of the repercussions. Our treatment goal was to help him feel comfortable enough within himself and his identity to come out to his family.

The second theme involved a complex array of dynamics that entailed Raul's relationship patterns with the men he became involved with. As a result of his still feeling somewhat uncomfortable with his sexual orientation, his propensity was to engage in self-destructive and unsettling brief encounters with men. Raul shared that he wanted a partner; a committed relationship. As a result of his discomfort, his pattern was to engage with men on a purely sexual level. Essentially, he was promiscuous; often Raul would have two or three different partners a week — and sometimes without protection. Although he was cognizant of what he was doing, and even recognized how destructive and unsafe his patterns were emotionally, he felt he couldn't stop. This is where we were in our treatment when something unpredictable happened.

Raul was invested in his therapy; he never missed a session, was always on time, and continually brought in relevant clinical material. So, when he called to reschedule his Monday appointment to Tuesday because he was behind on a paper he needed to finish for class, I was a bit curious. Tuesday was my busiest day — Tony, Garry, Tess, Rudy, and Anne — but I managed to squeeze him in during my one free hour after Garry — one of the other of my three gay patients — Rudy being the third.

Garry had to cut his session a few minutes short. He had a lunch meeting with someone on the Lower West Side, and since my office was on the Upper East Side, he needed a few minutes grace to allow for subway delays. It worked out perfectly, giving me a 20-minute break to make up for the free hour I gave up for Raul. But when I went into the waiting room to get Raul for his session, he hadn't arrived yet, which was highly unusual because he was always ten minutes early. *First he cancels. Then he's late. VERY out of character.* As I turned back into my office, I noticed a blue and yellow umbrella in the stand. *Someone's getting soaked today.*

I returned to my desk to jot down notes from my last two sessions. Almost ten minutes passed before I heard the outer office door open. I put away my notepad and went to the door. When I opened it, Raul was sitting in a chair twiddling his thumbs and looking quite anxious.

"I'm so, so, so sorry I'm late. I feel awful, especially since you were doing me the favor of squeezing me in."

"It happens, Raul. Don't give it another thought." Raul walked by me as I held the door open for him. As he got close, I noticed a heavy sweat beaded on his forehead. *He must have sprinted here. So unusual for him to run late like this* As I closed the door, I noticed the blue and yellow umbrella was no longer in the stand. *Hmm.*

Raul sat quickly. I felt a sense of urgency emanating, which was also unusual for Raul. Despite his struggles and conflicts, he was typically well-contained. He asked for a cup of water. I handed it to him, he gulped it down, took a deep breath, then immediately started talking. And boy was I going to get an earful.

Raul began explaining that over the weekend he met a "hot and sexy" man in one of the dance clubs he frequented. They made eye contact and instantly started dancing. Raul described feeling more attracted to this man than any other man since his high school soccer crush. Mike (the "hot and sexy" man) initiated foreplay on the dance floor, which ultimately led to Raul inviting him back to his apartment on the Lower East Side. *Hmm, why is Raul so anxious? Did he instantly fall for this guy? This narrative of events is not atypical; what has him so uptight?*

I wanted to ask Raul these questions, but the sense of urgency I felt in the room stopped me. I sensed that he needed to tell me what happened before he could even tolerate a line of inquiry. So I listened, bubbling with curiosity. Raul indulged me.

"Mike stayed the entire weekend. We didn't leave the apartment once. We drank scotch and beer and ordered food and had oodles and oodles of sex. I met Mike on Friday night, and he stayed with me until 11:00 Sunday night. Omigod, it was a glorious weekend. Well, except for when he left. That was disappointing." He took a breath here, so I thought I should say something to be supportive of what seemed to be an important event in Raul's life.

"I guess anyone would be hard-pressed to want such a magical weekend to end."

"It wasn't *that* he left that was weird. It was *how* he left. We were lying in bed, snuggling, watching *Desperate Housewives* on my DVR when, out of nowhere, he jumped up and said he had to go. He offered no further explanation. He dressed in a flash and was gone. It was all so sudden." *That is a little odd. But at least this explains why he didn't get his paper done. But I'm sensing something else. I just can't put my finger on it. Raul never spends the entire weekend with any man and he's always the one to end the liaison. Something here is remarkably and undeniably different.* I was leaning forward, literally on the edge of my chair.

"Raul, something seems different about Mike than any of the other men you've been with. Can you tell me what it is?"

"This is the first time I've felt this way about a guy, and I'm not sure Mike feels the same way. Yes, he gave me his phone number, but the way he left — so abruptly — it made me think he was only interested in sex," I could feel Raul's agony. It was palpable. And he felt genuinely heartbroken at the thought of this being a one-weekend stand.

At first I was imagining that this might be an emotional and therapeutic breakthrough for Raul, as his treatment goal was to be able to attach and form a lasting relationship with a man. I was just about to open up the therapeutic space for inquiry about his wanting to pursue something with Mike, something that was probably causing him to feel simultaneously fearful and conflicted. And then he dropped a bomb on me.

It is not common for me, especially with my experience working in forensic settings for many years, to be shocked and/or jarred by what a patient shares with me. Raul succeeded at nearly knocking me off my chair.

In contrast, to his nearly not being able to get the words out fast enough, I noticed there was something else he wanted to share, but was tentative. *This must be the real origin of his anxiety today.* In my most soothing and empathetic tone, "What is it, Raul?" We sat in silence for a few minutes, and then with slight caution came his big reveal.

"Mike's your patient, too."

My mind was spinning through all the possibilities. I was treating two other gay male patients at the time, Garry and Rudy. Both were significantly older than Raul, in long-term relationships, and both had been in treatment with me for a few years. I couldn't imagine either of them engaging in the way Raul described. I felt pretty confident that it was not either of them. *Wait, I don't have any patients named Mike. Then who?* My immediate association after this thought was: *Oh, my gosh, it's Tony! Wait, that's a ridiculous conclusion to jump to.* But still, my heart was racing.

Jacquie, calm down before you make a technical error. This is a delicate situation. And I had the sense that there was still more to the story. "How did he come to tell you he's one of my patients? I can't imagine it's a subject that comes up during the heat of a passionate weekend." I gave him a friendly smile to let him know there was no judgment on my end.

"He di-didn't have to t-tell me. I fi-… I figured it out." *Huh?*

"How could you figure that out?"

"I, um, I just ran into hi-him in your waiting room." Raul tensed up. He looked so anxious. *No, Jacquie, he looks guilty. But of what?*

"Tell me more, Raul. It's obvious you're upset about something. What is it?"

Raul diverted eye contact, which suggested that what he was about to share was causing him grave shame; it was only when Raul felt ashamed that he couldn't maintain eye contact. I glanced at the clock. We only had ten minutes left in the session. Raul started to tear up.

"I just... I just had sex with Mike in the... in the bathroom."

"In the bathroom?" *In MY bathroom?!* Yes, I was surprised by Raul's behavior, but I wasn't really angry. I was more curious about what would make him do something so out of character. I mean, I'm not naïve. People have sex in bathrooms all the time. And having a number of gay friends, I know it happens in clubs every night. But this is Raul. And this is my office. The two didn't add up to therapist office bathroom sex. I tilted my head, suggesting that I wanted him to elaborate.

"Really. Just n-now, here, in the... in the bathroom!" he couldn't stop stuttering.

This is a first. How do I handle this? And we only have about five minutes left. My heart was racing even faster, but I believe I maintained my composure. I needed to contain Raul and soothe his anxiety.

"You're dis-disappointed in me, aren't-aren't you? And upset."

"Not at all, but I am concerned about you, and we only have a few minutes left. Can you come in tomorrow? You seem upset and I want to help you through this."

Raul agreed that he needed an extra session. When I asked him if he felt calm enough to leave, "Yes, I'll be okay," was his response.

I usually try to keep my appointments on the hour to leave myself a few minutes between sessions. After seeing Raul, I felt like I needed a full hour to recover. I felt confused and slightly off-balance. With moments to spare, I ran to the bathroom to freshen up and allow my mind to ruminate over the information Raul shared.

I was so disoriented I tripped and fell, having missed the small stair in the waiting room. *Lovely Jacquie; how graceful;* thankfully I got up unscathed. *Who is Mike? I'm going to assume he really is my patient if Raul ran into him in the waiting room. Which means that one of my patients is lying about his name. Raul could be covering up his real name to protect him. But that doesn't make sense. Why bother giving me a name at all? Could it be Garry? He did have the session before Raul. But he's in a committed long-term relationship. And he never talked about wanting to cheat on his partner. Not that that matters. Even nice guys cheat. But the behavior that Raul described sounds nothing like Garry.*

It could be Rudy, but he doesn't have an appointment until later today. Maybe it was Garry. There was that umbrella that was there before Raul showed up, but gone when Raul finally arrived. Maybe Garry forgot it, came back for it, saw Raul and they were so aroused by seeing each other, couldn't help but "take care of business." But it's still so out of character for Garry.

Is it possible that it's Tony? He does seem to always be wary of his behavior and duplicitous with what he shares. He's never indicated any homosexual feelings, but that would be indicative of someone living a secret life. Was he the patient who had sex with Raul? And it would fit his profile to lie about his name. I thought back over the year-and-a-half treatment with Tony trying to figure out if I missed something. Tony always felt manipulative, mysterious and guarded, but it had never entered my mind that he was having sex with men. Usually I would at least have a sense that this was a possibility. *Did I miss something? If it is Tony, is this the reason his dialogue and way of relating felt so contrived? Is he struggling with his sexual orientation and too uncomfortable to share this in therapy? Or as a result of the betrayals he suffered indiscriminately having sex with men and women? I can't ask him. What Raul shared is confidential, and I cannot use any of the information he shared to inform my line of inquiry with Tony or any of my other male patients. It'll reveal itself in time, Jacquie. Just breathe. But boy, am I itching to know.*

Tess's session was minutes away, so I had little time to regain my composure. This was going to be a full day in many respects. Sure enough, when I returned from the bathroom, Tess was early and eager to get started. So eager that as she entered the room...

"Honestly, Jacquie. Not even any eye liner today?" *Not even the fear of cancer can shake this woman of her critiques.* A long day indeed.

Before Tess even sat down...

"What did I tell you, Jacquie, this is it, the end, the death sentence has been handed down from above, I don't even know how much time I have left, probably little, and the doctors will make me go for chemo and radiation and I'll lose my hair, MY HAIR, Jacquie, I love my hair, and I'll be exhausted and gaunt and do you know how much makeup you need to cover gaunt skin, and now they want me to go in for a biopsy." When she stopped her rapid-fire rant to breathe, I jumped in.

"Tess. I know you're upset, but I need you to slow down so I can help you."

Tess took a few calming breaths. "Do you think I can have a glass of water?"

I retrieved the water for her. Her hand shook when I passed it to her. She took a sip, then let out an audible sigh. "They definitely found a mass on my lung. The doctor wants me to have a biopsy to determine a diagnosis and to figure out the best treatment options. My luck is it's not benign." *You just took your glass-half-empty and dumped it on the floor.*

"I truly hope the biopsy shows it's benign." I leaned forward and patted her clenched hands. I wanted her to feel assured I was "with" her in the room.

We spent the next half-hour exploring her deepest fears and it became amply clear, as she stated when she raced into my office at the beginning of the session, that Tess truly believed she had just received a death sentence — she was terrified!

I also noticed that Tess was avoiding something. Throughout the session, she would begin to ask a question, "Would you..." but then would hold back. After a moment, she would return to the topic of the impending biopsy. On the fifth time...

"Jacquie, would you..." then nothing. "Um, could I have more water?"

I looked at her. *That's not what you were going to ask.* "Of course." I took her glass and filled it from the water bottle sitting on my desk. When I passed it over, her hand shook.

"Thank you." She sipped the water, then instead of putting the glass on the table, she held it, focusing on the rippling surface. *Should I ask her what's on her mind? Should I let it go?* "Jacquie. Would you, um, would you be able to pick me up at the hospital after the biopsy and bring me home? I'd also need you to stay with me in my apartment for a couple hours. You know, to watch over me, make sure I don't have a bad reaction after the procedure."

"I've been waiting this whole session for you to tell me what's been on your mind."

"The thing is, this will be an invasive biopsy. If I can't find someone to pick me up, they'll insist on keeping me in the hospital for overnight observation."

I didn't respond immediately. *This is definitely walking the line of appropriate doctor/patient behavior, and yet...*

Tess's voice took on a pleading tone. "I know this isn't what therapists usually do, but... I'm all alone. I don't have anyone else who can do this."

I knew immediately that I wanted to go, but I was still unclear about whether this would be appropriate. And I had other concerns. *How is this going to affect the boundaries of our relationship? What would my going or not going communicate to Tess? Who am I kidding? Now that the question has already been put out there, there's no going back from this no matter my decision.*

"When is the test scheduled?"

Tess seemed a little relieved already even without a positive answer. "For Friday."

In the fleeting moments after, I tried to figure out all the permutations of a positive and negative answer based on our unique dyad, the timing in the context of our relational process and the boundaries that we as clinicians are taught to abide by. I also needed to process if my mother's recent death from cancer was affecting my decision. *What should I do? Picking her up, that I can do, but staying with her in her apartment for two hours?* I was trying to imagine what that would look and/or feel like? *Maybe I should ask her the same question.*

"Tess, before I give you an answer, I'd like you to imagine what it would feel like to have me in your home. To muddle our professional boundary." She didn't hesitate. And I guess there was really nothing for her to process. Her needs were a priority to her, and any other thought was an extravagance she couldn't afford to consider.

"I have no one else." Every time she repeated this, my heart sank; I could feel how alone and scared she was.

"Tess, I really want to do this for you, but I need to think about it."

Since I was meeting with Tess again on Thursday, I would have a chance to process the best option with my own therapist during my session on Wednesday morning. I told Tess that I would let her know at our next session. She pleaded a bit, but eventually conceded.

Walking home that evening, my thoughts raced about my head. I was in the midst of a complex internal dialogue involving my human proclivities versus my psychodynamic inclinations. *The truth of the matter is that she's alone and her request doesn't feel like some underlying dynamic communication. The fact is that she needs me. She has no one. This could even show her for the first time that she's important and lovable; it even could be an emotionally corrective experience. But I've got to consider if there'll be repercussions to crossing this boundary. Based on the circumstances alone, I feel the right thing to do is to be there for her. To be with her, simply as a caring human being, seems to outweigh the boundary violation this would entail. We can process her experience of having me in her apartment as it arises during session.*

Jacquie! Stop it! You'll figure it out in therapy tomorrow.

My internal quandary exhausted me. I needed a swim to relax and shut my brain off. And it helped. I was able to go to sleep, pushing my thoughts aside, knowing I would figure out the answer the next morning with my therapist. In hindsight, I had made my decision before I even stepped into my therapist's office the next day, but I was afraid to admit to myself that what I really was looking for wasn't an answer, but rather approval from my therapist for this unconventional activity I would be participating in.

I spent most of my session exploring all the different possibilities that might arise as a result of either accepting or declining Tess's request. I also talked about what it was like for me to bear witness to Tess's experience only two short months after losing my mother. My therapist was empathetic and supportive. She allowed me the room I needed to come to my own decision; I would pick Tess up, bring her home, and stay with her for two hours. My therapist disclosed to me that she, a seasoned analyst, had made clinically informed decisions to cross boundaries a few times before. I left my session feeling better knowing that I, like my therapist and many others, sometimes need to step out of my professional and well-defined role to engage and support a patient.

Later that day, I let Tess know that I would pick her up and stay with her after the procedure. I immediately heard the relief in her voice as she endlessly thanked me. I knew then that I truly had made the right choice.

The next day, I tagged on Raul as my last patient of the day, so when he walked in, I already felt a little drained. Though I had just seen him the day before when he disclosed the circumstances with Mike, I was truthfully glad he agreed to come in for an additional session; I wasn't sure I could have waited another day to see him. I couldn't stop thinking about it. I still wasn't sure how I would handle asking about Mike's identity; I wanted to know, but the real question was if knowing if it was relevant to Raul's treatment. In the long run, it was probably more relevant to "Mike's" treatment and my insight into his character. Whoever it turned out to be, I misjudged him. I decided to do my best to be open, and allow the session to unfold naturally.

Raul appeared much calmer than the previous day, but I still felt the pressure of his need to talk. So I sat back and listened empathically. He shared that he had spent the night with Mike; he described feeling completely enveloped in the relationship already. And this frightened Raul.

"I've nev-never felt this way be-... this way before; I feel swept, I feel swept off my feet and attached to him." *Okay, Raul has never stammered before, and this is the second day in a row that he's doing it. This Mike character has some effect on him, and I don't think it's good.* "I need to talk about my feelings about him, but I have to admit I'm a little uncomfortable because I know he's your patient, too. And he's probably going to talk about me." He paused. "How um, how does this confidentiality thing work? Am I even allowed to talk about him?" *Oh my gosh. He's so sweet and sincere. I feel like hugging him.* I leaned forward hoping to ease his anxiety.

"Here's how it works. I can't share anything you disclose to me with Mike. Nor can I share what Mike tells me with you. The only circumstance where this confidentiality could be violated is if either of you are a threat to yourselves or each other. I can't even acknowledge to him that I know you two are dating unless he mentions it to me." I saw an almost immediate reaction in Raul — his shoulders, arms, hands, everything just relaxed.

The real dilemma for me now, which I did not share with Raul, was that the second-hand information provided by Raul and possibly Mike could eventually affect my objectivity. And for me, as the treating clinician, this was where I imagined I would have the most difficult time. At some point, I figured I'd have to tell Raul that I didn't have a patient named Mike. *Maybe I should look into the professional appropriateness of that kind of disclosure.* It was rather naïve of me to think this, but how was I supposed to predict the chaos that would unfold?

After reassuring Raul that what he told me would remain confidential, he became reticent again. *At this point in our relationship, he shouldn't feel ashamed to share something with me. This Mike is definitely not good for him.*

"Raul. Please. Tell me what's on your mind."

He sighed. "Mike isn't his real name." *I already knew that. I'm just glad that he does. But I wonder when he found out.*

"I'm curious why you initially told me his name was Mike?" But as soon as I asked the question, I knew the answer. Raul looked down for a moment; he seemed to be deep in thought. We sat in silence for a few minutes, until Raul, eyes red, looked up at me — and started crying.

"Because that's what I thought his name was when I first told you about him," he bawled a little harder here, "after the bathroom sex."

"When did Mike finally come clean about his real name?"

"When *Tony* showed up at my house." *I knew it was Tony! Well, I wasn't positive, but that's what my gut kept saying. Wait. Holy crap! This puts a whole new spin on things with Tony. But what if he doesn't disclose this to me? How will we engage the subject? Something that explains so much about his behavior.*

"Raul, I'm curious. Did Tony give you a satisfactory explanation about why he lied to you about his name?"

"It was kind of sweet, actually. He said that he never gives his real name with hookups. But he had such a good time with me, he wanted to tell me his real name, but didn't know how to tell me he had been lying all weekend. When we ran into each other in your waiting room, he said he was kind of relieved because it forced him to come clean with me. He said that I was the first guy he's liked enough to want to see again." *Makes sense since he never wanted a long-term relationship with a woman.* Raul rubbed the space over his heart. "And it touched me right here because you know how much I want a long-term relationship."

We sat together for a few moments as Raul continued to cry. He finally calmed down, reached for a tissue, and looked up at me. I felt sad for him; I knew he was really struggling. I also was afraid for him. He was quite a vulnerable and sensitive young man, and Tony was not a safe, or at least truthful, person; I knew that much. We explored what his tears meant.

"I'm still kind of afraid. I really like him, but... Tony does seem interested, I think he is, but he also isn't open about our relationship. Part of me thinks he's just seeing me for sex." *Wouldn't be the first time.*

We continued to process Raul's feelings throughout the session. I was curious about Raul's sudden attachment to Tony. *Was he immediately attracted to Tony because he sensed Tony's emotional unavailability, thus making him a safer choice? Was it Tony's seductiveness?* The biggest question I was struggling with was what it meant that Tony was engaging in a homosexual relationship. This was an extremely complex situation, and I knew I had to proceed with great caution.

Under "normal" circumstances, I wouldn't know Tony and would be able to stay with Raul and empathize with *his* feelings. I might question some of Tony's intentions as Raul presented him, but I would only know Tony through Raul's experience of him. Unfortunately, because I did know Tony, thoughts of him and his manipulative, detached ways of relating were interfering with my ability to listen with complete openness to Raul's narrative; I couldn't help being worried.

Raul and I would spend the next few months exploring his anxieties and insecurity surrounding his ongoing relationship with Tony. We were attempting to understand why he felt so instantly attached to Tony, and why despite Tony's growing ambivalence, Raul continued to see him. I sensed that Raul was engaging in this apparently dysfunctional relationship as a means of working through his own shame and confusion surrounding his sexual orientation. When I finally brought this up with him, Raul conceded. Essentially, Raul maintained a relationship with Tony as a way to externalize his own unfortunate uneasiness with his homosexuality.

Well, if nothing else, I feel like I'm ensconced in an afternoon soap opera.

At around 2:30 on Friday afternoon, I received the call from the hospital that Tess was awake and ready to be picked up. I walked over to Slone-Kettering and followed the nurse's instructions of where to meet Tess. As I walked through the hospital, the signs directing visitors reminded me of my own devastating loss. Despair and anguish overcame me for a moment; I missed my mother so much, and sometimes the genuine recognition that she was gone would become too much to bear. I stopped to gather myself in order to be strong for Tess, and then proceeded to the outpatient, post-surgical recovery floor to pick her up.

Once I arrived outside Tess's room, I could hear her carrying on a conversation with the nurse. Her speech was accelerated. *She must be nervous about the test.* I entered to find her impeccably dressed, makeup on, and ready to go. When she saw me, she introduced me as her "friend" to the nurse. *Her friend? Let it go, Jacquie. How else could she have chosen to introduce me?* I rationalized to myself, but I did have a sense that the choice of introduction held some clinical significance. *Just let it go; you can process it in session next week.* With the air freezing, and the wind even more bitter cold, I made haste finding a cab for us.

Tess often spoke of the beauty and spaciousness of her apartment; she hadn't exaggerated. Once inside, I fell in love with it. Next to my small, albeit cozy, pre-war walk-up, hers felt like a mansion. The large picture windows and enviable balcony provided an amazing, scenic New York view.

Wow! How does she afford this? Tess seemed relatively relaxed, particularly for someone who had just undergone an invasive test and now must await worrisome results. Tess offered me a glass of Pinot Noir. I declined. When she offered me tea, I felt she might take offense from my refusal, so I accepted. She brewed a couple mugs of Sleepytime for us, my favorite. She gave me a tour of her apartment, then indulged my unsolicited (though ever-present) curiosity by sharing an interesting piece of information about her financial situation.

When Tess was diagnosed and treated for her occult breast cancer, the doctors informed her that she only had about two years to live. The news was devastating. Her cousin Marc, a wealthy lawyer living in California, agreed to pay her rent, affording her the luxury of not having to work and to live freely for the two remaining years she had. That was 16-plus years ago, and Marc was still paying her rent every month.

Throughout her story, I must have been staring at a specific painting for some time, because Tess remarked, "That's an original."

"What's an original?"

"That painting. It's an original Chagall. I've almost gotten rid of it a half-dozen times over the years, but when it ultimately came down to it, I couldn't part with it. I've always loved his use of colors. Especially on this one. And the brushstrokes. It's not quite an impressionistic work, but not quite surrealist."

Tess was right. The colors jumped out at you. "It's striking, Tess. How long have you had it?"

"Oh. Forever. It was a wedding gift to my Aunt Contessa from my father."

Contessa? "Was she your father's sister?"

"My mother's."

And then it hit me. It explained so much about her distaste for the name.

"Your mother's sister? As in your father's first wife?"

Click-click-click-click. Tess's nails started on overdrive. And then… *click-cli—*

Stopped as suddenly as it started.

"More Sleepytime?"

"Thanks, Tess. Please."

I thought about pursuing this name thing, but decided to let sleeping dogs lie. Tess was recovering from a surgical procedure. The last thing she needed was undue stress. And honestly, I don't think much more needed to be said. In a number of sessions, she had explained in detail to me her feelings about feeling unloved growing up, about her father caring more for the dead than the living. The name "Contessa" was just another layer to that. A reminder she has carried with her since birth. *Why beat a dead horse?*

Tess returned with the piping hot tea. We enjoyed it with a few Lorna Doone cookies that Tess insisted on serving despite my earlier protests.

Tess spent the majority of our remaining time that afternoon advising me on how to meet a husband. It was a bit difficult and confusing to try to negotiate our conversation outside of the therapy room. Though I remained in the role of therapist, this was not a session. I was mindful that she was still scared, and this coffee klatch was her way of dealing with the fright she was fending off; but nevertheless, I tried to say as little as possible to keep my role professional, and not be enticed to engage in what felt like a casual conversation.

Any questions I had or interpretations I might make while in session, I made a mental note of; I would return to them once back within the boundaries of our therapy session. It was not an easy task, particularly since I had been living with my boyfriend for about a year, and suspected that we would become engaged relatively soon. The intrigue of sharing this information with Tess was quite intoxicating; I noticed I was literally biting my lip. I held steadfast to a non-disclosure position. Once I became engaged and Tess saw the ring (which I knew she would immediately and vigilantly notice), we could then process her feelings in a more clinically appropriate manner. Until then, though, "mum" was the word.

With just a tad more than two hours having passed and Tess appearing fine, I decided it was time for me to leave. I reminded her that she should call the hospital or me if she felt sick. I ended with "I will see you Tuesday at 1:15." As I walked home, I thought a lot about Tess's condition. *I wonder what the test results are going to be. I'm so glad I went; it was the right thing to do. But what's with her obsession with me finding a husband?* It finally hit me. Tess now identified with me and, as a result, she was unconsciously trying to work through her own regrets by guiding me and ensuring that I did not make the same mistakes that she made.

And no matter how hard I tried, I spent the weekend fighting off intruding thoughts of Tess, Tony, and Raul, wondering what the coming months held for each of them.

The following week, Tony showed up for his appointment right on time. When I went to retrieve him in the waiting room,

Tony — true to his character — was waiting while casually flipping through a magazine. Walking to my office, I was filled with curiosity. *Is Tony going to share his experience with Raul? He's so ingrained in his heterosexual history, will he ever admit to it? And does he know that I know? He must. Raul must have told him that he talked about them in his session. But I can't bring it up. It's Tony's place to do so.* As Tony sat in the patient's chair, he put on a devious smile.

The session began as his typically do. Tony discussed in detail his feelings about the woman he was currently "dating." He was discussing that after just three dates he was beginning to lose interest. *Three dates. Can he be talking about Raul? Were all his women really men?* Again, with his customary way of expressing himself, he was listing, without any affect, all the things that were wrong with her. I was so distracted, but tried hard to stay focused. So, I asked Tony, "This is exactly the same thing that happened with the last three women you talked about with me. Do you have any thoughts about this?"

Tony began a long-winded diatribe of how every woman he meets never lives up to his expectations. "Once I know a woman is interested in me, I get turned off," he repeated for the umpteenth time.

"Tony, you say you want a committed relationship, but your thoughts and behaviors seem to suggest something different," I was starting to get pissed. I still remember sitting in my own therapy trying to figure out why I was once unable to engage in a healthy relationship. Part of me could still align with Tony, but because of his lack of sincerity, it was nearly impossible to empathize with him — and I was really trying.

Tony was exceptionally brilliant; he was studying philosophy and was extremely well-read. He also had the remarkable talent of being able to read people; it was this strength that afforded him to get what he wanted from women. Now, in this session, for the first time, he used it with me. He started asking me questions about my own relationship status. In all his brilliance, he knew this was a source of angst for me; he knew asking me these questions would make me uncomfortable.

He succeeded. I looked at the clock; still 15 minutes left. I felt exceptionally hot; I was flushed and perspiring.

Tony and I were in a silent power struggle; and we both knew it. *Hmm, this is an opening. Should I introduce this relevant relational process? He'll likely deny it, but should I at least try to address it. Allowing it to remain lingering in the room was antithetical to the way I usually conduct therapy, and likely it is not good for Tony's treatment. But just like all therapeutic techniques, I need to think about our unique dyad. I'm not certain that this is the best time to bring in this clinical material. On the other hand, I'm not sure it will ever feel right beginning to address our relational process. Maybe I should just go for it.*

"Tony, I'm not sure answering your questions about my personal life will benefit your treatment. I'm also wondering why now; why after working together for over a year and a half have you decided to ask me this today."

Tony slyly smiled as he ran his finger over his lips and stared at me with penetrating eye contact. Finally, "I think you're single, and I believe you engage in casual sex, too." He winked at me; I felt exposed, vulnerable and metaphorically "penetrated." "I have fantasies of us having sex."

I was repulsed, just thoroughly disgusted. My stomach suddenly queasy from his come-on, I fought the urge to throw up. *His provocations toward me are getting worse. Maybe it's a projection. Yup, bet it is. Tony feels exposed and vulnerable because I'm not giving up my power and falling under his spell as other women do. And men!*

Although I was quite uncomfortable, I was also curious and really wanted to begin exploring what Tony just shared with me. Using the relationship and the process between us would provide me with great insight. I also hoped, but wasn't too optimistic, that it might create some curiosity for Tony. The session was nearly over, so we didn't have time. I was both frustrated and relieved simultaneously. I also wondered if he would ever admit to his liaisons with Raul. I ended the session by acknowledging the importance of talking more about his fantasy, despite my distaste of the thought.

"Let's explore this on Thursday." Tony nodded and left my office with a swagger in his step. *He must be really pleased that he thinks he got one over on me.* I felt as if I needed a shower; I wanted to wash him off of me.

Later that afternoon, with Christmas just days away and the holiday spirit in the air, Tess came to our session following her doctor's appointment. She was shaking. My heart sank as I gleaned the results before she could tell me, but I waited for her to start anyway. The results of the biopsy revealed that the mass on her lung was indeed cancer.

She explained that the doctors thought it was Stage 1; it was large-cell lung cancer, a less aggressive type, and, thankfully, it was operable. The doctors wasted no time. She was scheduled for surgery on Friday. Though the doctors were quite optimistic about her prognosis — confident they could cure it — Tess, having taken the initiative to go online to do the research and discovering that lung cancer often had only a five-year survival rate, did not share their optimism. She was distraught, terrified and deeply concerned.

I found myself wanting to soothe Tess with statements of reassurance that she was going to be okay; however, I recognized the real possibility that she might not be. Even if I knew she was going to recover from her illness, I knew that supporting her with reassurance would invalidate what she was experiencing in this moment. I decided the most appropriate clinical intervention would be to sit with her while she described her very real fears, and simply empathize and validate her emotional experience. Though it may seem counterintuitive, sitting with patients and experiencing their difficult feelings usually provides more support than trying to comfort them with soothing statements. Perhaps this occurs because when a patient expresses and shares those difficult feelings, the energy of those feelings become somewhat diffused, having been spent rather than repressed. I had originally hoped to process Tess's experience of having me in her home, but I pushed the relationally relevant material to the side; what she was bringing into the room surrounding her diagnosis was a crisis and this needed to be addressed first.

We spent our two sessions that week, just before her surgery, exploring Tess's fears. She explained how this was much more frightening than her breast cancer and how she felt ostensibly alone this time. The recovery period from this surgery also lasted longer. Tess would remain in the hospital for four to five days after the surgery; a full recovery, if she remained diligent with her breathing exercises, could take up to six months. At times, I found it nearly excruciating to inhibit my own emotions as I sat with Tess and contained all of her feelings, since they inevitably triggered feelings about my mother, as well as the existential awareness that we, as humans, are all vulnerable and have little control over some of the most difficult things in life. I've grappled with this existential crisis since college — and it never gets easier. *Ugh, my stomach is killing me!*

Complicating things — *could things get more complex?* — I had plans to leave on Friday, the same day as her surgery, for a long weekend to spend Christmas with my boyfriend's family in the Midwest; even my dad was joining us. Under "normal" circumstances, there would be no clinically relevant reason to share this with Tess. So when she asked me to accompany her on Friday and wait with her until she was admitted, I felt I probably should tell her the truth. *Would she have asked me to be with her on Friday if I hadn't picked her up last week? Is she going to continually ask me to step out of my clinical role to support her through this? I need to address this as soon as possible, but definitely not before her surgery and my trip.* My neck tightened up. *I need a massage. Focus, Jacquie.*

Tess had one friend that she had met at a support group for breast cancer survivors. Although they rarely saw each other — Amy was married, quite wealthy, and traveled a great deal — she seemed to provide Tess with *some* support.

"What about your friend Amy? Do you think she might be able to help you out?"

Tess frowned. "I doubt she and her husband will be in town." She opened her mouth to continue, but stopped herself.

"It couldn't hurt to ask." I tried to keep my tone even.

"No, I suppose not.'

Thank goodness I escaped that confrontation.

"Why won't you bring me?" she blurted. I could hear the slight irritation in her voice.

So much for thanking goodness. Though I faced an uncomfortable conversation, I felt it important to touch on the therapeutic framework. "Tess, I'm here for you, but given the boundaries of our relationship, I cannot act as a friend would. I was happy to help you last week and to be there for you, but we really shouldn't make a habit of doing that."

"I know, but… I wish you could."

"Most anyone in your situation would feel the same."

"The few people I have in my life are… rarely present. In times like this, I feel more alone than ever. What if Amy can't take me? Would you do it then?"

Ouch, that loneliness again. "Tess, even if no one else is available, I won't be able to take you. I'm going away for a long weekend, but I'll absolutely be available by phone if you need me." She seemed soothed by my offer. I wondered, though, if my excuse for being out of town didn't play into her relief even a little; that perhaps she no longer felt rejected because I wouldn't be around to take her rather than simply not wanting to take her even if I were available to. Regardless, she left the session seemingly calmer; I, however, looked and felt the worse for wear.

Done with sessions for the next several days, I closed up the office, excited for my respite. When I got home, I took a long run — I delight in how the cold December air chills my cheeks. With my therapist on vacation and my departure for the Midwest scheduled the next morning, I tried to use the run to work through how the events occurring between Tess and me were affecting me. I let my thoughts wander and eventually the endorphins cleared my mind.

After the run, I went for the massage I had scheduled to help me relax for my time off — something I love to do to start my vacations with a sort of clear mental and physical state. And it was working, until…

The massage reminded me of a sordid comment Tony muttered to me in session earlier that day. Something to the effect of him knowing the "special spots where his fingers can work their magic." *Gross! I should have had a swim instead of a run.*

Maybe the chlorine would have helped "disinfect me" of Tony's bawdy behavior.

Try as I might, I could not shake what was happening with Tony. Nor could I grasp what he was really getting out of therapy. Thoughts of the possibility of a budding relationship between Tony and Raul entered my mind. *Maybe Tony is really struggling with his sexual preference. That would help explain his womanizing proclivities. Should I confront Tony about this? Maybe I could just suggest it without bringing up Raul. I don't know what to do.*

Utimately, the massage did help me relax, but my mind was obviously still processing the events of the day; I woke up at 4:00 a.m., still ruminating about Tony's fantasy of us having a sexual encounter and what it meant. *Was he just playing with me? Is he truly in denial about his relationship with Raul? Is it something that he can't recognize outside of their time together, like a bubble in the universe?* I sensed that Tony shared this fantasy just to make me uncomfortable; he was attempting to control me because he felt powerless in the sessions. And maybe in the façade of life he'd created to gussy up reality.

I began to think about a patient I treated for three years during my internship and post-doctoral fellowship at the clinic. He had also told me vivid and disturbing stories about his domination over women. As the treatment unfolded between us, I felt his aggression toward me in the room. As a neophyte therapist, I was working hard with my supervisor to address his anger toward me. I was a representation of a woman he couldn't dominate. He was quite resistant to acknowledging his sense of powerlessness and emasculation in the treatment room. He always displaced his anger whenever I tried to probe him.

The Friday following 9/11, Orie, who emigrated from Eastern Europe, came into session and began to share how excited and happy he felt about the terrorist attacks. Having lived on the Lower East Side, he had the "perfect view." He explained that after the first tower collapsed, he ran up to his roof. "I didn't want to miss the second one falling!" he stated excitedly and aggressively. "Corporate America deserved it!" He declared this with a rush of power. I became so enraged, speechless. I couldn't even open my mouth. I was afraid if I did, I would verbally attack him. I tried to stay professional and hide my emotions about this, not wanting to feed into his performance, but I'm sure he could sense that he got at least a little rise out of me. And I still felt a surge of rage when I thought back on this. *I think I need to get up and go for another run. These ruminations are not helping.*

Once my plane landed Friday afternoon, I called the hospital to check on Tess's condition. Even though my vacation had officially begun and I was taking a break from analyzing the Tess/Jacquie dyad, I couldn't help but be concerned for her well-being following such a serious surgery. I felt relieved once the nurse informed me Tess successfully made it through surgery and was in recovery. This good news allowed me to fully enjoy my weekend, including the momentous occasion the next evening.

As it turned out, that Saturday night, my boyfriend proposed to me. I had turned my back for just a moment, and when I spun around, I found him on one knee holding out my mother's engagement ring, on which he had set a most stunning diamond. Even though we had talked marriage, the proposal still caught me off-guard. He left me speechless, a relatively difficult task to accomplish. My dad was there for this special occasion, and I wouldn't have wanted it any other way. My boyfriend's family was there, but my people were back on the East Coast — so my dad and I called family and friends to share the news.

With all the excitement, I needed air. I took my champagne and cell phone into the freezing Minnesota air. I stood there feeling like there was someone I forgot to call. As I scrolled though my contacts, I saw who was missing: my mom. Though still filled with excitement, I stood outside, alone, freezing, with my champagne, and let myself feel the emptiness of not being able to call her. These are the moments I need to recognize her absence, to help me to continue process my grieving.

Once I arrived back in New York and got settled at home, I called Tess at the hospital. While I was away, she had left a voicemail message on my cell phone to let me know that she was recovering well. She left the phone number for her hospital room, but said that she could wait to speak with me until I returned from my trip. Her message relieved much of my concern regarding her respect for the boundaries of our relationship: She knew I was away and did not impinge on my time outside of session.

When we spoke, she sounded weak and tired, but I did notice cheerfulness in her tone. Glad to hear from me, she informed me that she would be released the following Monday and that Amy was able to pick her up. *Great! She understands my picking her up after the biopsy was a response to a specific event and not something I could or would do on a regular basis. I'm glad I thought of having her call Amy.* As much as Tess complained about Amy and her lack of time for her, she did seem to be a relatively supportive person in Tess's life.

She also stated that it was not necessary for me to come visit her. "I don't even have my makeup here. I don't want you to see me like this," she explained to me. *Typical Tess.* I chuckled under my breath. I asked her to call me later in the week, after the doctors delivered the prognosis of the results from the latest CAT scan and biopsy of the surrounding lymph nodes. I explored her emotional state, trying to gauge how she was holding up. She was tired; hated being there; hated being labeled as a lung cancer patient; but from the information the doctors provided her thus far, the prognosis seemed hopeful.

Later that week, Tess called with good news. They had been able to remove all of the cancer and it was not in her lymph nodes. She should have a full remission.

The next morning, I awoke and laid in bed thinking about Tess's news of a full recovery. I realized that I was experiencing a somewhat paradoxical and complex reaction to her exceptionally good news. Though relieved and elated by Tess's excellent prognosis, I kept replaying in my head what my mother's oncologist had said: If my mother's metastatic cancer had originated in her lungs rather than her pancreas, she would have had a better chance of survival. Memory flashes of my mother's rapidly declining health brought me to tears, and soon after, hysterics. I forced myself out of bed and then to eat despite having no appetite. I went out for a run; I needed to blast music on my MP3 player to clear my head. It helped. *I can't wait 'til*

Dr. Gwen's back from vacation. Boy, do I have a lot to talk about!

Once Tess was home from the hospital, we agreed to have twice-weekly phone sessions for the first two weeks; she would be stronger after that and able to resume our regular bi-weekly office appointments. I don't particularly like conducting phone sessions; I always feel some of the essence of the engagement within the dyad is lost when working on the phone. Given the unique circumstances, I decided that temporary phone sessions were better than no sessions. Good call because Tess had a lot she needed to talk about following her arrival back home.

The content of these sessions focused on Tess's frustrations that she was not immediately able to resume her normal activity level; she felt tired and weak, and she had moderate pain at the incision site. Amy generously offered to pay for a home aid for Tess, who would help Tess three times a week for five hours. Tess also found companionship through this new relationship with Helena; having Helena's company three times a week seemed to be more helpful than any of the chores she was actually doing for Tess.

During these two weeks, I thought a great deal about how Tess would react to my engagement. I knew she would notice the ring immediately; I had the sense that she might be angry that I hadn't shared with her that I was dating someone for the past year-and-a-half. After all the time she spent in our sessions priming me to meet a husband, I never shared that I believed I had found him. She was in therapy with me twice a week for more than four years, so unless a patient is emotionally closed off, it's inevitable that a profound intimacy would develop. If we didn't share a comfortable and, at times, reciprocal relationship at this point, I would be analyzing the dyad and wondering what was wrong.

Two weeks passed and Tess finally felt strong enough to come to session; Helena walked her to my office on her first day back. I felt a bit anxious about her noticing the ring; I had been working through all the possible scenarios that might arise. After many years of clinical practice, I knew that going through all the exchanges that I imagined might happen was an attempt to suppress my own angst; truthfully, one can never be quite sure how the unique dynamics will manifest.

Tess entered looking fragile, but clearly happy to see me. As usual, she dressed impeccably with flawless makeup. I smiled. *Back to her old self.* The first fifteen minutes of our session, she spoke about her frustration with feeling weak. "I can't walk far. I get so tired and out of breath." We explored her feelings. Tess knew rationally that her recovery would take time. Her doctors clearly informed her of the lengthy recovery period, but it didn't lessen the irritation she felt. "I hate this. It's much worse than breast cancer." *Sure. Scarier. Harder recovery. Difficulty breathing.* "When I go in for my follow-ups, you should see how old and wrinkly the patients are in the waiting room. I don't want other people lumping me in with them. Damn it, they're all going to think that because I got lung cancer, I'm as old as them." *Yup, that sounds about... Tess-ish.*

But she was frustrated and impatient, too. She wanted to be better now, not later. And I truly empathized. After my hip surgery, I got so frustrated and angry because I so desperately wanted to run, sprint, race with the wind. But I ended up waiting six months. It drove me crazy.

"I feel as though I am never going to get better. I can't even write," she shared. We processed her feelings and discussed together that it was going to be a slow process, but eventually she would be able to do all the things she had before. She eventually conceded. Seemingly soothed, we sat in a comfortable silence for a moment, and then her face lit up. *She noticed the ring. Here we go.*

I had discussed self-disclosure with my therapist the previous morning. Once Dr. Gwen returned from vacation, I used my sessions to process and come to some comfortable understanding of how to negotiate the inevitable questions that would arise once my patients noticed my engagement ring. My usual therapeutic position was to assess each dyad separately, and respond and/or act according to each unique relationship. I always respond — or at least I try to — in the best interest of the patient; this is a sometimes complicated endeavor, as my responses to each unique dyad have a relatively wide range of variability. In the case of my engagement, my therapist supported me through my dialogue, which focused on two main themes. I sometimes felt that I betrayed Tess by never revealing that I had a boyfriend. Secondly, now that I'm engaged, what do I say when she notices the ring? Because of her investment in my "relationship success," she may take it as a personal affront if she learns that I've been hiding my engagement. She may even interpret it as lying. I talked this through every which way to Sunday, trying not to leave any stone unturned.

This method of working out my problems in therapy was my natural and spontaneous way of being-in-the-world. Not only did it work well for me, but in many ways it was effortless. It encapsulated who I was and enabled me to respond in a warm and genuine manner during my patients' sessions. I felt empowered as I left. *That was a great session. So helpful.*

"You're engaged?" Tess blurted, a combination of joy, mild surprise and less-mild confusion.

"Yes," I hesitated, not because I wasn't sure if I should answer "yes" — I had to answer "yes"; she saw the ring — but because she caught me off-guard, ensconced in another topic and unprepared for my prepared response. And then I felt flush. Something occurred to me that I hadn't been considering. How do I respond when she asks for more personal details. It wasn't a matter of "if." It was Tess. She would want all the specifics. But first…

"I can't believe you never told me you were even dating." *Just as I expected.* "How long? What's his name? How did he do it?" *Oh no.* "Can I see it?"

Before I could move, Tess had leaned in and lunged for my wrist to pull my ring and hand closer. Professional or not, I obliged. Not to sound sexist or set women back a century, but this is what women do. And to be quite honest, the engagement excitement still felt fresh, so I hadn't tired of others' fawning — fake or not — over the ring and news.

"It's beautiful. Just lovely. Where did your fiancé find the setting? It's divine. Actually looks vintage. It reminds me of jewelry from the '60s, totally my taste." Of all the questions I hadn't prepared for, this was the one I was most unprepared to answer. *I should've known she'd notice. She's so fashion-savvy. I can't tell her it was my mother's setting.*

"Thank you, Tess. That's sweet. And yes, it is vintage."

"Well, it practically screams 'Jacquie'." Her admiration was genuine. She then repeated her initial list of questions, and even threw in an extra few for good measure. "What does he do? Did you set a date? Have you started planning?"

Think quick. How much self-disclosure is appropriate? In that moment, I realized that attempting to understanding our relational process was more clinically appropriate. It would help me assess how much to disclose to Tess and what my disclosures might mean to her. *Be gentle.* "Before I answer any of these questions, Tess, I think it's important for us to understand why you're asking them, and how my answering them will help you."

As I expected, Tess's biggest question was why I had not shared that I was in a relationship.

"Honestly, I'm thrilled for you, I really am. But I feel a little, um… maybe rejected's the word I'm looking for. Here I am giving you advice on how you should look in order to meet a man and this whole time, you already had one." She sounded more irritated than thrilled.

"I understand how you might feel that way. I might simply have said 'Don't worry, Tess, I already have a boyfriend,' but I didn't because I feel that we're here to share and work through your experiences in your life, not worry about mine."

We continued to collaboratively discuss the boundaries of our relationship and how the therapy was her place to explore *her* issues. As we processed it further through a number of subsequent sessions, it became abundantly clear: Tess felt closer to me than anyone else in her life. My not sharing this major life change left her imagining that I did not find her important. Eventually, through examining our relationship and its inherent boundaries, Tess understood why I hadn't mentioned anything. She wasn't happy about it, but she did accept it.

On rare occasions, withholding information — secrets — from someone close is the best thing you can do to protect your loved one. But when I thought about the secrets lingering between Tony and Raul, I was sure nothing good would come of it.

Chapter 8:
No More Tears

"Once conform, once do what other people do because they do it, and over all the finer nerves and faculties of the soul. She becomes all outer emptiness; dull, callous, and indifferent."
—Virginia Woolf

Madison was my first appointment on Tuesdays. She was a complicated young woman, with little capacity for self-observation. When a patient is not capable of, or is resistant to self-observation, the treatment is always challenging. It also takes a lot to surprise me, and Madison, well, she dropped a bombshell.

At 30 years old, she had already had five different plastic surgeries. She shared that she had a rhinoplasty, two liposuctions — first her stomach, and then her inner thighs — breast implants, and lip enhancement. She wanted to have her breast implants done again, but her plastic surgeon responsibly refused to do any more surgery on her and instead referred her to me for psychotherapy.

Despite Madison's difficulty observing and being curious about herself, I still found her incredibly intriguing. Her stories surrounding her profession were fascinating to me, as well as her complete disconnection from her body and her emotions. During the first few months of treatment, I was working incredibly hard to establish a comfortable working alliance, which is an elemental first step toward a successful therapy. Madison's detachment made this basic fundamental prerequisite for a true engagement in the therapeutic process challenging.

Madison was referred to me for treatment by her plastic surgeon, who, I found out later, had slept with her. In fact, he had been one of her regulars.

Madison worked as a high-paid escort for more than five years. Once the doctor got married, he no longer solicited her services. Interestingly, it was only after this that he became her doctor. He phoned ahead to let me know she would be calling me. He believed Madison had Body Dysmorphic Disorder. He didn't share this with her, so in the beginning stages of treatment Madison was confused about why he referred her and what she should be working on in the treatment.

This created an intricate and complex clinical dilemma; at least for me and my way of conducting treatment. I heard through Madison's narrative many themes that were appropriate and important clinical material to be worked on. However, in order for the treatment to be successful, I needed Madison to experience some distress regarding what she was bringing in. There wasn't any; well, not for the first few months. For me, the real quandary was how much I should confront and attempt to create some distress surrounding what I thought Madison should be working on, because Body Dysmorphic Disorder was the least of her concerns.

Madison's "symptoms" were ego-syntonic, meaning they were integrated into her way of being-in-the-world and held no significant difficulty for her. In order for her to be motivated and engaged in treatment, the "symptoms" needed to become ego-dystonic, meaning Madison needed to experience some uneasiness. Without internal dis-rest there was basically no real reason for her to be in treatment. And she made this quite clear to me.

She continued to be baffled as to what she "should" be working on, and basically spent her sessions indulging me with incredibly compelling stories; I felt like a voyeur. I listened completely engrossed in what she was sharing, but any time I tried to intervene clinically, she ignored my inquiries and simply continued her dialogue. Though Madison wasn't my first prostitute patient, much like Kristy, her high-class clientele made her unique compared to the majority of my previous prostitute patients — I'd been working with sex workers for years — I knew I could find some answers if I dug deep enough into my past work.

Before my doctoral training, I had the pleasure of working with a struggling young woman who was a "sex slave." Basically

Wanda's story was that she entered the world of prostitution purely to support her crack addiction. She was arrested and sentenced to an 18-month drug rehabilitation program where I was working as a Masters-level psychotherapist. We worked together in twice-weekly psychotherapy for close to a year.

Wanda was the first sex worker I encountered in such an intimate setting, and through our treatment I learned a great deal about the complex psychology of the sex industry. I was curious, fascinated, and hungry to hear more. Sadly, just when I thought we were making real progress, Wanda was caught "prostituting" herself out to some of the male patients in the rehabilitation program. She was sent to jail, having violated her court stipulations. I felt I had failed her; I missed something vital. *What was it?* Looking back, I now understand that we were making progress, and ironically, it was the progress that terrified her. Unable to process her fears, she sabotaged herself by relying on former maladaptive behaviors; unconsciously, she placed herself back in her previous role. It was safe and familiar.

I felt sad when I thought back. I remember Dr. Mike, my supervisor at the time; in fact, he was my first supervisor. Dr. Mike told me something that morning, which over the years I have accessed to help me with other patients.

"Jacquie, you are a talented, caring young woman," he said. "Let me tell you something about addiction. You're going to find that it's a difficult problem to treat, and you'll see many patients fail to succeed in their recovery the first few times. Just remember, you planted a seed; you helped her see there was a different way to live. She just wasn't ready."

My work with Wanda enabled me to help the numerous sex workers I have treated in therapy since. They were all different — diverse backgrounds, different underlying reasons, a wide range of emotional repercussions — different all around, but with two common threads: detachment and shame.

All possessed the ability to detach from their bodies and engaged in sex with their clients in a perfunctory manner. And they all suffered from deep-rooted shame. Madison's detachment was familiar, but it was the pervasiveness and lack of psychological insight that made her uniquely difficult.

So as I sat with Madison, my thoughts drifted for a moment to Wanda. *Where is she now? I'll never know if she's dead, in prison, addicted, or finally in recovery.* I felt my jaw tighten.

With Madison, it was simultaneously perplexing and intriguing; and I was uncomfortable. So I began to try to understand Madison via my experience of her. I spent time exploring my discomfort in the room in my own treatment. My therapist helped me recognize what I already knew, but was unable to completely formulate because I was so enveloped in her world of escorting; Madison was detached from her internal discomfort and I was the container for the dis-rest that she was unable to let herself feel. I had many options on how to engage her. I began by using some defense analysis; instead of creating curiosity surrounding her unconscious process, I began to peel away and gently approach Madison's resistance. It was not easy, but eventually we made progress.

As for Tess's progress following her surgical procedure, the next six months of her cancer treatment essentially had three main themes. The first was Tess's unrelenting frustration surrounding the slow recovery from her surgery. The second, which related to the first, was her profound difficulty with the aging process. Lastly, was her persistent and determined focus on giving me advice on how to have a good marriage; more specifically, she was providing me insights on how to "keep a man."

I still believed Tess giving me advice was her way to try to undo her own mistakes and regrets, but it confounded things for me. I did not want to undermine Tess's attempts to feel she could help me in some way, as I sensed that it helped her feel more powerful and in control — something she desperately needed to feel as a result of the helplessness she experienced surrounding her health and aging. On the other hand, at some point I would need to address the underlying relational dynamics that were being communicated via her advice-giving. *It's too delicate right now; I need to wait until she's physically stronger.*

She has a lot of regrets, but I need to address this in order for her to move on. I hope I find an opening soon.

While Tess slowly recovered from her surgery, we began discussing her feelings about aging. Now 66, Tess felt deformed, old and worthless. These feelings slowly emerged when at 49 she lost her breast, but became increasingly prominent over the last 17 years. I noticed that when I encouraged Tess to speak about her experience of aging, she would speak about her feelings for a few moments, and then try to shift the focus of the session onto me and my upcoming wedding. *Okay, I need to confront her resistance.* I opened up the therapeutic space by helping Tess recognize her resistance to discussing her feelings, pointing out how she tried to place the focus of our therapy sessions onto me. Tess repeatedly discussed how depressed and alone she felt; I explained that in order for her to feel better, we needed to address what aging meant to her and explore her associated feelings.

We rehashed her mother's harsh criticalness and emphasis on Tess's appearance. I was persistent in my guiding her to explore and garner her inner strengths. The pain from her surgery was experienced as a constant reminder of her being "damaged goods." She wanted to meet a man, but her doubt that someone would find her desirable was a constant and unrelenting theme. My frustration grew as she remained steadfast in her resolve that she was old and her life was over. She also shared with me that she planned on rewriting her will and leaving everything to me! From a therapist's perspective, I wasn't immediately sure how to respond.

Personally, however, my feelings came through loud and clear. Images of me sorting through her apartment and her things repeatedly popped into my head. I almost felt like an intruder in her life, left alone to pillage her existence. The thought jolted me. *Tess is a fighter; I won't have to deal with this for at least 15-20 years.* Then came the clinical perspective: The idea that she would will everything to me communicated something vital — I believed she was trying to express to me how alone she felt. It worked.

Collaboratively, we explored things Tess could become involved in to meet new people. She resisted at first, but as her body recovered from the lung cancer surgery and her physical state improved, she started to open up to these ideas. Most significantly, she was writing again. This always implied that she was on the upswing. Tess even expressed that she felt alive and purposeful. Consequently, as she internalized some of her inner strengths and attributes, her anxiety around aging grossly diminished. Her self-esteem was on the mend. The next hurdle that faced me: the dynamics between us.

Tess continued to fixate on my upcoming nuptials. She provided a relentless barrage of advice on how to maintain a healthy marriage. Her anecdotal relationship stories held my interest for more reasons than my own benefit. Her advice clued me in to new sides of Tess and her perspective on things, particularly since her marriage had failed and her long-time lover Barry had left her for another woman. While thinking she was helping me, it was amply clear to me that, subconsciously, she was working through her own regrets. But as much as her motherly advice to me was helping her resolve her issues, I felt the time had come to address our relational process. I sensed that Tess had finally gained enough ego strength to tolerate being open to further exploration of our relationship.

The night before our next session, with Tess prominent in my thoughts before bedtime, I dreamed again of the psychoanalytical conference, though this version modified itself to concerns foremost in my mind.

En route to the event, I saw myself clad in my smartest cocoa pants suit. I always felt confident in its warm tone. Yet, when I arrived at the important conference prepared to present my new paper on self-disclosure in the treatment setting, everyone milled about clad in formal black (mostly suits), while I entered wearing my wedding gown. I could feel my face flush with horror, embarrassment, and confusion. I was at the wrong event hall for our wedding, and in the entirely wrong outfit for a conference. I couldn't find my fiancé anywhere. I was sure he had arrived with me, but now he was gone. Wedding. Conference. Both. Neither. All seemed lost in turmoil.

I woke up in a panic, drenched in sweat. The dream was so vivid. I found myself, barely conscious, reaching over to my fiancé's side of the bed to make sure he was still there. As soon as my hand brushed across his chest, the panic subsided, but I was still shaken. I got out of bed, washed my face, and tried to calm myself. *Wow, I could use a Valium right now. I'm really letting her get to me.* I called a friend; it was only 6:30 a.m., but I knew she would be up. We talked for a bit — peer supervision is always helpful — and when we hung up I felt mollified, calmed, and ready to start my day.

After eating and showering, I approached the closet to find something to wear. I was in a skirt-and-sweater mood, even though the cold weather called for pants. When I opened the closet door, there, front and center, hung my cocoa pants suit. And next to it? A billowy white dress, the one I called my "elf bridal dress" because when I purchased it, I imagined an elf or pixie wearing it in a forest wedding ceremony. *Am I still asleep, dreaming?* That elf dress had been relegated to the back of the closet the last time I checked. Really, it should have been put in storage at my father's house. *How did it move here? And next to my cocoa pants suit, which I swear was at the dry cleaner?*

Now they both hung there, taunting me. I shuffled through the clothes searching for a skirt, but kept coming back to the dress and suit. *No, Jacquie, ignore them. Just find a skirt.*

"What are you doing?" The voice was deep, gravelly. My fiancé was awake.

"Huh?"

"You've been standing in front of the closet for five minutes, staring."

"My elf dress."

"I took stuff out of the closet yesterday to straighten up, fit more things. Oh, and I picked up the dry cleaning yesterday."

I lifted the dress off the bar and moved it back to its rightful place. *Screw the skirt.* I grabbed the cocoa pants suit and ripped off the clear plastic bag.

Walking to my office, I found myself ruminating over my dream. It was the end of the week and I had already had my two therapy sessions. I understood that Tess's advice on how to "keep a man," while simultaneously considering how and why her own marriage failed, left me feeling uneasy. Having grown up with two loving parents who were committed to their marriage and clearly loved each other, my own ideas of marriage contrasted Tess's — whose emphasis dwelled on her two lost loves and the associated feelings of abandonment. The contradiction left me feeling vulnerable. In addition, I believed that the dream was also about Tess. It is common for one person in a dream to symbolize another or even a few different people. Tess's experience of being deserted by her two great loves was also represented in the dream, in which Tess was me. I embodied her experience of being left and my astute and empathetic feelings of having to bear witness to her heartache.

After the first three months of her treatment, Madison began to obsessively discuss difficulties with a young man she was involved with. This is when I first saw Madison truly upset and not in control of her emotions.

"He's driving me nuts!"

"How so?"

"First he's available, then he's not. We spend a fun weekend together, then he ignores me for days, not returning any of my calls or texts. It's pissing me off." *Welcome to the world of every woman ever in the history of, well, the history of women.*

The truth was, I could empathize with her. I'd had my share of relationships with unavailable men. I was lucky that I finally found a great guy who opened up emotionally to me, but the memory of those past relationships were still clear in my mind. *I wonder if he knows about her current line of work.*

Eventually, her obsessions would escalate, burdening me with the ethical dilemma of "my duty to warn" a potential victim of assault. But for the moment, her ruminations about him were still contained to constant and intrusive thoughts about him. I had been having some difficulties understanding what was happening with Madison, and what was being communicated by her unhealthy attachment to this young man.

Many of my previous and current patients complained about choosing an unavailable partner. *But Madison's conflict feels different. I need to sort this out; I can feel the thinly veiled rage behind her ruminations. And that's not good. She doesn't have a history of violence — well, no reported history — so why are my associations going there? Why am I imagining her killing him? Is it just her rage? Or am I sensing a real potential to be violent? I definitely don't want a repeat of what happened with Anne. Relax, Jacquie, you will figure it out.* Finally, during our session on a gray Tuesday morning, after relentlessly probing for more information surrounding Madison's internal experience of her relationship with Brad, I got my answer.

Madison first met Brad at a dance club on the Lower East Side a couple weeks into her treatment with me. She gushed when she first told me about him.

"We had an immediate connection. It's like we could feel each other across the room before our eyes even met, you know? Electric."

I've heard this one before.

"We danced and drank all night. And made out on the dance floor. One thing led to another and we ended up back at my place." Madison smiled, satisfied, as she twirled her hair. Almost smug, but also somewhat vapid, which she certainly was not. *Is this what I look like when I twirl my hair?*

She seemed done with the story, but I was curious. "Did you have sex with him?"

She burst with a short laugh, a mix of a snort and chortle. "Seriously?"

I nodded. Madison stopped twirling her hair, uncrossed her legs, and poised her hands on her knees while she threw me a look of condescending superiority.

"You do remember my line of business, don't you?" Her response dripped with biting haughtiness. *Hmm. Defense mechanism?*

"And you do remember my line of business?" I smiled and gave her a laugh. Not a dismissive one, but something more genial to help bring down her offensive shield. "Just because you get paid to have sex doesn't mean that I, or anyone for that matter, should assume you're going to have sex as soon as you meet a guy." *Not that there's anything wrong with that.* "Not that there's anything wrong with that." And I laughed.

She was a *Seinfeld* fan, and though I preferred crime dramas to comedies when I would watch TV, my Miami roommate loved *Seinfeld*. So when that particular line from one of the episodes popped into my head, I thought I'd use it as a bonding experience.

And it worked. She laughed, too.

"Yes, we had sex. A weekend marathon of glorious sex and Piper-Heidsieck." *Champagne. Your drink of choice.* "We were having such a good time, I even canceled one of my clients."

"Calling out sick to work? I'd say that's a good time." Madison smiled at my quip, so I knew she had a sense of humor about her career — and it conveyed to her that I wasn't uptight about her line of work. Or judgmental.

"Dr. Jacquie. I really like him."

And at first, Brad seemed to reciprocate Madison's affection and interest. He called often, and the duo spent quite a bit of time together. It was actually quite intense, or so it seemed through Madison's narrative.

It was the first time Madison had been in any sort of relationship with a man that was not a "paying" client since she began escorting. I was quite curious about how she was going to explain her occupation, her lack of availability on some weekends, and her obviously incredibly expensive luxury apartment. I was a bit hesitant to ask; again, I didn't want Madison to feel judged. I also didn't want her to feel that I thought she was not worthy of an intimate relationship. I sensed, despite her disconnection, a real and fundamental experience of worthlessness surrounding her self-image. This worthlessness was also suggested by her numerous plastic surgeries at such a young age; yet, again, this was something Madison reflected no curiosity about.

I knew it would take a long time for Madison to become aware of this painful internal sense of self; I didn't even try to explore this with her. I knew it would not be received well so early in her treatment. It was this unanalyzed, deep-seated worthlessness that eventually caused Madison to completely unravel when Brad pulled back. She was unable to process her feelings internally, or even put them into words. This resulted in her frantically stalking Brad — not like Anne's delusional stalker, but the real kind — as their relationship unfolded. And after only several weeks, it would become unbelievably toxic. Her circumstances, paired with the eventual turn of events leading to the termination of Tony's treatment, made for quite a challenging time. It was a "clinical juncture" where I needed to make rapid clinical decisions concerning situations that could have deadly consequences.

When Tess came in for her next session, she provided me with a most opportune opening.

"I still can't believe you're engaged. Have you set the wedding date?" *Once again with the personal questions, but I'm going to give her this one.*

"We've been throwing around some ideas, but no, we don't have one set yet."

"So I've been wondering... am I going to be invited?" *Her timing's uncanny. First the dream and now this.* I had been seeing Tess twice a week for five years and we had been through quite a bit together, so despite how inappropriate it would be for a therapist to invite her patient to a wedding — and Tess knew this — I suspected, almost expected, that these questions were going to come. I needed to explore what the questions meant to her, particularly in regards to the boundaries of our relationship.

"I feel close to you. I'd like to see you get married." She waited to see what I'd say. I waited for her to continue to what she knew would be the logical conclusion. "I know you probably can't invite me," *See, I knew she knew the boundaries*, "but I thought I'd ask." *Jacquie, it's important to honor her feelings about our connection.*

"I also feel the bond between us, so you're not mistaken about your feelings." Tess perked up a little by this, almost seeming hopeful. "But you're correct about me not being able to invite you. Regardless of how close I may feel to you, this is still a therapeutic relationship and there are limits to what is appropriate."

As I watched what looked like her seeming hopefulness being deflated from her, she responded, "I know you're right. I don't like it, but... okay." And yet this didn't stop her from continuing to ask about the wedding details.

Only a few sessions later...

"So, have you two picked the wedding date?" *Here we go again.*

"Tess, are you going to ask me about being invited to the wedding, too?

"No, I've accepted that that's not going to happen. I was just wondering if you're going to have a spring wedding or a summer wedding or you know, whenever. Because you can't plan anything else without knowing the time of year. The dress colors and styles, the flowers, things like that."

Should I just tell her and get it over with? Is it appropriate? I can't keep putting off her question by saying we haven't decided. That can hurt the trust she feels with me. And I don't want her to feel more dismissed than she already does. Besides, she's going to figure it out anyway. I'm taking two weeks off and, when I return with a wedding band, she'll know it happened.

"It's in November, Tess."

"An autumn wedding." Her voice pitched up with delight. "Fall weddings are my favorite. Crisp air. So many deep, rich colors to choose from. The flower arrangements can be just gorgeous."

As the months, then seasons, passed, Tess continued to offer marital advice. But now she would also add a dash of tips for cooking up a November wedding. "Make sure the bridesmaids have a waist jacket or shawl made from the same material as the dress and that it matches the dress style. It might get chilly, and you want the girls looking their best and not wearing some random, awful denim jacket or hooded sweatshirt. Oh, your centerpieces could be delightful. Use small pumpkins and gourds with autumn leaves as a base, then have a spray of colorful fall flowers. On the gift and cake tables and at the head table, you can decorate the end with horns-of-plenty, and maybe even the space near you and your husband. You don't want a centerpiece spray blocking your faces from the guests. You can also put the horns on the Viennese table. Oh, you must have a Viennese table and an espresso and cappuccino bar."

I allowed her to provide uninterrupted guidance and opinions in the occasional session. They were mostly harmless, but as it got closer to the wedding, her marital — not reception — advice became more prominent. I was going over in my mind: What did it mean for Tess and our relationship for her to offer me her advice? How will I broach this with her? During one of our last sessions right before my wedding and two-week break, Tess expressed her beliefs with increasing fervor.

"Tess, I'm curious. You've been giving me advice about marriage for quite a while. Do you have a sense of why you're so focused, so concerned about my marriage?"

I noticed her ruminating deeply. She took a while before she said anything, but I didn't interrupt the silence. I didn't want to diffuse her thought process nor the energy she was building to her truth. Finally, "I don't want you to wind up like me. I don't want you to make the same mistakes." She hung her head low. "I have so many regrets. It's painful to look back. And now... I'm alone." *Ouch. But... it's a window of opportunity to achieve a breakthrough for Tess.*

I kept my voice gentle, soothing. "Tell me more about your regrets." After five years, Tess was finally able to face some truths about her past and herself. It felt like we flipped a lamp switch, flooding light on a darkened corner of her memories.

"It was my fault. I ruined my marriage."

"How so?"

"I never became involved with my husband's children. Quite honestly, I didn't really even like them."

"Why?"

"They had attitudes. I thought they acted entitled." *Interesting coming from her.* After exhausting her feelings about the children, she admitted to having depressive episodes so many years earlier. "I would lie in bed for days at a time. And when I suspected he was having an affair, I didn't like it, but what right did I have to complain. I was as guilty as he was with my numerous liaisons. I mean, everybody cheats." *So she's said before.* "But I feel like I didn't fight for him or the marriage. I just let him go." She bowed her head in shame.

Then she shared the details on her marriage's ultimate demise. Though Tess knew that she and her husband were on shaky ground, they never talked about it — so his horrible, thoughtless actions not only surprised and shocked her, they had repercussions on all her future relationships.

One evening after work, she came home to an empty apartment. Without informing Tess, her husband moved out and took most of his belongings with him. He left Tess for the woman with whom he was having the affair. He filed for divorce, then immediately remarried. I felt my eyes fill up, but Tess didn't shed a tear.

"How does it feel to finally share this story with me?"

"I have a knot in my stomach. I feel like crying. Like I should be crying."

"Then cry. Don't you feel safe crying here?"

"That's not it. I've used up all my tears. I don't have any more to shed for him." She focused on my mother's painting, took a deep breath, then let it out slowly and evenly. "I'm done crying about it."

We sat there for a minute. No words between us. I felt that she needed a moment to take in what had transpired. To feel the weight she'd been carrying, holding onto for so long, finally fall off her shoulders. To own the moment and the release.

Then she said something that she'd repeated to me on many occasions, but there was a poignancy in the words that had been absent all those times before. "Jacquie, I have had a dreadfully hard life. I say all these things to you, share my advice — because you are a good, loving person who deserves only good things. I just don't want you to end up like me."

My heart broke for Tess, and I felt close to her — if only for a moment — in this rare instance of openness from her. Despite her frankness in our sessions, she normally kept herself closed off, keeping even me, the person she should feel safest with, at arm's length. So when she revealed herself to me, I was able to readily empathize with her. I shared my feelings of sadness with her.

"Thank you," she softly retorted.

After this session, Tess began to ease up on the marriage advice. Her breakthrough finally enabled her to focus on her own shame and self-blame involving the ending of her marriage. This was great progress for Tess. At our last session before my wedding, when she stood up to leave, she had to get in one quick beauty tip. "Please, please, have your hair and makeup done professionally."

In an earlier session, I had shared — maybe mistakenly — that I was planning on doing my own hair and makeup. So when she gave me this last-minute advice, I repeated my steadfast position. "Tess, I like a natural look." Admittedly, in the moment I felt I was half-defending myself.

She smiled, then turned to leave. As she walked out of my office, her last statement to me was, "See you in two weeks." Not another word about makeup. Maybe I wasn't mistaken to share it after all. Maybe Tess was learning that we were two separate souls and she didn't need to protect me from her past.

Later that same day, while shoveling down my much-needed sandwich, I heard an annoying *Zzz Zzz Zzz*. A moth was flitting around my office, its wings buzzing as it flicked against the lights and walls. I do not like killing insects, but...

Ugh. This could be extremely distracting during session; Rachel loses focus with even the slightest disruptive sound. This could be quite complicated; an intrusion in the safety of the therapeutic environment. I opened the office door, hoping my uninvited visitor would take the opportunity to leave within the next five minutes. I hovered over my sandwich, continuing to eat and waiting for the moth to exit. *Bzzzz...*

It had been quite a journey with Rachel. She, like many patients, had been experiencing what I call an "identity crisis" for countless years. So after close to a year and a half of twice-weekly sessions, she sent an email that made all our hard work worth it; the email signature was priceless. She finally, after struggling for many months, signed the email "Rachel." I noticed it with her in session; and then the real work began.

It was three months following this first instance of recognizing herself as Rachel that what we now refer to as the "moth incident" happened. As our session began, our uninvited visitor landed on the area rug, directly between the therapist's chair and the comfy patient chair where Rachel was sitting. *Interesting landing.* We both looked down at the moth; It was obviously distracting both of us.

Silence.

Hmm, what to do? I was a bit anxious and uncertain how to handle this unsolicited frame break. We were both staring at it. I sensed that the complexity of how to handle the moth was simultaneously distressing and humorous to us both. I quickly decided to bring it into the room, and process how to handle the moth with Rachel. I looked at Rachel; she was wearing pretty pink nail polish, I asked, "How should we handle this situation?"

We were both leaning forward, staring at the moth; Rachel said, "I'll do it!" She swooped up her foot and then smashed it down, eliminating the moth. She picked it up with a tissue and threw it in the trashcan. I sat there, astonished by her sudden, decisive — and somewhat uncharacteristic — action.

Again, silence.

Rachel was a woman; a fabulous woman, actually, who sadly was trapped in a body that felt strange and unfamiliar.

"Small steps," was the way Rachel wanted to transition, and wearing pink was the first of many small steps to come. The moth afforded us a new opportunity to explore Rachel's transition, and I was curious about how she felt after destroying the moth.

"I wonder how you feel having to eliminate our guest, which placed you in a traditionally masculine role?"

She tilted her head and smiled; the smile was coy.

Silence.

I could tell she was in deep thought. I was a bit anxious, but I knew I had to give her space. *Whatever she's mulling over, don't interrupt her thought process by breaking the silence. This is a key moment in her identity formation.*

Finally after what felt like an hour, she looked up and laughed. I chuckled with her.

"I feel good, maybe even happy for the first time." Rachel acknowledged that her years battling with severe and practically incapacitating depression were a result of her struggles surrounding her gender identity. It was through our journey that Rachel, a thirty-five-year-old man, finally was able to recognize that he felt trapped in a body that wasn't right.

"I want ovaries," he shared only a month earlier. Robert was now recognizing that he was a woman trapped in a man's body; he hated himself for this. With the emergence of Rachel and the use of the pronoun "she," the depression was lifting. And she began to experience moments of actual happiness. The "moth incident" placed us in a situation where one of us had to take a traditional dominant role. I didn't want to impose this on her, and once she took care of it, I was a bit fearful that she would suffer emotional repercussions.

Remarkably, Rachel was able to experience the irony of the situation, and we shared a moment of humor together. We talked about the "moth incident" and how uncannily it happened during her session rather than another patient's. The experience of the moth would have felt and likely been different with each of my patients, but it was the most complicated with Rachel and ended up being a powerful moment in her identity growth. She observed this, and left the session that day with a skip in her step and a particular lightness I had not seen in her before.

Madison was my last patient before my vacation for the wedding and honeymoon. Things had not been going well for her. Within just a couple months of the start of her relationship with Brad, he started pulling back in a slow, insidious fashion that Madison only noticed after his retreat was well underway.

First came his remarkable inability to commit to any plans with Madison. Her schedule was busy, as she had many regulars — apparently she was in high demand in her profession — so in order for her to keep her occupation a secret, she really needed Brad to make plans in advance. He did in the beginning, but as soon as it seemed that their liaison was more than just a fun sexual relationship, he stopped making plans. His excuse, according to Madison, was that he liked things to be spontaneous, which also seemed to work better with his increasingly busy schedule as a new lawyer in a prestigious firm. Consequently, he was calling less and less, which prompted Madison to call him more and more.

Now she brought that anger into the room.

Madison exuded an exceptionally strong, powerful presence with her tall, curvy, perfect posture. Though ever-present at the start of her treatment, as our therapeutic relationship unfolded, I sensed that her commanding and dominant presence was actually a defense against how small, ashamed, and insignificant she felt. I found myself wondering how Brad experienced her. I eventually developed a theory. I believed Brad was attracted to Madison's demanding and strong presence; it was sexy. She also was quite detached, which would appeal to a man only looking for a casual, fun relationship — and I guessed that's what he was looking for. When Madison noticed Brad withdrawing, I can only surmise that he began to experience her as needy; and Brad, a young, attractive lawyer at the start of an exciting career, didn't want any needy strings hanging off him.

The pattern of their relationship, as it unfolded, was one that was quite familiar to me. The more Brad pulled away, the more Madison reached out to him. When Madison backed off, trying to get away from the toxicity of their interactions, Brad would reach out to her. The status of their relationship on this particular day was unclear to Madison. She ranted about how they had sex over the weekend, and he still hadn't called her since then, despite her numerous attempts to reach him.

"I understand how disappointing this is. Maybe even heartbreaking. But you're visibly enraged. I'm wondering if there is something more that's evoking such aggressive feelings." This wasn't the first time I had encouraged her to be curious about her feelings. But we had remained in stalemate all those weeks. And then she yelled loud enough for New Jersey to hear.

"I get $400 an hour for sex, and he's getting it for free!" *Wow! I'm sure this isn't about the money.* I suspected her underlying conflict was "Why doesn't he want me?" Escorting gave her complete control over men, and with Brad there was none; this enraged her. And then she stopped, not examining her emotions any further. *Well, at least I made some progress in understanding her better.*

As Madison stormed out, still worked up from her outburst and resistant to my attempts to calm her, I was left wondering about her family history. She provided so little information it was hard for me to formulate how her internal dynamics developed. It was something I knew we needed to work on. Actually, there were more questions than answers when it came to Madison's treatment. I felt confident that, given enough time and patience, I could help her.

I also found myself fantasizing about escorting; I was quite often ensconced in this fantasy world while absorbed in my clinical work with many of my high-paid escort patients. I knew I could never do it; I would not be emotionally able to handle it. However, it still intrigued me. My first and foremost thought on this particular day was how easily I would be able to pay off my student loans. At this point, I calculated that my last student loan payment would coincide with my first social security check. My second thought surrounded my fascination with the resulting emotional consequences of escorting. I tried to explore this with Madison, but her lack of insight and resistance to self-exploration left her little ability to indulge me with an answer concerning her emotional experience and/or resulting implications surrounding her profession. I only hoped that she would give in to therapy before she buckled under her pent-up emotions.

Upon my return from my wedding and honeymoon, Tess asked many questions about the events. I disclosed a small amount of information, relegating it to common wedding and reception details. I shared that it was fun, that everyone loved my dress, and that I was happy. Tess didn't know that, even still, I was carrying the sadness of my mother's absence at my wedding.

"Did you have your hair and makeup done professionally?" *I absolutely knew she was going to ask me this.* These questions had become so predictable that I began to find them entertaining.

"What do you think?"

"I know you like the natural look and I'm sure you looked lovely, especially with your figure, but you really *need* to start using blush." I smiled. Only two years earlier, these comments surrounding my appearance used to feel intrusive and even hostile; now I found them endearing. Still, I was not blind to the possibility that my more gracious reaction to Tess's comments could have stemmed from changes in my life. Could the relationship with my new husband, a steadfast bond these past two years, cause me to feel more secure? Could that be why Tess's jabs seemed more caring than meddling now? Or maybe, despite Tess's efforts to keep herself at an emotional arm's length from me, I was able to emotionally bond with her. I should be mindful of this, maybe explore it in my own therapy.

As for Madison, I observed a marked difference in her from how she presented herself before my vacation. She was beginning to really unravel. Her thoughts about Brad had turned into an obsession. She had just come back that morning from a long weekend in Miami with one of her regular clients.

"Do you go on these often?"

"More often in the winter. A few of my regulars like to get out of the cold, and they enjoy bringing a little company."

"What do you do on these trips?" She smirked at my question, and I immediately knew what her churlish response would be, so I added, "I mean besides sex."

"My men totally pamper me on these getaways." *My men. Interesting.* "They splurge on packages at high-end day spas where I get the most indulgent massages and beauty treatments. Upscale hotels. Expensive dinners on Lincoln Road. Drinks and dancing on Ocean Drive. All I have to do is have sex with them a few times and I get everything a woman could want." To Madison, sex was a way to "get things." It was a fascinating dynamic; her ability to completely detach sex from intimacy was remarkable. Of all the sex workers I treated in therapy, Madison without a doubt was the most detached.

"Your men really spoil you on these trips." Madison looked at me and pursed her lips. *That comment hit home. But what was the specific emotional trigger? "Your men?" Or the whole comment in general?*

"I call them my mini-vacations." Her tone clashed with the sentiment as her voice took a bitter turn.

"Well, it sounds like you always have a good time."

"Not always." She shook her head to flip her hair back, then folded her arms like an insolent little girl who didn't get her way. *I bet I can guess why. Brad.*

"Brad spoiled this trip for me. Ruined my good time! And almost made me lose a client."

"What happened?"

"Well, my client, I'll call him Rick. He was almost ready to put my ass on a flight back home. I had to sweet-talk him and turn his frown upside-down."

"No, Madison. I meant what happened with Brad. How is he responsible for spoiling your trip?"

"Brad put me in such a perturbed mood that I wasn't my bright, sparkly self for Rick. I couldn't relax. He asked me what was wrong. Why I was pouting. I had to make up a lie that it was family problems. Then I apologized and put on a happy face for him. But I could tell that Rick wasn't happy."

"I still don't understand what Brad did?"

Madison raised her voice, yelling at me almost as though I were Brad. "What do you think he did? Not return my calls and messages! I kept checking my phone for texts, emails, anything. But nothing. Not a peep from that bastard."

Honestly, her anger became so oppressive, I felt a bit suffocated. And then I imagined that this was how Brad felt. Had been feeling. And without any established historical information on Madison, it was difficult for me to know how to intervene effectively. I decided to use some psych-education with Madison.

"I'd really like to help you understand what's happening with Brad, but in order for me to do that, I need to understand your past and present relationships better."

She was pissed at me and replied, "What's to understand? I already know what's happening! He's getting sex for free and he doesn't appreciate it!" Then she looked me square in the eyes. "Got it?" And then leaned forward. "Dr. Jacquie? Hmm?"

Hmm, indeed. She's a tough one to break through to. I know I need to stay where SHE is, but I also need to pique her curiosity. How am I going to do that? There's so much important, compelling clinical material here. And where is she going with Brad? I feel an undeniable sense that her behavior could escalate; not good. I need to figure this out, and quickly.

I believed with certainty that her rage had to do with her inability to acknowledge her underlying shame and worthlessness, but I needed her to experience this; an interpretation on my part would definitely not be well-received.

Chapter 9:
The Dinner Fork in the Road

Life can be difficult at times, and many questions have no answers. The determination it takes to go on and the resiliency required of the human spirit to find joy, are integral parts of existing as human. Running is symbolic of this struggle. The joy and satisfaction come from meeting the challenge head-on and realizing that just when you think you cannot go on anymore, if you pull deep from within yourself, you will find strength beyond anything imaginable.
— Jacqueline Simon Gunn

August 16, 2008. Another hot and humid New York day. When people complain about how dreadfully muggy Miami gets, they're not lying. I lived there for three years. But to be honest, New York gets its share of oppressive, steamy, sticky summer days. The kind of weather that makes it difficult to run. Don't mistake me. We runners will still take to the pavement; we just sweat more and pray for an open hydrant. Normally, I run in the morning when the sun hasn't yet scorched the city air, but on this day, I had to push my run into the evening — and now I realized I was unconsciously rushing my pacing run to make it home for a sporting event.

Quite honestly, I don't particularly like watching sports on television. Baseball. Football. Basketball. Boring, boring, boring. But I make an exception for the Olympics. I guess most people have their favorite sport that they just can't miss. Me? I love watching the graceful performances of the gymnasts. It's pure beauty. The real kicker for me, though, is track and field — and more specifically, running.

When the track and field events roll on-screen, something happens to me. I lose myself, especially mesmerized by both short- and long-distance running. I'll even find my mind wandering, sometimes reflecting on my 20 years of competitive running, and wondering if, had my life taken a different path, I would have been competing on an Olympic level.

So even though I understood why my uncontainable excitement caused me to turn my seven-minute, 30-second-per mile training pace into a six-and-a half-minute racing pace — a mistake, considering that this day was my ten-miler — it didn't make it easier to ease up.

This year, the Olympics held a profoundly significant meaning for me, as earlier in the year I had the pleasure of treating a lovely young runner on her way to compete in the 800-meter Olympic track competition. And as it had turned out, her treatment was analogous to an 800-meter track race: it was short, intense, and painful at times, and the outcome was nebulous. My thought this night as I raced home was: sometimes life just doesn't go as you planned.

I have treated many athletes, but ironically never a runner. I thought about the phone call I received from my orthopedic surgeon, explaining that he was referring Samantha to me. Samantha was a young track runner who was supposed to be going to the Olympics in the summer, but she was injured. To top it off, he shared that she was restricting her food intake, which was causing a decline in her athletic performance. "I think you can help her. And if you can, not only will she recover from her injury, she'll be able to compete." Though his words inspired hope, his desperate tone suggested an opposing subtext.

So while watching the opening commentary of the presenters and losing myself in a bag of cherry Twizzlers, my thoughts drifted back to Sam, my own accomplishments as a runner, and the profound connection we had during our brief, but intense, therapeutic encounter.

The midwinter morning of Samantha's first appointment, I looked out my window to find large, fluffy snowflakes falling — a beautiful scene. I downed the rest of my coffee and layered up for what I hoped would be a great run. I love running in the snow. It creates an undeniable sense of peacefulness, like being wrapped in a soothing blanket of white cotton, changing the often shrill urban streets into a hushed cityscape.

I had finally fully recovered from my ankle break. My rehabilitation seemed to stretch on infinitely. I felt pretty defeated when, at the peak of competing, I suffered two major training layoffs. First my hip, then my ankle — and in between these two injuries, I lost my mother. I would have to say 2006-2007 ended up as, qualitatively, the most difficult time in my life to date. In November of 2007, I married, which is when my life seemed to balance out. Samantha came along only months later in February 2008.

My snowy run left me feeling invigorated. It never ceases to amaze me after all these years: I can wake up tired, drag myself from bed to bath, and push myself out the door after little sleep; yet, by the time I return from what should be an exhausting five-mile run, I feel more alive and rejuvenated than ever. Endurance running feels like a drug. If you're well-conditioned, it provides a natural high. The ability to stay relaxed and focused in the face of pain and exhaustion is essential to being a successful long distance runner.

This may not seem like much fun, but the sense of strength and power that comes from running is like nothing else I have ever experienced. For me, this is the psychological component of the "runner's high." When the pain seems most intense and you really want to stop, somewhere you find the strength to keep going. Continuing in the face of such a rigorous effort endows you with all the power that you'll need to push on. This, then, for me at least, supplies an inner strength that is needed to move past the pain into a sort of spiritual transcendence.

I have been running and competing for 20 years, and each run is a sacred part of my day. When I first started, I found it an easy way to stay fit; but after a few years of easy four-times-a-week running, it morphed into something else. Running became a part of who I am, a part of my identity. I'm a doctor. I'm a student. A woman. A wife. I'm a runner. I'm always thinking about my training. Of course I remember the many, many races I competed in, but I also remember and reflect upon some of my best training runs.

So this morning, as I dressed for my first session with Sam, I guess I wasn't surprised to be thinking about my running more than usual. I wondered how it would feel to sit with a younger athlete going toward a goal that at one time could have been my own. I thought about my life decisions. The path I ultimately chose led me down a different road, and now looking back, I felt the sense of loss that one experiences when contemplating a missed opportunity. Or was it?

Regardless, I felt excited at the prospect of working with Samantha, though I had to quell the many thoughts racing around in my mind. With running such an integral part of my identity, what was it going to be like to work with a well-conditioned athlete preparing to go to the Olympics to compete in a sport that was so close to my own?

Well, you'll certainly understand her struggles, and being familiar with her sport could be useful. I've helped so many athletes, but this is going to be different. Very different. She's obviously a much younger and better-trained athlete than I, and she'll be fulfilling a dream that I might've achieved if I'd been introduced to distance running when I was younger. Gosh, I hope I don't feel envy. Hmm, this last thought's a bit uncomfortable; the fact that my mind is going there means something. Whatever happens, Jacquie, you can handle it — at least I hope I can! Loss is a difficult thing for you. Well, good thing you've got your own therapy to work these issues through. This should be an interesting experience.

Samantha entered the session dressed in her Adidas athletic gear. *Hmm, my favorite brand. Wow, she looks strong.* I could see her athletic physique under her fitted pants and sweatshirt. Track runners are typically muscular and Samantha certainly had the prototypical track-runner's body. Even her cadence, particularly her posture, screamed "Athlete!" She had dark brown hair pulled into a pony tail, chiseled cheekbones, and the perfectly glowing skin that is a distinctive attribute of someone in great physical shape. I noticed her looking at my legs as she sat down in the patient chair. I had a skirt on with wool stockings. I imagined my lean muscular legs caught her attention; I was wondering what she was thinking, but it was far too soon to ask. I felt certain this would be brought into the room eventually, but definitely not in a first session.

"Samantha, if it's okay, I'd like to start with you telling me why you're here?

"Please call me Sam." Only slightly louder than a whisper.

"Absolutely. So tell me what brought you into therapy, Sam."

Confusion crossed her face as the muscles in her massive legs tightened. "Didn't my, um, didn't my coach tell you?"

I smiled, hoping to ease her obvious tension. "He did. But I'm interested to hear the story from you."

She related a brief explanation of her athletic history: her many years of training, her passion for the sport, how the Olympics became a possibility. As she told her story, I observed the incongruence between her strong physique and her shy and soft-spoken tone. She splayed her arms across her front in a V-shape, as though she were attempting to hide her legs.

"I've been trying to figure out why I feel so uncomfortable with my body. It feels like it came on all of a sudden."

I crossed my legs. As I did this, Sam looked at my thigh muscles again. "Sam, these things never happen overnight. It's a gradual progression of feelings that build up cumulatively. We're going to explore your past, and together we'll try to get to the bottom of this."

Her coach, Mr. Dawson, informed me via phone — we never met face to face — that she had been recovering from a stress fracture in her foot that her doctors and physical therapist astutely believed may have been caused, or at least exacerbated, by a restricted diet.

At only 22 years old, she had already been competing nationally for four years, and had suffered numerous stress fractures. More recently, her performance had started declining, which also suggested a lack of fuel. So, when Coach Dawson sent Sam for a bone density scan, the test did indeed reveal some deterioration in her bones. This is highly abnormal for a 22 year old, particularly for an athlete who consistently performs high-intensity, weight-bearing training exercises. Once given the results, Sam felt obligated — nay, forced — to tell her doctors and physical therapist that she was restricting her diet. This meant that she was eating, but not nearly enough to maintain the physical health of an athlete.

"How did that make you feel?"

She inhaled deeply, then released it in a sigh. "Well, when the doctors told Coach Dawson about the scan and my food issues, he wasn't happy. He wanted me in therapy right away." *Hmm... avoiding my question.* "So they referred me to you." She looked at her shoes when she said this. Then she added, and she honestly did appear concerned: "If I don't get control over this, I'll miss my chance to go to the Olympics this summer."

Hmm, this is gonna be a toughy. Disordered eating and body image issues are quite challenging to treat. It requires time and delicate handling — and we only have a few months. I've got to figure out when this started.

"Sam, think back. Can you remember when you first noticed feeling uncomfortable with your body? And take your time with this." And she did. We sat in silence as she ruminated over her past. Again, I noticed her looking at my legs. It was so penetrating; I felt the urge to grab the throw blanket in my closet and cover my legs. I didn't, of course.

While sitting in silence, my mind drifted off and I found myself thinking about the difference between long-distance running and track running. I had never competed in track in school, but I was familiar with the experience of training on the track. My running coach, Chantal, had me performing innumerable track workouts in preparation for my long-distance road races. They were painful; and the pain was different than what I experienced during endurance training and longer races. I was fast on the track. Chantal would often say, "J, you have natural ability. You have strong legs." This statement — combined with my determination and persistence to meet my pace goals — kept me coming back, but truthfully these workouts were not fun. I was in my own world thinking about Chantal screaming, "Let's go, J. Faster, you can do it!" She pushed me, and it was because I rose to the challenge that I started placing in local races.

On the track, Chantal had me running 800-meter repeats; basically, running full-speed twice around the track. I was averaging six-and-a-half-minute-mile splits — about 1,600 meters — a remarkable pace for a non-professional athlete. I hated every minute, and Chantal knew it; but it had to be included in my training to give me the speed endurance I needed to reach my pace goal for the marathon I was training for. Since 800-meter repeats were an integral part of my distance running training schedule, it was quite coincidental that Sam was racing the same distance.

Sam continued sitting in silence, her various facial expressions indicating that her mind was obviously working on her past. *How's she feeling? So close to the Olympics she can practically taste it, yet so far.* My thoughts moved to my training with the New York Road Runners' Club. The once-weekly training with them was brutal; but these workouts actually placed me in a new pace category. After two months of training with them, my splits during my long runs were averaging between seven and seven-and-a-half-minute miles. I felt great! When training on the track with them, I was always the lead runner and another club member asked me to join his competitive team. "Jacqueline, you have such strong legs. You'd be an asset to our team. I'll train you personally; your mile splits could get even faster."

I was 31 at the time; really, the perfect age to begin a more competitive distance running career. Between finishing my doctoral training and working as a pre-doctoral intern at The Karen Horney Clinic, I just didn't think I could handle adding more long-distance training. The internship was demanding and I was still writing my dissertation. I graciously declined, but mentioned my reasons, and said I would keep his offer in mind as a possibility once I achieved my academic goals. I felt knots in my stomach as I reflected on our now years-old exchange. When I finished my academics and could have accepted Bob's offer, I suffered from a serious hip injury. This set me back, and as I recovered, I lost my mother and then broke my ankle. I felt sad. As I shared all of this with my physical therapist, he said to me, "Jacquie, right now, just be glad that you're training again. Please don't push yourself too hard yet!" I learned to listen.

Finally, Sam looked up, knocking me out of my trance. She cleared her throat. "I never told anyone about this before. I feel ashamed, especially after what everyone's done for me."

"I can see this is difficult for you." She seemed a bit more comfortable as she began describing the earliest memory of discomfort with her body. She described running track in high school. Her strongest and most competitive distance was 800 meters — a half mile. She was the fastest of all her team members and won numerous races, but despite her accomplishments, she was always comparing her body to the other girls she trained with, as well as those she competed against. Her legs brought her the most unease; they were always bigger than all the other girls.

Hmm, okay, so this explains why she immediately looked at my legs when we sat down together. I'll definitely have to explore her awareness of my body sooner than I normally would. This is a big issue for her. That's when I fully realized the pressure to rush her treatment and began to feel it; I wanted her to be able to compete in the summer Olympics. *Jacquie, you can't rush this or just bandage her psyche so she can go; her health's at risk! And oh boy, she really does have strong muscular legs. But then again, all track runners do, especially short distance and sprinters, whereas long-distance runners tend to have longer, leaner thigh muscles. And it's her strong legs that have gotten her to where she is now — about to go to the Olympics.* I knew she was going to be tough, fully equipped to handle the emotional rollercoaster she was getting on; most athletes are, myself included.

Sam began crying. "What am I gonna do? I can't help myself. I can't stop restricting my diet and I'm beginning to lose my power," she whimpered, before exploding, "And to make matters worse, my legs are as big as ever. I feel crazy!"

I hadn't finished gathering the background information, but Sam's breakdown changed things. I needed to shift gears, be with her in the moment. There is no template for psychotherapy. In order to have an effective and successful treatment, one must be flexible and respond to the needs of each individual patient. This comes with experience. Empathic listening was what Sam needed in this moment. Sometimes simply reiterating what the patient just expressed and acknowledging her emotions is enough to calm her, even make her feel safe.

"I understand how you're feeling. You're afraid. You feel like your relationship with food has taken control of your life. You have no power over it." By the time I had finished speaking, Sam had calmed down and her eyes lit up.

"Yes, Dr. Simon. Yes, that's exactly how I feel!"

I noticed that our first session hour was coming to a close, and I wanted to give Sam something to help her emotionally and engage her in the treatment. "Before we end for the day, Sam, I want you to know something. We're in this together. You are not alone. We're going to work hard to figure out what's leaving you feeling out of control, and what's driving you to restrict your food intake." She tensed up a little. "Sam, I hear how hard this is for you right now, and I imagine you're feeling a lot of pressure to fix this."

"You have no idea!"

I thought for a moment, reflecting on my injuries and how it made me feel. Athletes usually pride themselves on the control they have over their bodies — I know I do. But perhaps she also felt she had relinquished control of her body to her coach and the sport. As a young woman, that can be powerfully traumatic. "You know, feeling like you have no control over your own body can be an emotional experience. Painfully emotional."

I sensed this experience of feeling out of control may have been the underlying reason Sam began restricting; it was a maladaptive way to try to regain a sense of control over her training, and also her life. It was a bit premature, but I was reminded that I was working under a time constraint, so I decided to try a bold tact.

"What are your thoughts about what I've just shared?"

Sam teared up. She hung her head, then nodded. "Yes, I think you're right."

We scheduled an appointment for the following week and still a bit tearful, Sam got up to leave. At the door, she turned and with her head down she asked, "Dr. Simon, do you think I can overcome this? Do you think I'm going to be able to go to the Olympics?" *Wow, talk about a loaded door-knob comment. I've been wondering the same two things. What am I supposed to say? "The onus is on you, Sammy-girl?" Of course not, but I need to say something! Okay, just be honest with her, but, for goodness' sake, be gentle, Jacquie.*

"Sam, people recover from discomfort with their bodies and disordered eating, so yes, it's possible. We're going to work hard to help you overcome this." Her glassy eyes darted about as she leaned against the door. "Sam." My eyes met her gaze, and then I smiled. "I'm hopeful." She let out a long exhale. *Was she holding her breath?*

"Thank you, Dr. Simon. I'll do my best." *That's all anyone can expect, Sam.*

And she closed the door behind her.

Tony, my next patient, had spent the better part of the past year continuing his covert relationship with Raul and overtly expressing his fantasies of having sex with me. A number of multifaceted, complex predicaments were happening concurrently, and I struggled with containing my own thoughts and feelings. In the last nine months or so, it seemed like we made more back slips than forward momentum. And still no mention of homosexual feelings. One could almost see his self-repression in the way he carried himself. So erect, stiff, every movement seemingly choreographed.

We continued, as we had discussed, to explore Tony's fantasy surrounding a sexual liaison between him and me. It became difficult to hold my knowledge of his relationship with Raul in abeyance; but I had to. And he didn't give me much information about his fantasy relationship with me. So finally, I decided to take a therapeutic leap and introduce the notion that it might be difficult for Tony to be engaging in a relationship with a woman he knew he couldn't have sex with; a woman who ostensibly was "controlling" the boundaries.

Tony appeared to mull over what I said. Rarely did he pause like this to process our discussion. But just as he had been doing for more than a year now in these atypical moments, he slowly, absentmindedly traced his lower lip with his middle finger, slightly pulling the flesh down. In these moments, he seemed both innocent and erotic. In the half-minute of unfamiliar silence we shared, visual images of Raul and him having sex in the bathroom flashed in my thoughts. *Oy! Stay focused, Jacquie.* Tony finally looked up, and in his usual constricted manner said, "Maybe, but there is something else I want to focus on today." It was the first time in a long while that I heard sincerity in his voice. However, I still proceeded with caution — and distrust. Tony excelled at manipulation; I imagined he could feign being genuine without effort.

Okay, he definitely needed to derail my question. At least I put it out there. Is he going to tell me about Raul? With his uncanny ability to read people, I imagine he knows that Raul told me.

"I met a woman a several months ago. I really like her."

"Interesting." Tony gave me a curious look, so I elaborated. "Interesting that you're just bringing this up now."

"No. Not interesting." Tony's pitch grew testy. "I didn't know if I wanted her to stick around."

In my attempt to regain my footing, my control in this therapeutic relationship, I didn't say a word. I stared at Tony, waiting for him to fill the silence with what I was hoping would be a big reveal: That the woman was really a man.

"I think she could be the one." *Does she have a name?* "Maybe these sessions have been working after all." *Should I say something or continue the silent treatment?*

"Tell me more about her."

Rather than give me her name, age, or details about who she was, he instead described in vivid detail the mind-blowing orgasmic sex they were having. As I listened to his bedroom exploits, I wondered if this new person was actually Raul. *Did he really meet another woman? Is he carrying on two sex lives? I can't ask him. All I can do is listen to his narrative and follow the line of inquiry that matches what he is sharing. Ugh! This is harder than I thought it would be.*

Then it occurred to me. *The times he described spending with the woman are different than what Raul told me transpired between them. Different dates. Different locations. Is he changing everything to play mind games with me? Did he really meet another person? And is this person really a woman rather than a man other than Raul?*

If it is a woman and he truly believes that he likes her enough to have a long-term relationship with her, is it really because he's otherwise fulfilled in his relationship with Raul? This guy's history has more layers than a bad pop singer's vocal tracks. I really feel for the women he dates. I had to laugh. If Tony is representative of the single men on the market, no wonder I had a difficult time meeting the right guy. And I wondered what Tess's reaction would be if she knew that guys like Tony are what single women had to contend with. *"Jacqueline, fix the makeup situation. When you've got the wrong curb appeal, that's the kind of buyer you're going to attract."*

Later that evening, I found myself wondering about Sam and her struggles. I didn't have enough information yet to conceptualize the exact reasons for the evolution of her symptoms, but I was toying with some ideas. Athletes and dancers often develop body image issues that eventually lead to restriction in their food intake. I have quite a bit of personal and professional experience with this. But as with any human struggle, each person is different. So I wondered about Sam's unique and personal difficulties. Her emphasis on her legs grabbed my curiosity. Runners, especially track runners, need strong legs.

I remembered my mother telling me what my ballet teacher said to her after class one afternoon: I had a good chance of dancing professionally because I had strong legs. I suppose it was easy for me to transition from ballet to distance running because of my muscular legs. I love my legs now; they are long, lean, toned, and super-strong. However, this wasn't always the case.

My thoughts drifted back to high school. My legs were much more muscular than any of my friends. Whenever we went shopping together, I would feel uncomfortable when it came time to try on clothes. While they all slipped easily into jeans and pants, I always had difficulty. I was small framed, but my legs were so muscular and strong, finding jeans that fit comfortably was a chore. I'd become self-conscious as we approached the fitting rooms. Once in college, when I became active again, dancing, cheerleading (that's not a misprint — yes, an existentialist cheerleader), and short distance running, I discovered that my legs were my powerhouse; the hallmark of all my successes in sports. I began to see them as my most treasured attribute; and slowly I became more self-confident all around.

As my thoughts moved back to Sam, I speculated if her experience was anything like mine. *Now you're just being ridiculous, Jacquie. If that were the case, she wouldn't be struggling so much. She's an athlete in a sport that requires tremendous leg strength — and her legs objectively look like a track runner's legs. So what is it, then? There's something more to her struggle. Hmmm, what is it? For some reason, she never developed the ability to emotionally integrate her leg strength into her internal organization of being a competitive athlete.* This aroused my curiosity — and my anxiety. *How the hell am I going to help her in just over two months? Two months! I know I can help her overcome this, but, c'mon. Two months? Ugh, what a dilemma!*

Tony continued to talk about his new relationship with "the woman," who he finally named: Eva. Within three weeks, Tony was referring to her as his girlfriend. He described Eva as exotic, sexy, and wild; she was sexually open, and Tony and she were having threesomes on a regular basis.

"With women?" I had to inquire.

"Whatta you think?" I didn't answer him. The space between us seemed to shrink and grow simultaneously. "Yes, with other women. I ain't sharin' Eva with another dude. Besides, two pussies are better than one."

I hate that word! And that wasn't the answer I was hoping for. There was so much silence between my question and his answer. Sure, it sounded convincing, but he had enough time to formulate a response appropriate for someone who's not attracted to men. Is this part of his façade? Then again, he didn't say he wouldn't have sex with another guy. He said he wouldn't share Eva with another guy. So in addition to his homosexual repression, he has major jealousy issues.

I would soon learn that I struck the bull's-eye with that jealousy assessment.

The sessions basically consisted of Tony reporting their sexual escapades. I was still perplexed as to why Tony was still in therapy. He did his best to avoid any sort of growth, and when he did experience it, he would put forth great effort to derail his progress. I also struggled with questions surrounding Raul and him. We were seeing each other twice a week for quite some time when I finally decided to just straightforward ask him.

"I'm curious about something, Tony. You've been in treatment for nearly two years, and I'm still unclear as to what you *really* want to work on." Frustration spilled out of his heavy sigh.

"Did you forget or were you not paying attention, because, honestly, this is bullshit that you don't know this." He gritted his teeth, his full lips tightly closed.

"Humor me."

"I'm here for two reasons. I need to understand my patterns with women; I wanna get married soon. I'm 37 and still living with my parents. I mean, c'mon. You know this stuff."

"Yes. I do know this stuff."

"So why are you making me rehash it."

"To remind you of your goals." He looked at me, defensive. "Every time you make progress, you do something to derail it. And I don't believe you're being honest with me or yourself."

"How can you say that? What about Eva?"

"Describe your relationship with her."

"The sex is great. Awesome, even. She's hot. Sexy. Easy to be with. Doesn't piss me off too much." He put on a self-satisfied smile.

"Tony, you didn't describe a relationship. You described a person and sex." From his look, I could tell he didn't get it. *I'm gonna have to spell it out for him.* "Just because it's lasted a long time doesn't mean that your interaction with Eva is healthy and productive. What you described to me was a series of one-night stands with the same woman." His eyes lit up, which I could only assume meant that he understood the difference between the two. *Wait a sec. He said two reasons. I don't remember him mentioning any other reason.* "Tony, you said you came to therapy for two reasons. What's the other one?"

He suddenly shifted in his seat and he began clenching his jaw. *Did I miss something? Say something else wrong to agitate him?* He appeared extremely uncomfortable, which was abnormal for Tony. *Oh my gosh! He's going to share his homosexual proclivity. Finally! If so, then this would be major progress. Whatever he's about to tell me clearly is true, or he wouldn't be displaying such atypical discomfort.* I noticed, as he was about to speak, his uneasiness led to his becoming constricted again about sharing. But this time I understood it as defensive, not manipulative; the restriction of his affect suggested he was sharing something that caused him grave shame.

"Tony, just let it out. It's okay."

"Part of the reason I came to therapy…" He took a deep breath. His hands were shaking a little. "The second reason was that I beat up my last girlfriend. Well, the last long-term girlfriend."

His confession came as a total shocker to me, more because he wasn't admitting his gay relationship than because he beat a girl. I always sensed an underpinning of violence in him. *Poor girl. I wonder how bad the beating was.* And as if he could read my mind…

"It was pretty brutal. I'm ashamed that I did it. And sorry. But when I found out that she had cheated on me, I just… What? I wasn't man enough for her?!" He was beginning to replay the anger he felt. I wasn't really prepared for this news, so I hoped

I'd be able to control the situation. "I mean, I freaked out. I-I just lost control. It was like I left my head, and when I got back, my body had beat her so bad, I broke her finger. "

What do I say to him? I can't excuse his behavior, but I need to empathize and stay with him in the moment. But again, as though he were reading my mind...

"I never thought I'd ever do something like that. I mean, sure I got in fights when I was younger, but it was with other guys."

"What were those fights about?"

"The usual. You know, 'boys being boys' kinda thing. Nothing that ever got me in real trouble."

"But this incident. This did get you in real trouble."

His head hung low. "I know. I woulda done time, or at least community service or something if Clarissa didn't drop the charges."

"The police didn't advise her to get a restraining order against you?"

He caught me eyes. "No, they did. And she did. But I guess she felt like, I don't know. I was just glad she dropped the charges." He then averted his gaze. *Something else?* "Anyways, that's when Mommy made me come to therapy."

His "Mommy" sent him; quite interesting based on their dynamics. Then, the reality of what he had just exposed really hit me. *Holy shit!!! He has a history of domestic violence! What is my responsibility here? Is Raul in danger? I can't even tell Raul to be careful because it would break Tony's rights to confidentiality. Because Tony has not revealed any relationship with Raul, and hasn't reported any violent fantasies about "Eva," I can't even disclose any possible threats to Raul under the ethical "duty to warn." I'm between a rock and a hard place here. And what if there really is an Eva and she's not Raul? I need to think this through carefully.*

And why didn't he tell me about this sooner? It's been two years? I mean, THIS is the real reason he came to therapy. And he only confessed it now?

And here's what I learned. Tony admitted that he was uncomfortable sharing this incident with me. He was afraid to tell me earlier in our therapeutic relationship; he didn't want me to judge him for what he did. I wondered with him that if he was truly ashamed of what he did, if he was actually judging himself.

"She was going to leave me; I couldn't control myself." *Kind of a half-answer, but I'll take it for now.*

"What was it like to share this sensitive information with me?"

"Relieved. I always knew I was gonna tell you, but um, I just needed to find the right time." After this reveal, however, his affect became grossly restricted.

Another grueling session with Tony had come to an end. When he left, I felt spent. Fortunately, I had a 45-minute break. I set my alarm on my phone, and napped on my couch for a half-hour. I awoke refreshed, ready, and emotionally available for my next patient, but with the remnants of a dream on my mind. One that focused on Ralph, my young Juvey client from Miami. Ralph was standing at a kitchen table while Tony and Sam were tied with rope to the chairs.

That's all I remembered from the dream. Just a fleeting image. But it got me to thinking about the symbolism of the image. Tony and Sam tied to a chair, maybe bound by their families' expectations? It certainly would explain Tony's resistance to admitting his sexual relationship with Raul. His Catholic family may frown upon homosexuality. But what about Sam? Maybe there's more to her eating disorder story than just self-image. Could it be inflicted by her own parents? That's definitely something to keep in mind.

But then my thoughts drifted to Ralph. He didn't have a family to be tied to. Yes, he had his prostitute mothers, but there were no legal ties, no solid home life, no foundation to lean on while he built himself up. And he wanted that desperately.

We, all the therapists on the unit, tried to help him. In fact, I was in the midst of advocating with the court system to place Ralph in a rehabilitation program where he would have a chance to pursue a more constructive path. Things seemed promising. And that's when something terrible happened on the unit that endangered this one chance he had to get out of the system, off the streets, and away from Miami. The images still haunt me.

Having grown up in a multicultural neighborhood in the Northeast, I was fortunate to not be exposed to too much racism. In many ways, before Unit 6, I would say, I was a bit naïve. Although south Florida had so many transplanted Northeasterners, I quickly learned that it was still the South. And I became privy to numerous firsthand accounts of what it was like to grow up black during Southern segregation. I felt the constant subtle attacks from the mostly African-American correction officers. I could feel the hatred. I felt on guard, but also, in a twisted way, guilty.

So, when Jacob, a Caucasian Jewish boy, was brought on the unit, I frequently heard the word "cracker." It was spoken right in front of me. There was a complete disregard for the effect a discriminating slur such as this might have on me. I never said a word. My empathy toward black people having to be subjected to such horrific attacks and events at the hands of white-supremacy ignorance left me feeling so sad for them. However, what the guards did to Jacob was not only illegal, but also inhumane and in violation of basic human rights.

Jacob was brought on Unit 6 after robbing a local grocery store. He was evaluated and brought to Unit 6 because he was threatening suicide. As a result, he was locked up and was not allowed anything in his cell, not even a blanket. He couldn't have anything that he might use to hurt himself. While in his cell, he was only able to wear underwear. The guards would give him his uniform when he was at school, and then take it off once he was back in his cell. He cried and screamed all the time. All the time. It was terrible. Our psychiatrist placed him on a mood stabilizer, which I was never quite sure he actually needed, but I had so little experience, I didn't feel comfortable questioning her decision. Now looking back, I know she was wrong. Jacob wanted attention and if the only attention he got was negative, well for him, it was better than nothing.

What the guards did to him only made him worse…

Ralph spent much of our session time talking about Jacob. His affect in sessions was usually pretty flat and controlled, but I began to notice that when he was discussing Jacob, his feelings were often accessible in the room. And they shifted dramatically as time went on. Through the eyes of Ralph, I would become privy to many things; Things I wished I remained unaware of. Looking back, I remember thinking of the irony of the term "Correctional System." *Hmm, maybe not the most accurate choice of words. If the system "corrected" criminality, then why is the recidivism rate so high?*

Ralph spent quite a few of our sessions describing his feelings surrounding the abuse Jacob was being subjected to every day on the unit. Jacob was being beaten up daily by the correction officers. Because it was juvenile detention and not an adult penitentiary, the officers were not allowed weapons, so they used their fists instead. They made it seem as though they were trying to control Jacob's outbursts.

The first few weeks Jacob was on the unit, the beatings almost always followed one of Jacob's outbursts. He would yell and shake the bars of his cell. This often created a chain reaction as the other boys rebounded by yelling and rattling their own cell bars. It was overwhelming; at times, the ruckus developed into a deafening noise sometimes lasting for hours with no respite. The guards' resolve was to go into Jacob's cell and beat him until he was quiet. It was done in such a way that when I secretly called Child Protective Services, the woman on the line said, "Miss... corporal punishment is legal in Florida." She gave me a real attitude.

At first, Ralph was irritated with Jacob. "Ms. Jacquie, this homey is getting the whole unit in trouble. Last night, they didn't feed us dinner because homey was makin' too much noise." I listened, leaning slightly forward, and nodded. The next session, two days later, Ralph went off on a tirade. It was the first time I saw him so engaged with his anger and sadness.

"Home boy's mother went to court yesterday to try to get him out. She said he needed to go to a psychiatric hospital." Ralph was fuming.

I responded, taking a slight risk, "Ralph, it's obvious this is upsetting you. Can you tell me about what you are feeling?"

"Feeling?" He raised his voice at least five octaves. "Home boy has a mother. She came to help him. She loves him. I got no mother. My ole' girl is on crack and left me. I got no one. Candy can't come to help me. She says she loves me, but she's a prostitute and I ain't legally adopted. What's homey got to cry about?!"

Despite Ralph's anger, I could feel his underlying sadness and overwhelming feeling of loss. Being relatively inexperienced, I was at a loss of how to respond. So I just sat with him, and stated, "I know, Ralph. It's unfair."

His shoulders relaxed and I actually think I noticed his eyes start to well up with tears. The whites of his eyes were turning red. He looked down and said, "Ms. Jacquie, can I go back to my cell?" *He doesn't want me to see him cry. I want him to feel safe enough with me to let his guard down. But I also don't want to push him too far. If that happens, he will disengage. What to do?*

I tried a compromise. "I can see you're really upset, Ralph. I'm here and want to listen, but if you feel that you need to be alone, I respect that," I responded.

"Thanks, Ms. Jacquie," Ralph responded, avoiding eye contact and already half-way out the door.

When Sam came in the following week, I kept the dream where she was tied with ropes to a family kitchen chair in the forefront of my thoughts. As she sat, I immediately noticed her looking at my legs again. The temptation to open up the relational space and discuss her experience of my body in the room gnawed at me. I held off. Although I knew I would need to bring this up sooner than I normally would, I felt we needed to establish an alliance first. I also wanted to better understand her difficulties. I did mention coming twice a week. Under normal circumstances I wouldn't immediately start a first-time therapy patient at twice a week, but with Sam, the pressure of time intruded upon my usual way of working. She agreed to come twice a week; she appeared anxious about the ever-present Olympic countdown, too. Thus began our twice-weekly therapeutic journey together.

I asked how she felt about our first session; I often do this, as it helps me gauge how my new patients experience the therapy. She looked at me, then she fixed her gaze on the wall for a moment. I could see her mind working.

"It got me to think about things. From the questions you asked, I think I figured out how it started." *Excellent!!!* "When I joined track in high school, I took to it pretty easily. My coach called me a natural. He even told my parents that between my ability and persistence, I could easily land a college scholarship, probably even make it as a nationally competitive track runner."

"How old were you at the time?"

"Fifteen."

"And how did it make you feel when the coach said what he did to your parents?"

"It psyched me up, you know? Really pumped me. I mean, I knew I was fast, but his confidence in me drove me to go even faster."

I listened, attentive to her story. Her coach, having his hands on an incredibly talented athlete, really did push her. And as a result, Sam earned a full scholarship and eventually began competing nationally in the 800-meter race. But I sat anxious, waiting to hear something that would help me understand her struggles with her body-image. I have to admit, I also was a bit envious of Sam's accomplishments. I began jogging right after college and evolved into a competitive runner over the years. Like Sam, my coach told me that I had natural ability, particularly with my endurance, and that through our training I would soon be winning races. My coach was right. I love running. Again, a stomach knot. I thought of the question that haunted me: *if my life had taken a different road, would I have been competing in the Olympics as a distance runner?*

By the time my talents for the sport were recognized, I was already committed to my academic pursuits and I was afraid to risk giving that up. In addition, the running complemented my academics by providing a great outlet to release stress and feel free. If I started to pursue running as a career, I felt fearful that it would no longer be freeing. The pressure of living up to expectations imposed by others would change the whole experience.

I got it! It was a Dr. House moment.

"Sam, after you started competing and winning regularly and you learned that earning a scholarship was on the line, how did that make you feel?"

"It made me a little anxious, but, you know, like, the good anxious. The kind that makes you train harder and run faster. That drives you to push yourself to the limit. My team was counting on me, just like I counted on them to do their best. And I didn't want to let them down. Or the coach. He had a lot of faith in me, and that made me feel kind of proud, so I didn't want to let him down, either."

"What about your parents? They must have been proud, too."

"Yeah, totally. Plus, we didn't have much money, so the possibility of a scholarship meant a lot to them. So when that news came about, my mom pushed me, too." Sam looked at her legs, then pulled her track pants away from her thighs. She quickly blurted half under her breath, "Sometimes, she was on my case more than my coach." She kept her focus off me.

I think we're getting closer. "How so?" Her wheels were turning, but she wasn't answering. *Give her a moment, Jacquie.* But I also felt that she had a certain momentum going and I didn't want that energy to diffuse, so finally, "Sam?"

She popped out of her trance. "You know, the usual 'mom' stuff. She made sure I didn't miss my training, but also that I kept my grades up, slept enough, and um, you know. Stuff."

"Like what other stuff?"

She sighed. "Like, um, watching what I ate." She quickly added with a joking tone, "You know, 'cause I love packing down the junk food." *She's deflecting. I think we hit on it.* "So, like, just keeping me focused on earning that scholarship."

Hmm, I wonder if... "What's your favorite junk food?"

Sam hesitated. "Um, like, you know, everything."

"Right? I love a good dessert."

She eyed my body up and down. "Really? You're so fit, you look like you never cheat."

"I wouldn't call it cheating. I enjoy having dessert every now and then. But cherry Twizzlers, now those are my go-to treat. Nobody comes between me and my Twizzlers."

Sam smiled at that. "I love peanut butter M&Ms. I used to have a bag every day. My mom would get so mad if she saw a wrapper in the garbage. I got in the habit of hiding them in my backpack and throwing the wrappers in the garbage at school." Sam laughed. "That worked until she put a book in my backpack and found my stash." She laughed again, but this time there was a nervous tinge to it. "She started smelling my breath after that. I finally stopped eating them after a while. I felt like I was always looking over my shoulder, so it got to where I just didn't enjoy them anymore."

"How many bags a day were you eating? Did she feel it was spoiling your dinner?"

"I'd only have the one bag. Not those ginormous ones; just the single-serving bags you buy in a 7-11. But she said I was getting f—, um, big, so she put me on a diet."

"Gosh, Sam. You were a teenager. You had the metabolism of an adolescent combined with the energy output of an athlete. You must have been eating an awful lot to gain enough that your mother felt she needed to put you on a diet."

"I didn't think I was. And the coach even suggested that I eat a little more carbs."

"Did *you* feel you were getting big?"

"No. I mean, I guess, a little. I don't know. My mother did have a point." Sam adjusted her sitting position and again pulled her pants away from her massively strong legs. She then waited for me to talk.

And I waited for her. I sat. I smiled. Sam straightened her shirt. She gave in. "By the end of my second track season, my clothes didn't fit me anymore. I had to buy all new pants."

"Just pants? What's a shopping expedition without new tops?"

"My shirts fit fine. Actually, better than ever. Only the pants were too tight."

"Around your waist?"

"No. Now that I think about it, the pants were loose around my waist. It was mostly in the butt and upper thighs where they were tight."

I crossed my legs. I was wearing a skirt, so my muscles were out there for the world to see, but mostly for Sam to see. And I did notice her examining them. And then she ran her hands over her own leg muscles.

"Did your coach ever show any concern about your glutes and thighs getting bigger?"

"Never a mention."

"But your mother was highly concerned. Do you think she was afraid it would adversely affect your running and ability to win at meets?"

Sam ruminated. She scrunched her face, looking like a pug, like she often did when she was trying to recall a memory. "Sometimes. It would depend. If I was ready to head out to a meet, she'd ask how I expected to beat all the pretty, skinny girls with my backside and thick legs, her way of saying big fat ass and big fat legs. 'Cows don't beat gazelles in races, Samantha!' is what she'd often say."

Oh my gosh. I can't believe her mother called her a cow. I felt sorry for Sam. I know parents can be harsh with their children. They want them to be the best they can be, but sometimes they don't use the best methods of communication to urge their children to improve. Tell the kid she looks awful and she'll want to make herself look pretty. *Um, yeah, right. Like that's gonna work.* But that often backfires. The girl may withdraw. After repeatedly being berated about her looks, the girl eventually comes to believe that she's ugly and no one will ever see her as pretty. Or the girl goes the opposite way. Maybe she becomes promiscuous in an effort to prove to her mother — but more to herself — that she can be wanted by another. *I wonder what Sam's mother looks like.*

"Is your mother a petite woman?"

"Yes. A few inches shorter than me. Slender. Always watching her weight. Seriously. She's relentless about it."

Hmm. "Why? Does she gain weight too easily?"

Sam shrugged. "I've only ever seen her skinny."

I'm pretty sure Sam thinks her legs — her muscular, athletic legs—are fat, and I'm also pretty sure that her mother, who may have some body issues of her own, has mistakenly put that fat-leg idea into her head. Now what do I do? Sam needs help, stat!

Sam's unique situation required that I follow a more short-term psychodynamic approach. This involved staying focused on this one specific issue, and intervening more immediately. It went against my every trained instinct. Rushing her therapy could cause me to miss the mark, skim over the precise issue that could result in permanent change. On the other hand, missing this Olympic opportunity could set in motion other psychological repercussions that might only exacerbate her current issues. *I've got to work fast, but fastidiously. I need to engage her curiosity about what she just shared.*

"Sam, looking back on that, what would you say to your younger self?"

Her face was already scrunched again when I asked the question, so I knew her memory recall was in full swing, but I wasn't sure she actually heard my question. I gave it a moment more before... "Sam? What do you think? Sam?"

She unscrunched and met my eyes, alert.

"Sorry, Dr. Simon. I didn't hear the question. I was just remembering a story my mom once told me after hounding me for the umpteenth time about my M&Ms."

"Do you want to tell me about it?"

"We had just finished arguing about the M&Ms. Well, it wasn't as much an argument, as it was me standing quiet listening to her go on and on about getting fat. Then she told me about when she was a schoolgirl, probably about twelve or thirteen. She liked this boy in her class and he found out about it. After school on the way home, he ran up to her, knocked her books down and yelled, 'How could I like you? How could anyone ever like someone who looks like a fat elephant!' The boy ran away. My mom said she picked up her books and cried all the way home. When she got home and her mom asked why she was crying like a baby, she told her mother the story."

I think I know where this is going, and it's not going to be happy. "What did her mother say to her?"

"She said to my mother, 'So stop being a fat elephant.'"

And there it is. That's quite a pearl of wisdom.

My jaw dropped low enough that it might have mistakenly appeared to unhinge. "Not that it's any excuse to say something unkind like that, but was your mother overweight when she was young?"

"That's the thing. I've seen photos of her when she was eleven and twelve and she wasn't fat at all. She did have a little, round belly, but it really was little."

"What do you thi-?"

"Holy sh-, I mean wow, Doctor Simon." Sam's face lit up and she sat forward. "I get it!" And I knew then that Sam had her own Dr. House moment. "This is my mom's baggage. And she put it on me. But how is this going to help me get to the Olympics?"

"Now the really hard work starts." I explained to Sam that with this new cognitive insight, we needed to uncover the consequential emotions.

Wow, it worked.

I did actually start to think it was possible to help Sam stop restricting her food intake enough that she could gain clearance from her coach to compete. She was remarkably insightful; and appeared to use her persistence and commitment as an athlete in the therapy room.

Walking home that evening, proud of the progress with Sam, I thought about the dream. The suspicion about her mother's unwitting involvement in Sam's eating disorder must have already been in my subconscious, so it manifested itself in my dream. My unconscious mind made the connection between Tony and Ralph's problems and linked it to Sam.

But what about Tony? I was processing the selective information that Tony shared about his past, and the even more selective facts about his present-day situation, and tried to make heads or tails of it. *Maybe his stiffness and lack of spontaneity in our sessions is a defense against characterological shame. Is he projecting his own shame onto me, assuming I will harshly judge him? This would make sense, given his history of boundary betrayals.* I was reorganizing and hypothesizing as I was beginning to integrate what Tony shared as a different and less pathological way of understanding his being-in-the-world.

I usually can conceptualize a patient's dynamics early in the treatment. I rarely rely on diagnoses. I experience them as limiting and dehumanizing; essentially, the criteria diminish each patient's uniqueness. I found myself using the cognitive toolbox — my personal euphemism for diagnoses — in trying to understand Tony. Whenever I find myself depending on diagnostic criteria to conceptualize one of my patients, it usually means that I am having difficulty grasping what is happening with him/her internally.

I knew from Tony's way of relating to me that his primary problem was pervasive, and grossly affected his way of relating to others; in other words, I was certain that his primary problem was a personality disorder. Tony's depressed mood was secondary to his character disorder; this is relatively common. Rarely do patients report their presenting problem as a personality disorder; it is quite common for them to come to treatment reporting depression as their primary reason for entering treatment.

When Tony first came in, I couldn't help but think of him as a psychopath. After all my work and training with forensic patients, I knew what it felt like to sit with someone presenting with psychopathy. I tried hard not to limit myself from understanding him based purely on this preliminary diagnosis; with great effort, I believe I remained open. Two key factors were now causing me to re-evaluate this original diagnosis.

First was Tony's disclosure that when feeling he was going to be abandoned, he reacted impulsively. Impulsivity indicates that a person is responding emotionally in a situation; and furthermore, one cannot (as Tony reported) control one's emotional "outburst." This is antithetical to a psychopath's absence of real emotion, extraordinary lack of empathy, and the ability to control how he will respond to others and his environment. Second was my intuitive sense that Tony's relationships with women and now with Raul — whether he was Eva or not — suggested some identity confusion. Identity confusion is common developmentally in teenagers and young adults, but usually suggests something significantly conflict-ridden in someone who is in his thirties, most apparently his secret homosexual proclivities. But what else was under the surface that I didn't know about.

He has borderline personality disorder! There's a psychopathic quality to the way he relates, but I think these traits are actually Tony's psychological defenses against shame, rage, vulnerability, and pronounced identity confusion. It's been more than two-and-a half-years, how could I have missed this! Ugh! I berated myself for at least an hour, and then I decided that at least now I had a better understanding of his internal processes and was better equipped to treat him.

Or so I thought.

Chapter 10:
Cuts Like a Knife

The next seven weeks were a real challenge. I sensed that Tony and Raul's relationship — or non-relationship — was growing increasingly stressful; if not for Tony, then at least definitely for Raul. Tess was doing better since her cancer procedure, thankfully, but I was working under the gun with Sam on her eating disorder to get her back in fighting shape for the Olympic trials.

Sam was fully recovered from her stress fracture and able to get back on the track. I decided to use running as a metaphor for Sam's therapy treatment. This helped to facilitate a level of comfort for myself as I began to make therapy interventions that felt premature. The endurance required for long distance running was analogous to long-term psychotherapy, but Sam was a track runner. I began to use my own experiences on the track to inform my interventions; I went into it with a swiftness and velocity that was immediate and painful, but short and efficient.

Sam was really restricting her diet. She was open with me about what she was eating, or should I say "not eating." I thought back to my first injury, a stress fracture in the neck of my right femur. I was on crutches for three months and unable to run for four; it was an absolute nightmare. I was so uncomfortable and out-of-sorts. My orthopedic surgeon's solution was prescribing Xanax, which I resisted. Eventually, though, my resistance lost out. I hated taking it, but frankly, it was the only thing that helped. Once I was ready to start training again, the doctor referred me to Chantal. He believed I was overtraining and needed coaching to prevent another injury. Chantal would also help me slowly and safely return to the level of training and intensity that I was running prior to the injury.

Chantal's motto during our early rehab training was "food is fuel!" She gave me a strict diet, or more accurately, rigid "nondiet." She had me eating so much I felt as though I was spending my days running and eating. She taught me one of the most valuable lessons to ensure peak athletic performance; my food intake was fundamental for training and the more I ate, the harder I could train. A year later, I ran my first marathon. I crossed the finish line of this 26.2-mile road race with such power and strength, I could have kept going!

I was in therapy one morning in March talking about my own anxiety surrounding what I began to call "the countdown." Sam and I only had three more weeks before her doctors and coach would make the looming decision about the Olympics. I pleaded to my therapist, "Three weeks, that's only six therapy sessions. Gwen, she's still restricting."

Dr. Gwen reassured me that I was doing everything I possibly could to help Sam. She reminded me how difficult disordered eating and body image issues were to resolve. She also made me aware of the over-identification I was experiencing with Sam.

"She's young, Jacquie, I understand that you feel pressured, but my sense is that you are almost imagining yourself in Sam's position. Your identity is organized around being a runner, and it appears to be affecting your objectivity with Sam. We both know that you've been remarkably effective in treating other athletes." Gwen waited to catch my gaze. "Sam is different."

She was right; I felt my tension ease.

"She's always looking at my legs. I want to bring it into the room." I was half-asking Gwen's permission. "I feel if she could organize her identity around her athletic endeavors, she possibly could begin to integrate her legs and overall body as that of an Olympic athlete."

Gwen agreed! On the subway ride back to my office, I began to think about the phenomenological aspect of Sam's dilemma. Sam was disembodied from her legs, insofar as they became the container for all her negative affect.

Two thoughts occurred to me. First, Sam's mother's body image issues and her disengagement from her psychology led to her imposing her issues onto Sam. The not-so-subtle remarks about Sam's legs being "too thick" eventually led to Sam despising her own legs. And again, with harsh irony, it was her legs that got her to the athletic level she had attained. In addition, and equally as damaging to Sam's already fragile sense of self, her mother never expressed any pride toward Sam for her remarkable accomplishments. This disallowed Sam from integrating her identity and experiencing her body as that of a strong, powerful and successful athlete. *Wow, Gwen really helped with this one. Maybe it was the hours of session time I used to describe my own experiences as a runner. She understood me; and inadvertently helped me organize my thoughts about Sam.*

Raul had a session the next day. Or should have had a session the next day, but he cancelled that morning. He was still having grave difficulty in his relationship with Tony. And honestly, it was painful to hear. Raul was a vulnerable and sensitive young man, with such genuinely painful struggles. I wanted to protect him from the wrath of Tony; but other than creating curiosity, and hoping my line of inquiry would help him decide to separate on his own, there was nothing I could do. *My adherence to the ethics code is making me nuts.* I had even called the anonymous American Psychological Association hotline to see if there was some loophole that would afford me the right to share information with Raul to protect him. There was nothing I could do unless Tony reported a plan to physically harm Raul. *Ugh!*

Tony was playing the "push-pull" dynamic. He would spend days with Raul and then disappear for days; when he pulled back, he wouldn't return phone calls. And when Raul would eventually hear from him, Tony would provide no explanation as to where he was or why he pulled back. Raul was so afraid of losing Tony that he never pushed the issue. Nor would he question Tony about if he ever spoke of him in therapy. So, our sessions focused on the underlying reasons Raul "loved" Tony, and why he cognitively knew he should leave, but emotionally couldn't.

I thought we were finally getting somewhere until Raul cancelled one of our sessions. This was quite unlike him. The only other time he had cancelled was because of Tony — so now that things had become more stressful between them, I grew even more concerned when he didn't want to reschedule, and simply left a voicemail message stating that he would just see me for his regular session the following week.

I became worried. My only option would be to call 911 and have the police take him to the psychiatric E.R. at a local hospital. But that would be an overreaction to the situation. Raul wasn't suicidal; so again, it was not ethical to call 911 under these circumstances. My thoughts were spinning, grasping for some way to handle this. I even sought out a consultation with a senior analyst, but there was nothing I could do. The only barely helpful suggestion was to increase my own therapy sessions to assist in containing my own anxieties.

Then, when Raul came in on Monday, I noticed he had a black eye. *I knew it. This is why he cancelled. He didn't want me to know.* When I asked Raul about the injury, he explained, while crying, that Tony punched him, and that he was afraid if I knew I would call the police and have Tony arrested. His next question left me with a knot in my stomach.

"Does Tony talk about me in his sessions?" His voice cracked from the sadness he could no longer contain.

"Raul, I'm sorry for what happened between you and Tony. Unfortunately, as I've explained numerous times, ethics rules are quite clear on this matter. I cannot disclose that sort of confidentiality." *Why am I talking like this with Raul? So proper. Like a textbook?* It might have been because I felt powerless. I so wanted to tell Raul everything, but I couldn't. And I didn't know how else to handle this trying and sad situation. *Unless...* "Raul, let me instead respond to your question with another question." I chuckled a little to ease the despondency in the room. "I know, just like a therapist."

"That's okay." Raul laughed a little, too, as he wiped that last tears from his cheeks.

"Raul, what would it mean to you if Tony *were* talking about you in sessions?"

"Then I'd know he cares about me, and I matter to him."
His answer broke my heart.

After discussing the events, Raul promised me this was
the first time Tony displayed any violent behavior toward him.
After Tony's story about Clarissa, I was rightly concerned. Raul
explained that he and Tony had a threesome with another man.
Threesome? Tony talked about having threesomes with Eva.
When this man left, Tony — in a rage — accused Raul of being
more attracted to this other anonymous man. Raul recalled that he
was crying and saying, "No, no, Tony, I love you and I only did
the threesome to make you happy. You were the one who wanted
to do it!"

With Raul's history of feeling dismissed, unacceptable,
and unlovable because of his father's grossly distorted — and
equally pronounced — prejudice against homosexuality, he was
immensely vulnerable to self-blame and self-deprecation. I
imagined that this was what was happening with Tony, whose
intermittent availability left Raul feeling unlovable. In an
unconscious attempt to correct historical issues with his father,
Raul needed Tony to love him. The whole dynamic between
them allowed Raul to repeat unresolved issues with his father and
reinforced his own perception of himself as worthless.

I wasn't sure if I should share my thoughts with Raul; the
timing of an interpretation is especially important. I had an
opening, but Raul was so upset, I wasn't sure if my interpreting
the underlying dynamics would feel like I was minimizing what
he was feeling in the moment. Aside from this, I was also angry
with Tony. And I did not want that to be apparent to Raul. *Gosh,
this is so complicated. I have to try to help Raul in the same way
I'd work with a patient in an abusive relationship where I wasn't
privy to the additional information I had from working with Tony
as the perpetrator.*

I decided to start by asking him about the threesome and
his black eye. If an opening was available through this line of
inquiry, I would interpret the connection between Tony, Raul's
father and the underlying feelings of being unlovable then. Raul
disclosed that this was the third threesome Tony and he had. He
shared that he didn't particularly like having them, but didn't

want to upset or lose Tony, so he would get drunk and participate. We spent the next few sessions processing Raul's feelings; he felt used. It was sad to see him like this.

I was going on a ten-day vacation the following week. Although I did have a covering therapist, my concern that Tony's abuse might escalate while I was away occupied my thoughts. *Raul, just stay away from him! Please.* I couldn't say this to Raul, but it was prominent in my mind throughout every session following the black eye. During our second-to-last session before my vacation, we discussed his need for external validation of his worthiness, based on his father's assaults to the core of Raul's being. Raul, who was impressively psychologically-minded, agreed that he was indeed looking for Tony to "love" him. He didn't feel lovable; but if Tony loved him, then maybe he would feel worthy of "love."

We then discussed the notion that Raul needed internal reparation; he needed to internalize self-love. Without this he would never really feel that he was loved. Raul processed this information, but wasn't ready to get fully on board with it yet.

"I agree with and understand everything you're saying, Jacquie, but it's just an isolated idea right now. The emotional pull to repeat what my father made me feel for so many years. It's too strong. I'm not ready to break up with him."

Thank goodness. At least I've got you talking about it.

"What if something happens while you're away?"

"Raul, I'd like you to make an appointment to meet with Dr. Jane. She's my covering therapist while I'm away. So if anything happens, you know her and feel comfortable with her."

He agreed, which provided me with some relief, albeit short-lived.

That night while soaking in the relaxation of the after-run bath, I was thinking about life in general. I felt nostalgic; this feeling was occurring quite frequently since losing my Mother. Life seemed oddly different, and the emotional experience was inexplicable. I felt lost in an abyss, at times, but also strangely okay, too. I have always pondered life; I was and have always been precocious. I began asking existential questions as a child before I even knew what the word meant. I must have driven my parents nuts. How does a parent respond to questions that don't have answers?

I thought about all the different paths, options, decisions that are open to us as human beings, and how one small moment, decision or experience can affect the rest of one's life. It was then that I realized why I felt so pressured with Sam. Of course, there was a legitimate and rationale component to the way I felt, but I also began to acknowledge and integrate what Dr. Gwen had pointed out to me earlier that day. I was aligning with Sam, and feared that if she didn't make it into the 2008 Olympics, her entire athletic career would be finished. Although this was a possibility, it was also entirely possible that Sam would recover from her psychological struggles with a longer treatment and compete in the 2012 Summer Olympics. I felt relieved and actually more secure with my ability to help her.

The following week, Sam came in for her appointment, predictably looked at my legs, and sat down. I took the leap, and opened up the analytic space so we could process Sam's experience of my body in the room.

"Sam, I've noticed you looking at my legs." *Gently, Jacquie, gently.* "I'm interested to hear what your thoughts are?"

Silence.

I have often wondered if silence is a sound. In the context of the therapeutic relationship, I eventually decided that silence is indeed a sound. And a loud one at that. Sam's silence "sounded" contemplative; I could tell by her eyes and body language that she was thinking. I'd wait as long as it took for her to process and form what she wanted to express.

A few minutes ticked by without a word passing between us. Suddenly, "Break My Stride" burst from my cell phone. *Damn!*

"I'm sorry, Sam. I forgot to turn the ringer off." I glanced at the number and saw that it was Sam's coach. With Sam's consent, I had been communicating with her coach and doctor on a weekly basis. We were all working together to help Sam be physically and emotionally prepared for the Olympics. Her coach was anxious; he really was quite pessimistic. Sam's strength and athletic performance continued to decline as a result of her lack of fuel. Sam had also lost weight, and now was below her ideal training weight.

Training weight is athlete-specific and tends to differ depending on one's sport. As a sports psychologist, it is important to understand what the difference is between training weight and healthy weight. Many athletes struggle with training weight, myself included. This is one reason why I always go to doctors who treat athletes. Athletes' bodies are essentially quite different than non-athletes' bodies, and therefore it is important to have a doctor that understands the intricate nature of these differences.

I remember the franticness of the triage nurses when I was brought to the emergency room the day I oh-so-gracefully broke my ankle. Despite my high blood pressure resulting from the physical pain I was in, my heart rate was 42. A normal heart rate is about 62. They initially thought the low heart rate was a symptom of something systemic and unrelated to the ankle break. Then I informed them that I was a distance runner. "Oh, wow, you're in great shape," the nurse remarked. Essentially, for an athlete, a lower heart rate is normal. It basically means that one's heart is well-conditioned, and therefore doesn't have to work so hard.

Training weight is a similar phenomenon. Essentially, it is the weight that an athlete must maintain to be able to train rigorously and to ensure peak performance. Often, this weight is slightly lower or higher than what would be considered one's healthy weight; it is sport-specific and different for each athlete. The emphasis on one's weight, particularly for younger athletes, often leads to body image issues and disordered eating. When treating athletes, it is quite common for me to be privy to the painful struggles surrounding one's ideal body versus the training weight that one's coach suggests or sometimes insists upon.

For Sam, this was always a difficulty; Sam's training weight was higher than she was comfortable with. She described her endless comparisons between herself and the other runners she trained with. She knew rationally that she was sabotaging her potential career as a runner, but emotionally she couldn't stop restricting. And this created a major problem. If she did not get back to her training weight, she definitely would not be going to the 2008 Olympics and she knew it; and yet, her restricted eating persisted and her performance continued to decline.

I also began to wonder if Sam really wanted to compete at the Olympics. Was this really what she wanted or was it something she thought she was "supposed" to want? *It's interesting and notable that her symptoms appear to be getting worse the closer we get to the ominous decision day. If, in fact, she does have her doubts about wanting to go to the Olympics, how am I going to explain it to her coach?*

I heard the beep on my phone indicating a voicemail. I dreaded the message. Sam's coach had been putting a lot of pressure on me and it was beginning to piss me off. I felt like saying, "I am a psychologist, not a magician, and I believe you're more concerned with your Olympic team than you are with the emotional health of your athletes!" I was indulging myself with these fantasies when Sam finally looked at me and began to speak.

"Your leg muscles are so long and lean, that's how I want my legs to look," she softly shared. "Are you a dancer?" *Hmm, responding to personal questions is always a toughie. And the dual process that is occurring within our dyad is quite complicated. We are both sitting with envy. How do I navigate this one?* I wished I had a moment to think, but I didn't.

I relied on my clinical intuition in the moment and responded with a technique I often use in these situations. "Sam, I will answer your question, but first please help me understand how a direct answer will help you."

Silence again. I was wondering in this moment if I should disclose my own envy about Sam's accomplishments, and my feelings about what I experienced as a loss and a missed opportunity. It was tricky.

But finally, "When I look at your body, I feel the same way I feel with my teammates who have leaner muscles." *Yikes! I definitely could identify with this painful experience. And as uncomfortable as it was to sit with, I was glad it was out in the open.* I decided that a disclosure of my own envy would not be appropriate and would likely complicate things at this point; maybe another time, but not now.

Instead, I encouraged curiosity. "Sam, thank you for sharing this. It's courageous of you." *Now's the time, Jacquie. Make the connection between her strong legs and identifying as an athlete.* "Sam, I'm curious. As a track runner, isn't it an asset to have strong legs?"

Sam nodded, though looked a little apprehensive. *Tread cautiously, very cautiously.*

"Since it's your legs that have given you the ability to train and excel as an athlete, I'm wondering if we can work together to help you experience your legs as a fundamental strength as an athlete. They are your powerhouse. A symbol of all your dedication and perseverance as an athlete."

And she got it! The thing that makes her different is the thing that makes her special. She did understand what I was saying, and explained that she was fully aware that her legs needed to be strong. The real difficulty, as I began to understand it, was that she felt so much pressure from her family and her coach; she just could not take it anymore. Sam's food restriction and performance decline was her only way of maintaining control over her own body. Albeit, not the most constructive approach, but the only option she felt she had.

It also functioned as a form of communication; unfortunately it was a strong statement, but one that neither her parents nor her coach could hear.

"I feel like they own me, and to them all I am is a pair of legs that can run." Sam raised her voice. "And to my mother, a fat pair at that!" Honestly, it was the first time I remember seeing such involved, energetic emotion come from her. *Just "a pair of legs that can run." Ouch! She felt she wasn't being treated as a whole person. What an inordinately painful experience.* Having felt pressure from her coach myself, I completely understood what she was saying.

My role was to hear her. Listening and being heard are two different things. The former is simply allowing someone to talk, where as the latter involves really listening and suspending one's own judgment in order to identify and truly empathize with someone else's emotional experience. I heard Sam's message loud and clear. We only had five more sessions left before "judgment day," so I began to address issues that if I had had the luxury of time, I would have filed away for another day.

"Sam, I'm sensing that you feel your coach and family don't see you as a whole person."

"Yes, yes, Dr. Simon, this is exactly how I feel! No one else seems to get this." Even though her body had quickly relaxed, her eyes held a particular sadness.

The session was coming to an end, and there was something important I needed and wanted to ask Sam to think about between sessions. I was a bit tentative, as I had the intuitive sense that I was really opening up "a can of worms." However, I felt that if I didn't bring it up, I was not only doing Sam a disservice, but I would be colluding with her parents and coach. I had to intervene; it was in Sam's best interest. *In for a penny, in for a pound.*

"Sam, there's something I want you to think about before our next session."

I paused. Took a deep breath. She leaned forward in her chair, eager with the headway we had made. *I hope she's strong-willed enough to come to her own conclusion.*

"Do you want to compete in the Olympics this year? Is this something you want, or is it something that you feel you should want?"

I observed her pupils dilate immediately after I finished my question. She looked at me long and hard, then rose to her feet.

"I promise to really think long and hard about it, Doctor Simon." Then she left the session with a sprinter's kick.

I had fifteen minutes before my session with Tony, and I knew I should really return Sam's coach's call. I knew what his voicemail was going to say; his messages were always the same. He wanted to know how Sam was doing in therapy, and if I thought she was making progress. In the beginning, the weekly contact with him felt reassuring; I wasn't in this alone. But as time went on, he began to irritate me. This particular day, following what was revealed through my session with Sam, while listening to his predictable message, I was annoyed. I decided he could wait. I wanted to give myself a chance to think about how much I should share with him. Truthfully, I also wanted the precious fifteen minutes to decompress, eat my lunch, and emotionally prepare for my next patient. *He can wait; I'll call him later while walking home.*

In Tony's next session, he continued to discuss his growing feelings for Eva. *Eva is really Raul. She has to be. How would he have time to be so involved with both of them? Well, Raul did describe his intermittent "disappearing acts." Trust your intuition, Jacquie.* The dilemma here was that if Raul wasn't my patient, too, I would never think that Tony was engaging in a homosexual relationship. I needed to try to listen to Tony's narrative about Eva openly, without focusing so much energy on if she was, in fact, Raul.

I wonder. Does the real identity of Eva matter for Tony's treatment? Yes, Jacquie. It most definitely does! Tony hasn't been disclosing an integral piece of information about himself. And I can't say anything, nor question anything relating to Raul's disclosures. Even if Raul asked me to break our confidentiality and confront Tony, I couldn't. This is becoming way too confusing. Do I need to refer one of them to another therapist? And if I did decide to do this, how would I present it? I'll think about it over my vacation and make a decision based on what is best for both of them. Ironically, I would never have to make the decision that plagued me so.

Later that day, I received a voicemail from Sam; she had never before called between sessions. I grew a little anxious as I listened to her message. *Maybe I pushed her and/or confronted her with material she wasn't ready for. What choice did I have; we only have five sessions left before "judgment day."* Sam was calling to cancel our Thursday session; she was taking some graduate courses and had forgotten she had a test on Thursday. She said that I need not call her back; she would see me next Tuesday. She never cancelled — and she was fully aware of the "countdown."

I always wonder if there is some sort of communication when a patient cancels a session. Unlike some shrinks, I am not so rigid that I can't accept that sometimes when a patient cancels, the reasons are true. In Sam's case, I pretty much was convinced that she needed space. What I had introduced at the end of the session was too much for her to bear. I wondered if I had made a mistake.

What else was I supposed to do? It was important to acknowledge her as a whole person, and one who was fully capable and had the right to make her own decision. I was trying to soothe myself and rationalize a possibly huge clinical error. I really wanted to call her back, but I knew it wasn't the right thing given the circumstances; she needed the space and regardless of the "countdown," she had the right to take care of her own needs. I decided not to reveal the cancellation to her coach. Not yet, at least. I didn't think he'd understand the psychology behind her non-verbal communication; he would insist she came in, and I knew from my expertise, that this wasn't right for Sam. She could not advocate for herself to her coach or her family. I needed to respect her as a person in charge of her own life and her decisions.

In that moment, I associated to Robin Williams' character as a psychologist trying to help Matt Damon's character in the movie *Good Will Hunting*. I had watched the movie several times, and I was really impressed with Sean's (Robin Williams) extraordinary talent as a clinician. He was able, through his own disclosure, to form an alliance and ultimately free Will (Matt Damon) from his past.

What stood out for me, as I was thinking of Sam, was Will's superior talent in mathematics. Like Sam, he was endowed and gifted. As a result, a professor of mathematics at MIT wanted and expected Will to take a prestigious position where his skills likely would advance the entire field. This professor didn't care what Will wanted and he pushed him. It was Sean who stood up for Will and forced his former college friend to listen to what Will wanted.

Ultimately, the relationship between the dyad changes both of them, affording each of them the opportunity to follow their true desires. The metaphorical "hurdles" were gone and they each individually "swiftly" and "gracefully" pursue what they really want. I always cry during the part of the movie when Will finally has an emotional breakthrough, and then the moment when Will, once tough and defensive, becomes vulnerable and cries as Sean holds him. It is profoundly moving.

My association to this movie encouraged me and made me think that what I had suggested to Sam was actually the truth. She started out loving the track races, but once she was discovered as an exceptional athlete, the pressure from others left her fragmented and disengaged from her own desires. She was pursuing a path that she wasn't certain she wanted. The Olympic goal eventually was no longer her goal, but rather was the goal of her parents and coach.

This eventually resulted in her alienation from her true self, and she was stricken with the "should." Although I imagined the body image issues were not related to the aforementioned formulation of Sam's psychology, her food restriction was. My role was to help Sam find her way back, and begin to integrate her own identity apart from the imposition of others. My sense was that she would ultimately decide to compete once she felt it was her own decision.

So using my formulation, I tried desperately to explain this to her coach, but as I suspected, he was having a hard time grasping the complexity of the situation. I felt like Robin Williams' character in *Good Will Hunting* as I relentlessly tried for a half-hour — exhausted at 8 p.m. after a long day — to really get him to grasp the essence of what I was saying. It was hopeless. He just didn't get it. So I tried a different approach.

"Jack, you need to back off!" This uncharacteristic, harsh conviction temporarily shut him up. "Now please listen to me. You and Sam's doctor have sent Sam to me to help her, and you need to listen to me. Back off me and… back. Off. Sam!"

He got it. We hung up. I was tired, hungry and frustrated. *He is tough; poor Sam.*

I knew I could help Sam; she was insightful, reflective, curious, and seemed to really take in what we were exploring. The real dilemma was the limited time we had. A truly effective treatment to relieve Sam from her internal struggles, usually takes quite a bit of time. On the plus side, because of Sam's cancellation, my fiancé and I would be able to leave earlier for our weekend trip, beating some of the rush-hour traffic out of the city. The downside? Samantha and I had just two weeks; that is only four sessions now that she canceled her next one! And the "countdown" was on.

As I thought about this, it reminded me of the anxiety I always feel just moments before the buzzer goes off, indicating the start of a race; And with Sam, the "race" was really on. There was no holding back, as we experienced marathoners learn. Go easy in the beginning, and take time to increase one's pace. The race really starts at the 20-mile mark. With Sam, though, her therapy really was an 800-meter race; there is no time for an easier pace to start. A runner needs to put everything out there as soon as the buzzer goes off. And basically we were at the 600-meter mark. With only 200 meters to go, we would need to push this therapy to its "physical" limits.

As I was packing for my vacation, I pondered what Tony expressed in our last session. He was feeling closer to Eva. Usually, when a patient is presenting with conflicts surrounding the ability to engage fully in an intimate relationship, this would be great progress. This instance was different. Extrapolating from what Tony shared about his violent assault toward his ex-girlfriend, his growing feeling for Eva, and the assault toward Raul left me uncomfortable. The closer he became to Eva, who, by this time, I was convinced was Raul, the greater the likelihood of another attack; it felt imminent. The risk of Tony losing control became heightened the more intimate and closer he became with his partner. I also was concerned that my vacation was unconsciously perceived as abandonment for Tony; this again, placed Raul in a high-risk situation.

Once I was in Vermont, I felt much more relaxed. The mountain air and the nostalgia of annual ski trips with my family when I was a child afforded me peace of mind. This was also my first big trip with my husband as a married couple, so it was important that I be present. I consciously put my concerns and repeated reviews of their case aside. The second day of our trip, we returned from an invigorating day of skiing. I felt so relaxed and was looking forward to some hot chocolate and a warm bath, when I noticed that I had a voicemail message.

I noticed on my caller ID that it was Tony. Tony rarely made any contact with me outside of the session hour; my heart began racing. *How odd.* My husband tried to convince me not to listen to the message, reminding me that I had a covering psychologist to take care of any patient-related issues while I was away. He was right, but I did feel a sense of obligation and responsibility to listen; so I did. Tony's message: "Thank you for all of your help, Jacquie, but I need to go now. I just wanted to say goodbye."

I had an immediate visceral reaction. My hands started shaking. *He's calling to say "goodbye." He's threatening suicide? No, Tony has no history of suicide attempts. At least none that he reported.* I tried to talk myself out of the idea that he was going to hurt himself, but I knew intuitively that that's what he was implying with his message. *Jacquie, you know this is serious. You need to do something. Now!* I looked again at my phone. The call had come in only about 30 minutes earlier.

Should I call Dr. Jane? No, that doesn't feel right. How about his mother? She is his emergency contact. No, call Tony first. He could just be trying to provoke me and intrude upon my vacation. Punishment for "abandoning" him?" Then calling him colludes with what he wants to enact with me. Jacquie, forget the dynamics here; you can process this later. Even if he's just trying to be sadistic, the message implies a suicide threat and you must respond regardless. My husband noticed the look of horror on my face and asked what happened.

"It's a patient emergency. Sorry, hon, I'll be right back." I threw my hat, gloves, and ski jacket on, took my phone and patient address book. I was already dialing Tony as I walked out the door.

There was no answer on either of Tony's phone lines. *Should I call his mother or Dr. Jane? Tony probably wouldn't have contacted Dr. Jane. I'll call his mother.* I had barely completed this thought when my phone started ringing. It was a blocked number. Usually I don't pick up blocked numbers; I wait to see if the caller leaves a voicemail. Based on the current circumstances I was facing, I answered the call. I had knots in my stomach; I really sensed somatically and intuitively that something "bad" had happened.

I was right.

It was the police. *Not good.* They asked if I was Dr. Jacqueline Simon and if I was the psychologist currently treating Tony. I responded, breathless, "Yes," to both questions. I really felt weak. They were so formal and spoke officially as they informed me of the events over the last 45 minutes. All of my forensic research and clinical experience did not prepare me for what I was about to hear. *Are we, as clinicians, no matter how experienced, ever really prepared for some of the experiences we are exposed to when working clinically? I think not.*

The police informed me that Tony was just arrested and was being escorted to one of the psychiatric forensic wards in Brooklyn. Basically, Tony attempted to kill Raul and then kill himself. "What happened?!" I almost didn't believe them. A neighbor had called the police when she heard screaming outside. She saw Tony take a knife and jam it directly into his own stomach. Raul was already lying on the sidewalk. Tony had stabbed him in the stomach first.

I learned that Raul was alive and was rushed to the hospital by the EMTs that arrived at the scene. They didn't have any information concerning the severity of Raul's condition and suggested that I call the hospital. Tony's wound was not deep; the EMT that was with the police said his wound was superficial. They suggested calling the hospital's forensic ward in about an hour. They also asked if I could meet them at the hospital. I explained that I was out of the area and on vacation. They agreed to give my phone number to the attending doctors or residents on staff, and have them call me as soon as possible. They apologized and we hung up.

During the call, I could hear Tony ranting and screaming in the background. "Get your fucking hands off me, you pigs! Now! Don't fucking touch me!" I later learned that although it was in the middle of the winter, Tony was outside wearing only his boxer shorts.

I sat outside for a few minutes to collect my thoughts before returning to the hotel room. *This is literally "insane." I think Tony purposefully did this when I was on vacation.* I was going back and forth in my mind, driving myself crazy, wondering if I should go back to New York. We still had three more days of skiing in Vermont. I called Dr. Jane; she didn't know anything until I called her. When I hung up with her, I felt a bit calmer, and was able to recognize that it was important for me to stay *and enjoy* my vacation. While still in Vermont, I spoke with the treating clinicians and physicians treating both Tony and Raul.

I spoke with Raul's doctor first, as I was extremely concerned about the severity of his injuries. I was relieved to find out that although the knife did almost puncture his internal organs, he didn't need surgery, and medically would have a complete recovery. Tony was being treated in the psychiatric ward, but medically would also recuperate. *Well that gives me some relief, but what am I supposed to do now in regards to their treatment with me? Jacquie! Enjoy your vacation! This dilemma can be dealt with on Monday.*

Despite my propensity to ruminate, I did manage to compartmentalize the events and enjoy my vacation. Thoughts of both Tony and Raul did fleetingly come into my mind, of course, but I was able to contain them. Toward the end of my trip, I received a phone call from Raul. He was distraught, emotionally broken, and crying uncontrollably. I managed to calm him down a bit. He was being released from the hospital, and we made an appointment for Tuesday afternoon.

Sam came in on Tuesday and immediately apologized for missing Thursday's session. I decided simply to ask her if everything was okay. A delicate compromise; I didn't interpret or confront her, I simply asked. She revealed that she was quite anxious about what was brought up at the end of her last session. *Wow, she's so open, reflective and self-aware.* I felt hopeful. I acknowledged and validated that indeed it was a difficult question. I then asked her for her thoughts. Her eyes became heavy and moist. "I gave it a lot of thought and you're right, Doctor. Simon." She started to cry. "What should I do?"

If we were at the 10-mile marker of a marathon or even the five-mile marker of a half-marathon, there would be many options on how best to explore this, but we didn't have the time or space for that. So I went in fast, much faster than I was even comfortable with. But it was her only chance of winning. We were sprinting to the finish line at this point. So I pulled the psychologist's famous modus operandi of turning the question back on her.

"No one, not I or your mother or your coach, can make this decision for you. What do you want, Sam?" I leaned forward. "Do you know what you really want?"

Silence. I realized that there was no way to guide Sam through a self-exploratory journey of accessing her own desires, increasing her awareness surrounding her own goals versus those enforced by others, and/or helping her make a more integrated decision. All I could do at this point was confront the situation vigorously and help her feel comfortable and free to share what she wanted with me.

It was nearly five minutes when Sam finally looked up. At this point, I didn't know what to expect her to answer. She appeared emotionally exhausted. She opened her mouth and my stomach suddenly sunk. *Oh, no!*

"I want to go to the Olympics!"

Wait. What? I immediately noticed a change in her intonation. I heard her "strength" and "power" for the first time. *Here is the track runner I have been looking for!*

"I just want my parents and Jack to leave me alone," she stated, tears in her eyes. "I can do this, but the pressure from them is just too much!" I really felt for her. I know her coach was a hard-ass, but you have to be to be a good coach. Her mother, though, when she delivered those snide digs about being fat, they were not helpful to Sam. Those comments cut deep, like a knife — sharp and painful.

"I know, Sam, I know." She looked up and smiled through her tears. "Sam, you're a strong young woman, and whatever you decide to do or whatever path you choose, it's your life and your choice!" I took her hand. It's not something I make a habit of doing with patients, but I felt she needed it. "I support whatever decision you make!"

She smiled.

After this session, Sam began to eat more. Consequently, and as we had all hoped, her strength and speed returned quickly.

When I met with Raul later that afternoon, I could barely contain my curiosity about what had transpired between him and Tony that led to such a pronounced escalation of violence. On Tuesday morning, Raul explained that he and Tony were having sex in Tony's room. In the year they had been dating, this was the first time Tony ever brought Raul to his home.

Tony's mother, true to her character, knocked on the door and then quickly opened it before receiving permission from her son. She witnessed both Tony and Raul completely naked, Raul's hands were tied up, and Tony was on top of him. Tony's mother stood there with the door open staring for a moment, and then started screaming that they were both "dirty, filthy men." She did not close the door; she afforded them no chance of any privacy, but rather insisted that Raul get dressed and yelled, "Get the hell out of this house! This is your fault! My son is not gay. Get out! Get out now!"

"And then," Raul continued, "Tony's mother stepped aside. Some girl named Eva was standing behind her. That's why Tony's mom came to the door. To let his girlfriend into his bedroom! After all Tony's paranoia about the other guys in the threesomes, *he* was cheating on *me*. With a *woman*! Did you know?"

I gave Raul my you-know-better-than-to-ask-me-that-question look.

Raul described feeling violated, horrified, and frightened. Tony quickly untied Raul's hands while his mother and Eva yelled at him. Eva threw something at Tony, then ran out.

"That's when Tony was shouting at me, repeating, 'You ruined everything.' So I got up, grabbed my clothes, and bolted out of the house while tripping into my underwear."

Raul heard Tony's mother screaming after him, but he was so traumatized, he had no recollection what she was saying. His next memory was Tony running out of his house in only his boxer shorts. And he still had a full erection. *He was aroused by his mother's intrusion. Yuck!* I had chills.

"I thought Tony was coming to apologize. For his mother. For the girlfriend. The lying. Everything." Raul swallowed hard, his eyes reddening. "Instead, he snapped open a switchblade he had palmed from view and stabbed me. The next thing I remember is being in the ambulance." He began sobbing. "I don't know. I must have blacked out. But when I came to, my stomach was stinging bad and there was blood everywhere."

I felt sick to my stomach. *There was nothing you could have done, Jacquie.* The whole story was so unbelievably disconcerting and upsetting. I think the part that made me the most sick was the visual of Tony's mother in the doorway watching them and violating their privacy, especially Raul's.

The images of the scene were running through my mind throughout the session and for days to follow. I now knew for certain that Raul was not Eva, not that this piece of information was even important at this point. Raul disclosed that he wanted to see Tony, but they would not let him. *Okay. This is not good.* Raul decided not to press charges against Tony. We spent some time exploring this. Despite everything that happened, he still was "in love" with Tony and he did not want to do anything to hurt him. *This is partly how these people become repeat abusers. Their charm over their victims is so strong, the victims don't want to press charges. And hope they will still be loved by the abusers.* We were at the end of the session, and I asked Raul to really give some thought to the idea that he appeared to show more concern with protecting Tony than taking precautions to protect himself from harm. He seemed to take this in. His response, half out the door, was, "I will."

Once Tony was released from the hospital, he was placed in an inpatient forensic psychiatric hospital. I never saw him again. My hypothesis surrounding his violent act toward Raul was that Tony was struggling with his own homosexuality, but could not take ownership of those feelings. His behavior suggested two things to me. First, having sex with Raul behind a door with no lock in his intrusive mother's home was his unconscious way of attempting to show her that he was actually gay. Secondly, his attempt to hurt or possibly kill Raul was an externalization of his desire to "kill" his own homosexual proclivities. He was truly conflicted. And despite the terrible things he had done to Raul — and his ex-girlfriend Clarissa — I felt sad for Tony.

Raul spent months processing what happened; he was more symptomatic during these months then he was when we first started treatment. Slowly through processing the events, he started to get better. The incident forced him to reveal his homosexuality to his family. At first, his father threatened to disown him as his son. Through his mother's more sympathetic position, she finally convinced Raul's father to go to family therapy. I made a referral, and the three seemed to be getting to a place where Raul was accepted for who he was — a fabulous, warm, intelligent gay man.

Tony and he were still engaging by phone for the first few months following the incident. After many sessions of exploring the self-destructive nature of maintaining contact, Raul was finally able to stop taking his calls. About eight months following the incident, and through his diligent and hard work in his individual and family therapy, Raul finally met a man that he really liked and felt safe with. At the time of his termination, about a year later, he was living with his partner, maintaining a close relationship with his family, and was comfortable with his sexual orientation.

I would miss him. We shared a long and complex journey, but, unlike Tony, who was trapped in a conflicted cycle of denial, Raul did meet all his treatment goals. I was so proud of him.

My last session with Sam was quite compelling. She fervently thanked me over and over. I smiled. She did inform me that as a result of her inability to train efficiently leading into the Olympics, she would be going as an alternate. She expressed disappointment, but also shared that it would be a good experience. "Regardless, I know I'll be competing in 2012, so this is just practice." I sensed that some of what she shared was a rationalization to cover her disappointment, but I simply validated her. It wasn't the appropriate setting to start exploring her defenses. I did share that she could call me at anytime if she wished to return for treatment. She nodded in acknowledgement.

As she was leaving, she turned around and said, "Jacquie, I know you're a runner, too. My coach told me last week. Good luck with your training."

I nodded in recognition. Then I stopped her before she closed the door behind her. "Sam, did knowing I was also a runner help you in anyway?" I was curious, but also thought this was a good opportunity for my own growth as a clinician.

"Yes. It helped me realize that you knew what the pressures of competing were like, and it explained why your legs are long and lean." She smiled again and I smiled back. She came back toward me as I was sitting in my therapist's chair. She leaned down and we hugged. "Thank you," her voice broke a little, "for getting me back in the race." Then she turned and sprinted out.

That night I was thinking about Sam. She was an amazing young woman. She was able to translate her skills as an athlete into her therapy. I began to think of the therapeutic process in general, and what strengths a person needed in order to have a positive and constructive response to therapy. Both Sam and Raul easily engaged and were able to form a therapeutic relationship. They trusted me and the therapeutic process; were reflective — thought about the therapy outside of sessions — and showed the capacity for insight. Additionally, both really showed an investment and desire to feel better; and they each respectively rose to the challenge.

Tony was on the opposite extreme. I knew from the start of Tony's treatment that he would be a challenge to engage in a trusting, genuine therapeutic encounter. When I hear narratives from patients involving their interpersonal relationships, it gives me an excellent sense of how easily they will be able to form a therapeutic alliance.

It was abundantly clear from Tony's relationship with his mother and woman in general, that the first few years of his treatment would involve trying to help him engage — genuinely, openly, and with self-reflective curiosity — in a therapeutic dyad where he would feel safe enough to make himself vulnerable. Sadly, Tony and I never got to this point. I hated thinking about it, as I always focus on patient's strengths, but I wondered if he ever could; or if he even really wanted to — begging the question: Are some patients so resistant that they can't be treated?

Chapter 11:
"I'm Sorta Pregnant…"

Over the next two years of our twice-weekly treatment, I worked hard with Tess to increase her self-worth, based on her many pronounced internal attributes. She finally seemed more confident. Her obsession with aging had lessened, and it seemed that she had an increased sense of comfort with her stage in life. She was writing a lot, which always helped her feel vibrant and alive.

She also appeared to really experience me, her therapist, as a whole person, and began to develop a real sense of admiration toward me. I particularly noticed that she no longer was trying to change who I was, but rather relished in my ability to maintain a strong sense of self. This was major progress for Tess. There was always the transient "you need to wear blush" comment, but aside from that she was more complimentary of my appearance than ever before.

I did wonder, *why blush? Why is it that this is the most important type of makeup she thought would enhance my appearance? The irony is that even when I do put on a bit more makeup, I never wear blush. In fact, I cannot even remember ever owning blush. Should I be curious with her about this? It must have some metaphorical significance.*

"Tess, why do you always say I need blush?"

"Well, you always look pale, blush would give you nice rosy cheeks. You would look more alive." My association to her response was that she was projecting her own need to feel more "alive" onto me. I thought about this. *I can be on the lighter side, especially in the winter, but I wouldn't say pale. My running always leaves my skin with a healthy glow and a little color from the sun. Yes, I'm sure she feels deadened inside.*

When I thought about the beginning stages of our therapy seven-and-a-half years ago, I truly was amazed at Tess's progress. It felt good to see her doing so well. But as it often is in life, something unexpected happened; Tess spiraled down. Tess's cousin Marc had not been well over the last year, and things were only getting worse as he struggled with heart problems. As the weeks went by, Tess grew increasingly worried about him — and increasingly depressed. He wasn't taking care of himself or his condition. Marc continued to smoke and drink, didn't take his medication, nor did he exercise.

In the two months prior to this particular session, Tess also learned he hadn't been eating much, either. She was concerned about Marc, but she also felt virtually helpless. Marc was always relatively irritable and he never listened to anyone. While Tess pleaded with him to see a doctor; Marc petulantly brushed her off. And because he lived in California... "There's nothing else I can do." Tess would throw her arms in the air, frustrated.

When Tess came in for her session one day and flopped down in the patient chair, I knew things took a turn. There was an all-encompassing ominous feeling in the room.

"Marc's dead."

My jaw may have dropped. The way she blurted it out was nearly as shocking as the news. As I probed Tess for more information, it became evident that Tess only sensed he was gone, but had not received an actual phone call. She felt it. The session was incredibly difficult, insofar as Tess didn't have any concrete evidence that Marc was actually dead, yet she was already mourning his loss. I sat with Tess as we processed his demise, and her resulting fear and loneliness. Although she hadn't seen Marc in many years, they spoke on the phone nearly every day.

"Of my surviving relatives, I feel closest with him. And now I know he's gone," she blurted out as she walked out of our session, head down and shoulders' slouched.

Later that day, I received a phone call from Tess. When she arrived home after our session, there was a message on her answering machine from Marc's wife, Stacy, calling with sad news. Stacy's message confirmed Tess's fear. Marc had indeed died late the night before. When Tess came in two days later, she seemed broken, detached, and removed from her affect surrounding her loss. In my attempt to help her access her feelings, I noticed and was curious with her about the pronounced incongruence between the content of what she was sharing and her affected state. Tess's eyes were vacant as she shared that she did feel sad, but that her primary affective experience was numbness. Her clinical presentation, as well as her description of feeling "numb," indicated that Tess was in shock and traumatized.

Tess was having great difficulty accepting Marc's death. Stacy and Marc's brother, James, held a ceremony in New York in remembrance of Marc. Tess hadn't seen either of them in a long time. "It was good to see them," she shared at her session following the ceremony. It was difficult for Tess to accept Marc's death, particularly because he lived in California; and other than his phone calls, he wasn't part of Tess's daily life. Stacy continued to pay Tess's rent, as Marc had requested in his will. I could sense Tess's struggle with her deep sense of loss, but after the first two weeks of talking about it in therapy, she would briefly mention Marc and then quickly change the subject. She was so distraught; she just could not process the loss. I could feel the heaviness of the burden she was carrying in the room. The sessions became so draining.

Unfortunately, one cannot get away with avoiding such a deeply traumatic and painful experience. As a result of Tess's difficultly expressing her feelings surrounding her significant loss, she slowly began to have numerous somatic complaints. She complained of back pain, stomach pain and headaches. The most distressing somatic expression was her considerable weight loss. I attempted to gently broach the subject with her; I even explained that these symptoms were most likely a result of her grief. She just could not elaborate on what she was feeling. I really began to worry when Tess lost so much weight that she became too weak to walk to session; the only way she could make it to session was if Helena escorted her. She could barely get up from her chair after session, and even while talking she was breathless.

After a month of really pushing Tess to confront her feelings surrounding Marc's death, and as her physical health declined, I finally decided that in order to continue treating Tess, I needed her to see her medical doctor. I felt strongly that her physical decline was a direct result of her loss, but with her medical history, I felt it would be irresponsible on my part not to consider that her symptoms could represent a medical illness. She agreed to go — I didn't give her much choice.

On my walk home, I reflected on Tess and her frequent resistance to change and how it manifested in her treatment. At nearly every turn, she seemed to take the path of least resistance, even if it meant not improving her status. It's human nature, so I shouldn't be surprised. Tony did the same thing. With every easy choice, he dug himself deeper into his hole of homosexual denial.

Then I experienced the opposite with patients like Sam, whose desire to achieve something pushed her to make the difficult changes she needed to succeed. Ralph was another of these patients. He came from awful surroundings, and though he did awful things to survive, his desire for a family, for a better life, pushed him to improve himself, to make real changes.

He was on the brink of succeeding, of getting out of Miami and off the streets that put him in juvenile detention, when something happened that nearly derailed his one chance for happiness.

I arrived on the unit one morning and was immediately overcome by a stench like I had never smelled before. *What the-?* My olfactory system was in overdrive. I was greatly curious, but also mildly concerned that I might faint.

There were a few guards inside of Jacob's cell, the bars were open and I saw Dr. Jerry standing outside the cell — I assume looking upon the white Jewish boy who did not belong in this detention center. I buzzed myself into our locked office; I was hoping the stench would be less potent in there. My hopes were quickly dashed. And I felt the buzz on the unit. Then it hit me — the boys weren't in class either. *What's going on? It feels creepy in here.*

I stepped out of the office to try and figure out what was going on. I kept my hand over my nose and mouth; it smelled like shit!

Because it was.

Basically, Jacob had smeared his feces all over his small cell. I peeked in; the unbearable odor overwhelmed me. It was like nothing I had ever seen or smelled before. In addition to smearing his entire cell with feces, Jacob had spelled out S-A-T-A-N with his own shit. I'm not exaggerating when I say that it literally covered the walls. My eyes widened; they felt like they were popping out of my skull. *Was he secretly collecting his shit? There is soo much of it.* And then…

I ran into the bathroom and threw up. To this day, I don't know if it was the smell or the horror that I witnessed that made me sick.

And yet, despite the stench that permeated every corner of the cell block, I saw Ralph, subdued, reading in his cell; the other boys were screaming vulgarities at Jacob and "bar shaking." *What a fucking nightmare!* The whole scene felt surreal and somewhat akin to a bad dream. Back in the office, Dr. Jerry explained that Jacob was going to be placed on Unit 12 for the day; that unit was solitary confinement, the Juvey's equivalent to the infamous adult penitentiary's "hole."

"But what happened?" I sort of figured it out already, but wanted the details from Dr. Jerry.

"Well, Jacquie, the morning shift came in at 6:00 a.m. and basically found Jacob lying in his own crap, with his fecal matter spread all over his cell."

"But it's noon. Why did they wait so long to start cleaning," I asked. Two guards were escorting a chained-up Jacob to Unit 12, and three other guards, wearing some sort of hazmat gear, were cleaning the cell.

"There is protocol, Jacquie," Dr. Jerry said kindly and gently. I could tell he was really upset. But he also seemed to be holding back, hiding something. He forced out a smile. "Why don't you take the day off. Go home, go for a run, get some work done, or just relax by the pool. It's going to smell like this all day."

"Okay, thank you, Dr. J. But what about Ralph's session, and the group later?" I asked. I was especially curious about Ralph. Why, while the other boys had been making such a racket, was he so quiet, just sitting in his cell reading? He must have been angry about the disruptions Jacob caused, as well as him getting the guards riled up, which is never good for any of them, and creating the putrid smell he had to sleep with.

"The boys aren't allowed out of their cells today. Given the situation, this could cause a riot on the unit. There is nothing for you to do today. Go home," he again stated.

"Can I at least see if Ralph is alright?"

"I'm sorry, Jacquie, no. Right now we have to let the guards take over," he stated. I heard a bit of defeat in his voice. I imagined he was advocating for the other boys, but as always, the guards' "rules" superseded ours.

I looked at Ralph in his cell from afar. He never even looked up. I left. I was glad to be away from the smell. What a relief I felt when I finally opened the unit's door into the fresh Florida air. But I was simultaneously upset. *Something more happened. Something provoked Jacob. And I'm sure it was bad. Was Dr. Jerry trying to protect me from any liability that would come with the knowledge of what really happened? I have the feeling he was.*

I tried to get the images of what the fecal-covered cell looked like out of my head. And I tried to get the images of what the fecal-covered Jacob looked like out of my head. And I tried to relax by the pool. But I failed on all accounts. I couldn't shake my restlessness. I eventually decided it was useless and went up to my apartment to take a nap.

For Jacob to act out in this manner, something awful must have triggered his behavior. Maybe one of the other boys on the unit pushed him to the limit. Jacob wasn't from the streets. He grew up in a stable home, and ended up in juvenile detention for a one-time offense that was neither violent nor drug-related. He probably just wound up with a judge in a bad mood. Because of his relatively cloistered environment, Jacob couldn't handle himself with the other detainees. He needed to get out of juvenile detention, but behavior like this wasn't helping his cause.

I finally fell asleep, hopeful that things couldn't get much worse for poor Jacob.

My hopes were soon smashed to bits.

Despite her anger toward Brad, the lawyer who seemed less interested in her than she was in him, Madison continued to contact him. He responded intermittently. Madison began to exhibit rather disturbing behaviors that unveiled themselves in a slow and insidious manner. When Brad didn't respond immediately to her solicitations for contact, her rage led to impulsive and self-destructive actions. Toward the end of her most recent session, she revealed that she showed up at his place of employment dressed in a revealing, somewhat erotic outfit. She walked in, insisted on seeing him, and confronted him in front of one of the partners at his law firm. While telling me the story, she laughed with a maniacal tone that barely veiled her rage. Brad took her outside, told her he could no longer see her, and asked that she not contact him again. And then things became frighteningly serious.

While walking home that evening, thoughts of my other sex worker patients marched through my mind. I find the nature of their work fascinating, as well as the extraordinary stories I have been privy to. My thoughts suddenly focused on the two years I spent in my clinical internship and post-doctoral fellowship training. During that time, I took on a number of patients that were either in the sex industry or were struggling with sex addiction. My supervisor's comment came to the fore of my thoughts: "You work well with these patients, Jacquie, I think because you're exceptionally open. You just may have found a niche for yourself."

What came to mind immediately following that thought was my month-long obsession with The Bunny Ranch just outside of Las Vegas. This brothel is a relatively well-known high-end escort service, where one can peruse a roomful of escorts and choose who they would like to be with from that group. Ironically, prostitution is not legal in Sin City, but it is in many counties in Nevada, and therefore the ranch has received quite a bit of media attention.

I had just finished my post-doctoral fellowship and was living in a sublet in downtown Manhattan. There was an HBO special about The Bunny Ranch that was on almost every night for a month. Prior to this, I had never even heard of the ranch. I found myself incredibly intrigued by the women who worked there, and the interviews about their experiences. There was one interviewee that caught my fascination. I still remember a statement she made during the course of her interview: "I don't have a boyfriend, so this is my sexual outlet." It seemed so ordinary; unusually normal, and simply a different and unique way of living for these women.

When my first student loan payment came, I started to have fantasies about working there for a month. Based on what the women shared with the filmmaker, I could go for a few months and completely pay off my entire loan. Pure fantasy, of course, as I knew I could never bring myself to do it, but the idea of it intrigued me nonetheless. I watched it over and over as I attempted to grasp how these women were able to participate in these relationships. *What made them different? Would they have any emotional repercussions?* The whole concept captivated me.

So when I listened to the countless stories I was privy to, they just seemed so ordinary; but emotionally, when I really, really thought about it, I was stuck. *Why couldn't I do it? Had I really become part of the "herd?" Were my thoughts really so infiltrated by mainstream societal notions, which I had spent years trying to disengage from, that I was brainwashed into thinking it was wrong for me to engage in a sexually contracted relationship? Or is there something deeper within each of us as individuals that makes the idea of having sex for money difficult?*

That morning seemed like a typical Thursday. But as I've come to learn, in the world of a clinical psychologist, "typical" in the traditional sense of the word doesn't apply. The day can start out easily and predictable, and then suddenly something unexpected happens and the entire day is different; maybe even the world or one's perspective of it is changed. One must be prepared for anything.

This particular Thursday, I shared two immensely profound moments with two different patients — both with the pervasive dread of death in the air.

While in the midst of my morning shuffle, I had almost forgotten to put the beautiful watercolor painting in my bag. I had planned to give it to Kyle — a thoughtful, authentic twenty-something. I had considered what it would be like to give Kyle a "gift." *How would Kyle react to my giving him the watercolor painting? How might it affect our relationship?* I intuitively sensed that presenting him with this minor, yet metaphorically significant, concrete object was clinically correct given where we were in our therapeutic journey. The gift was meant to be a powerful non-verbal communication. As I nearly went flying across my apartment, "Snoopy, please, Mommy already fed you," — because my cat was underfoot — I reached into my closet, grabbed the painting, and left for the office.

Once in session together, Kyle began crying. Over the many years we had worked together in twice-weekly psychotherapy, Kyle never once cried. Until now, that is. His tears over the past three weeks were continuous, palpable and incredibly genuine; I felt a burning sensation in my own eyes and a big lump in my throat as I sat with him in all his pain. His father had died after a year-long battle with brain cancer. Kyle took care of him, and now he was gone.

And the loss, well, it was overpowering. Kyle, who once used illicit substances to mask his emotional pain, was now drug-free; his tears represented years and years of suppressed emotion. His only respite at this vulnerable time was his therapy sessions with me.

"Jacquie, I spend every day a wreck," he shared with tears in his eyes. "I'm torn up inside, but when I get off the train and know that I'm coming to see you, somehow all the tension in my body just disappears."

"Kyle, I'm happy I can provide you with some relief."

For a little over a year, Kyle had been the primary caregiver for his father, who was displaying ominous neurological symptoms with no diagnosis. Kyle and his father had a terribly complex relationship, as his father never really accepted his son as a gay man; he often made backhanded, insulting comments about Kyle's sexual orientation. This left Kyle shame-ridden to the core of his being.

Over the last year, as Kyle cared for his father, there was some reparation; his father began to open up to Kyle. He recognized and apologized for many of the mistakes he made and tried in the best way he could to express to Kyle that he loved and accepted who he was: a profoundly sensitive, kind and supportive person.

Just two months prior to this session, after what felt to Kyle as an inconceivable amount of time, the doctors discovered that Kyle's father had an inoperative brain tumor; he was placed in hospice and died with Kyle at his bedside.

"He was finally the father I always wanted." He choked on his words, "We just didn't have enough time." My eyes burned from his confession, and finally a tear trickled down my cheek; I felt heartbroken for him.

Kyle was leaving on Saturday for Vermont. His father had a second home there, and Kyle often found some peace while spending quiet time surrounded by the breathtaking mountains. This trip was different; Kyle was going to make a decision about his father's assets. I was leaning far forward in my therapist's chair, listening intensely and honestly, really feeling Kyle's pain. We planned to have our twice-weekly sessions by phone during his two week trip, but I was concerned about Kyle's ability to soothe himself without the reprieve of our sessions.

I looked at the clock; only five minutes left. I felt the stillness in the room as time seemed to freeze. There was such intensity between us as Kyle cried uncontrollably. With only minutes left, I made a clinical decision that I had been processing since our Monday session, when Kyle shared that he would be away for two weeks. He was describing fantasies of having me go with him.

"I know you can't, but thinking of you there with me makes the trip feel easier."

"I want to give you something Kyle, but I need you to tell me how you feel about accepting it," I said, ready to take a bit of a clinical risk. He nodded. The tears stopped; and time marched forward again. I went into my office closet and got the watercolor. I sat down again, as I gave Kyle the beautiful, soothing painting. "Kyle, I want you to have this. My mother painted it. When you're feeling alone, afraid, in need of support, I want you to look at this watercolor. Think of it as a representation of me and our therapeutic relationship."

"It's beautiful," he said with his usual sensitive tone. "Jacquie, you really want me to have this? But your mom created this. Are you sure?"

I nodded. "She would've approved."

"You don't know how much this means to me. Thank you." When I handed it to him, his arms enveloped the painting. I really wanted to hug him; I held back. The potency of this shared moment was so intense, it felt as if we were already hugging.

Later, when Tess came to session after her doctor's appointment, she had bad news, which she delivered with flat affect. "Jacquie, I'm dying." *More death!*

I let out a barely discernible gasp, but my body was visibly shaking. This had been something I considered a real possibility when I required the medical exam, but hearing these words come out of her mouth made my worst fear for Tess a reality. *Is it cancer again? Or something worse? Is there something worse? Poor Tess. Stay calm, Jacquie. Deep breath.*

I sat with Tess for a moment; my thoughts were spinning. *How do I proceed with this?* I had to remain as calm as possible to provide a contained safe environment for us to explore this news. Finally, I broke the silence, "Tess, I'm so sorry — please tell me everything the doctor said."

Tess was not typically a drama queen. Actually, she was the antithesis; her affect was usually relatively flat. "The doctor said that if I don't gain weight, I'll die. He told me that I was killing myself."

Relief washed over me; she only needed to gain weight and then she would be fine. My neck and shoulders were so tight. *I am without a doubt, going for a massage later!* And then… *Wait a second. Why did she disclose this information in such an ominous, dramatic manner? She must have known news of her dying would upset me.*

"Tess, why would you give me the doctor's prognosis as though he handed down a death sentence? All you need to do is gain a little weight. You love a good French meal. Enjoy!"

"I feel like I'm dying. The weakness is so unbearable. I don't even have the energy or desire to read or write or go window shopping on Madison Avenue." *That's like me saying I don't feel like running. Hmm… a new bout of depression rearing its head.*

As I left my office that night and leisurely walked down an unusually quiet Madison Avenue, I still felt the intensity of what happened. I helped free one patient from the death and sadness of his father's passing, of losing him just when they truly became a part of each other's lives, while I knocked heads with a stubborn patient who was nearly ready to choose death rather than face her own loneliness. Tess and I had a new road to hoe, it would seem.

We spent the next few sessions exploring if, in fact, Tess did want to die. During this difficult time with Tess, I thought of Ralph frequently; and about my mom. Life can be so fleeting; this was something I have always known, but never quite grasped experientially until I lost my mother so quickly. We as humans are vulnerable and life is unpredictable. My mother wasn't ready to die, but she truly had no control; the decision, in the end, wasn't hers. Ralph didn't choose the circumstances he was born into, but he did have some control over the choices he made that would lead him toward a more fulfilling future. He was resilient and pushed himself into unknown territory, somehow knowing there was a better life for him out there.

Tess, sadly, thought her life was over. She really had been feeling this way since her "Fall from Glory," at 49 years old. She had overcome many challenges, but it felt like she was a cat with nine lives. She didn't triumph, as Ralph did. Instead, she went through the motions and somehow without any emotional volition surpassed many difficulties. Sometimes it felt that she was trying to die, but her body wouldn't let her. It was oddly confusing. Early one morning prior to one of our sessions, I realized that Tess did have a spark; there was a will to live. Despite her communications that she thought her life was over, there was still a will to live. She just didn't know what Ralph did — she did have some control over changing her circumstances and her future.

Since Marc's death, I strongly sensed that she lost her will. We discussed her feelings. At first, she explained that, yes, she did want to die. As we continued processing her passive suicidal ideation, over the course of several painful sessions, she eventually concluded that she actually wanted to live. Losing Marc had temporarily left her feeling despondent, helpless, and emotionally dead. The potent message from her physician helped Tess acknowledge the reality of her current self-imposed declining health.

It was the impetus she needed; Tess began eating more and she slowly put weight back on. She was feeling stronger and stronger. Within only one month of her latest breakthrough, Tess had most of her strength back. And she was writing again. In fact, as I had come to learn some time earlier, Tess's ability — read: desire — to write became an accurate assessment tool in gauging her emotional state.

It was around this time that I was deeply ensconced in the process of writing my first book, *In the Therapist's Chair*. At first, I hadn't mentioned anything to Tess, but when I decided to write a small vignette about something interesting that occurred within our dyad, I had to have her sign a written consent form. Tess consented without hesitation, but knowing that I was now writing a book introduced a multitude of interesting, yet, at times, powerfully difficult dynamics.

Tess couldn't contain her curiosity about my book. With all her questions, I found it increasingly and inordinately difficult to manage all the different relational processes that were happening simultaneously. Tess made it clear that she was a great writer and editor; she reminded me many times that before her "Fall from Glory," she was employed as a writer and editor. She came to the session following our discussion about my book, and made an unexpected offer.

"Jacquie, I would love to co-author your book with you. I really am a good writer." *Here we go.*

I had been imagining all the significant feelings that might arise surrounding Tess's reaction to my book, but this was not one of them. And I sensed some envy. I knew that I had to negotiate my responses to Tess with graceful delicacy. To this first offer of help, I replied, "Tess, I do know you're a writer and editor. I'm so flattered by your offer to co-author my book, but I feel it'll be a violation of our professional boundaries."

She was quite forceful for a bit; reminding me again and again what a great writer she was, but I held steadfast to my original response about our boundaries, and reminded her that the book was nonfiction. It was an experiential book, revealing a behind-the-scenes look at what it is like to work clinically with patients. Eventually, she conceded.

As I was going through the editing and publishing process, Tess continued displaying curiosity about my book. She shared that she was excited for me, but simultaneously felt somewhat supplanted by my decision to start writing. In one difficult session she shared that she wished I had chosen painting, rather than writing, as a creative outlet. It was even affecting her writing. When exploring the difficulty she was experiencing, she explained that she wished she was as young as I and that she had my credentials. "With your doctorate and all your experience, your book will be a smash."

The combination of admiration and envy turns out to be a common pairing. I knew my job was to hold these two mutually exclusive positions for her. I also encouraged her to focus on all that she had to offer as a writer, regardless of her level of education. "Tess, you write fiction. Do you need credentials to write novels? A doctoral degree?" I wanted her to feel her own value without comparing herself to me.

"No, I guess it doesn't matter."

Since her previous session when Madison informed me that Brad insisted that she no longer contact him, she ignored his request and attempted to re-engage him with obsessive stamina. I sensed that his rejection triggered her unprocessed shame and humiliation; as a result of not being aware of these feelings, she experienced rage. Her need to reach out to him had little, if anything, to do with him, but rather was a defensive reaction to her own internal process.

After a few weeks of phone and email stalking, without a response from Brad, Madison turned desperate. Her franticness, her distress, possessed a profound, underlying sadistic quality — and this worried me. I took a risk that under other circumstances I probably would not have, but I was concerned about her propensity to react violently. I thought it was my ethical responsibility to confront her. So, I opened up the relational space in the room and noticed with her the rage and viciousness she had been demonstrating. Interestingly, Madison was able to respond with some awareness. She did admit that she was enraged and had fantasies of hurting him. *Great, I opened up a can of worms here. I know I needed to, but if this goes much further I may have to call Brad and warn him of the possibility that Madison could potentially assault him. Oy!*

I had to do a risk assessment. That is, I needed to understand if Madison's fantasies of hurting Brad were purely an outlet for her aggression, or if she harbored real intent to harm him. Madison reassured me that she wouldn't do anything to physically hurt him; I believed her. *Whew, okay, good.* I then took another leap and began to ask questions about her family relationships. She was resistant. I explained to her that I needed to have some background information if I was going to continue to treat her. She finally conceded. And with the information I gathered, it all began to make sense. Eventually, she did do something soon after that left me astonished.

The next few sessions with Madison were difficult but enlightening. She persisted in reaching out to Brad. Instead of desperation, I felt her attempts to get his attention to be extremely provocative and sadistic. She was quite overpowering, even in the room with me. I felt myself retreating and holding back from any interventions; her rage scared me. Fortunately, I was able to gather the basic information I needed to help me understand her underlying dynamics.

Madison was born in Russia. Her father was emotionally abusive; during her adolescence he ruthlessly criticized her appearance. He also diminished any of her achievements. She reported that his "favorite" verbal assault was, "Natasha, you are big-boned and dumb. No man will ever want you." She shared that this was his daily diatribe to her. Her mother didn't, or more accurately, couldn't help her because Madison's father assaulted her mother, too.

I looked at her, tilted my head and asked, "Natasha?" Madison then shared some shocking information; something that I would never have imagined.

At sixteen years old, Madison couldn't take it anymore. Her friend was leaving Russia to come to New York as a mail-order bride. Madison was lost, confused, and beaten down; she surmised that her friend afforded her a way out. A few months later, with her friend's help, she came to New York as the young bride of a wealthy banker 25 years her senior. She just left Russia. Picked up and disappeared, not even informing her parents, and basically took on a new identity. She changed her name to Madison; it was another way to avoid any affiliation with her country and her family. In fact, Madison even took dialect lessons, which explained why she spoke with absolutely no accent. In this way, she was able to emotionally dissociate any connection with her painful past.

I was shocked, but also sad for her. She was alone in the world, and as a result of her childhood trauma she emotionally defended herself by completely detaching from people and dissociating from "Natasha," her childhood and adolescent identity. *This is incredibly powerful.* I had a feeling that any probing for her emotions surrounding this experience would likely be met with resistance, but I tried anyway.

She gave me nothing.

"Dr. Jacquie, I did what I had to do, and there's no reason to go back there." She added with conviction, "There's nothing to figure out!" Her claws were out; and I took her lead and backed off.

Later that evening, I began to make some connections between Madison and some of my other escort patients. Of course, I still needed to learn how Madison made the transition from mail-order bride to high-paid escort. I did have a viable hypothesis about this, but I still needed more information.

Most of my escort patients were far more accessible and unafraid of experiencing and sharing their emotions; Madison was almost entirely detached from her emotional world. It was intriguing that these patients shared similar experiences of emotional abuse and the resulting shame. I was left wondering if and/or how this may have guided their paths. Was it the repercussions from the emotional abuse that enabled them to engage in sex for money? If so, how?

Just prior to the real escalation of Madison's obsessive ruminations and stalking behaviors, she indulged me with the information I needed to confirm my hypothesis. About two months into her new marriage, Madison's husband displayed controlling and emotionally abusive behaviors. Based on the inherent dynamics of the arrangement of her marriage, her husband was able to exert complete control over her. He told her what to wear, how to act and when they would have sex. Essentially, she was a prisoner in "their" luxury apartment on Central Park West. Madison described that her only sense of solace and comfort was her ability to sit on their outside balcony and watch all the people roaming freely in Central Park. She wanted to get out, but didn't know how. She had no money, no citizenship and absolutely no support.

There were echoes of her father's verbal assaults in the insults that her husband imposed on her throughout their marriage. She "hated" him, but felt trapped. Madison lived like this for nearly ten years. One important thing Madison learned from her marriage was that one way she was eventually able to control her husband was through sex. The more she gave him, the more money and indulgences he provided. This information led to her escape. One morning without any forethought, she broke into her husband's safe, stole fifty thousand dollars in cash, packed some of her most expensive clothing and jewelry and left him.

I was so completely engrossed in her story that when I finally glanced at the time, I realized that we had gone over the allotted session time by ten minutes. I recognized my own desire to just keep going on with the session; I felt like I was at the climax of a fantastic story and the novel was being ripped from my grasp. *Face facts, Jacquie. The session's over and Madison is in no distress. Time to wrap it up.*

"Madison. I hate to do this — and in the middle of a remarkable breakthrough — but we've already gone ten minutes past our session."

Madison smiled, This time it was genuine. "Dr. Jacquie. You forget the line of work I'm in. I'm all about the time limits."

"Thanks for understanding. I look forward to continuing next week."

"Me, too." Madison got up to leave. With her hand on the doorknob, she turned back and said, beaming with pride, "I didn't even have a chance to tell you what I did to Brad this week." And just like that, her sadistic edge returned. "We're back together. I told him I'm sorta pregnant."

And then she was gone.

Before I went to retrieve my next patient, I lifted my jaw off the floor.

Madison cancelled our session the week following her disclosures about entering the world of escorting, and her door-knob comment. She left a message on my voicemail that she would be away all week on a job, and would see me the following Tuesday. Madison rarely cancelled. I didn't believe her this time; I felt she was avoiding the session. I wondered if she was feeling too much shame surrounding what she had shared about her life. It took a long time for her to tell me and it was a struggle for her. My other more disturbing thought was that something happened with Brad that she didn't want to tell me. Again, I was a bit concerned about the possibility that her emotional assaults could become physical. I couldn't call Brad; there was no evidence that would imply a "duty to warn." So, I sat anxiously until the following Tuesday.

I was on edge Tuesday morning; thankfully, Madison showed up for her session. She brought me a cup of coffee; we were seeing each other for nearly two years and she never brought me coffee before. So, I was quite curious about what this gesture meant. So I brought it up.

"Thank you, Madison. I'm wondering what made you bring me coffee today?" I pretty much knew Madison wouldn't be able to look for the deeper meaning of her actions in the room.

"I got one for myself, so I thought I would bring you one, too."

I was right.

I truly couldn't be sure what she was communicating. My immediate association was that she felt guilty for avoiding her session the previous week. I didn't probe further. Based on Madison's internal dynamics and the co-created dyad, I knew we wouldn't get anywhere. Madison was just unable to work this way in therapy. I let it go, but made a mental note, and would listen for derivatives during the session. I thanked her again, and took a sip to express my appreciation.

Ugh, there's a ton of sugar in this. Does the sugar mean anything deeper? Probably not, she didn't know I drink my coffee black. Yuck! Stop, Jacquie, don't get derailed with this. You need to know what happened with Brad. Oh, maybe Madison is unconsciously attempting to distract me from the content of what she discussed in our last session. Stop analyzing. Just sit and wait for her to start.

There were a few moments of silence before she started. I felt so anxious and eager waiting for her to begin, I found myself about to ask again. I held back and waited.

She explained that Brad believed that she was pregnant. She chuckled; again, I felt the profound sadistic quality in her laughter. It was so disturbing. Now that he thought she was pregnant, he was engaging with her again. He was still only intermittently responsive and it was driving her really crazy. She was enraged, but completely disconnected from her affect. I felt it; it filled the room. I felt so uncomfortable.

I gently asked what she was going to do when he found out she wasn't pregnant. Maybe I have watched too many Lifetime movies; I imagined her stealing a baby from the maternity ward at New York Hospital. Goosebumps crawled across my arms. She explained that she planned to keep up her lie for a few months and then say she had a miscarriage.

In the meantime, Brad was begging her to have an abortion. He made it clear that he didn't want her or their baby. She seemed completely removed from his clear and absolute rejection, instead she was focusing on the control she had over him. She was threatening to tell his well-to-do Jewish family. And *this* was freaking Brad out, forcing him to continue to see her.

Madison was fully aware that Brad was only seeing her and continuing to have sex with her because he was afraid she would tell his family. She didn't care; it was all about having control over him. I attempted to help Madison be curious about the connection between her earlier experiences and her need to exert control over men. She just could not think this way. I believed her past was just too painful for her to allow any relationship between her past and present into her conscious awareness. It was amply clear to me and I was deeply distressed. I just didn't know what else she was capable of.

I also had the sense that Brad would figure out she wasn't pregnant before she told him about her miscarriage. From what I understood about Madison, if this were indeed to happen, I felt she could really lose control. My immediate association was what happened with Anne. Or worse. What happened with Tony and Raul. *Not good!*

I knew I couldn't contact Brad. Aside from Madison's emotional manipulations, there was no concrete evidence that would warrant a "duty to warn" Brad of a potential physical assault. I felt trapped and jittery. I have a rather humorous affinity for the overly dramatized Lifetime movies, but this was not a movie, although at times it felt like one. This was real, and I was in quite a predicament with Madison.

Later that night I went for a second run; I needed to clear my head and really think through how I could help Madison, and also figure out what my ethical responsibilities were. I had fantasies of terminating the treatment. This is unusual for me; I normally become attached to my patients and work with them for years. The fantasy was an indicator that Madison placed me in the role that she unconsciously split off. I now occupied her role as the distressed person who felt a complete lack of control. I was experientially experiencing what Madison had endured most of her life. And it was a horrific feeling. It did help me empathize with her underlying process, though, which is always helpful.

I hadn't felt like this in some time: torn in how to proceed. There are certain moments in the life of a therapist when you are faced with a difficult decision. Like with Anne. In retrospect, I shouldn't have let her leave my office. Or with Tess when I called 911. I still live with regret that I let Anne leave. Sometimes I think I wanted to believe she was okay, so I didn't have to watch her being escorted out of my office against her will. In Tess's case, I knew I had to call, she might have died had I not, but dealing with her anger afterward was delicate and complicated. It never gets easier.

Another example I was thinking about was when Ralph disclosed information about a criminal act that I felt needed to be reported. But if I did, it could jeopardize his one chance to get out of the juvenile detention system and off the Miami streets. It happened a week or so after the incident when Jacob smeared his feces in his cell.

On the day following that incident, the unit felt incredibly strange; no one mentioned anything. Jacob was escorted back to his cell mid-day. I watched as the guards dragged him in. No one even looked up. I really wanted to discuss the whole incident with Dr. Jerry; I was concerned, but I could tell by the loud silence that I wasn't "supposed" to ask.

Later that day, I met Ralph for our session. He didn't mention the incident either. I wanted to probe him, both to indulge my curiosity, but also to explore any feelings he might have about it. When Ralph didn't bring it up, I realized that there were unspoken rules in the correction center; it was a subculture and one in which the walls kept secrets. I did not want to compromise our therapeutic rapport. I also did not want to leave either of us in what I imagined could be a "dangerous" situation.

I began to notice, following the incident, that Ralph displayed remarkable amounts of empathy toward Jacob, a 180-degree change from his ranting envy for Jacob's family life. A few days after the incident, he shared that after the therapy staff left, two or three officers were beating Jacob at the same time. There was bruising on Jacob's body to prove it. *Hmm, Ralph knows something more. Maybe he knows what caused Jacob to act out?*

The next day, Ralph returned to session and he seemed markedly agitated. "I want to tell you something, Ms. Jacquie, but I don't want you or me to get in trouble," he said with just a touch of uncharacteristic hesitancy. I reminded him that the content of our sessions were confidential, with the exception of a disclosure of suicidal or homicidal thoughts and/or through a court subpoena. I barely finished my sentence when he blurted out, "Jerome and Mike raped Jacob last night." Chills ran up and down my body. I tried to stay calm or at least give the semblance of calmness, but my thoughts were racing; my heart was too. *Shit! I have to report this, but I don't want to breach the promise I just made to Ralph, and I certainly don't want the guards going after him. Shit!* I needed to think this over to determine how I should proceed.

Regardless, something must be said. How to do it without compromising Ralph's trust and safety was the real issue.

Earlier that day, the results of the court advocacy for Ralph's discharge arrangements had come through. After all my hard work, Ralph was going to be released from Juvey in two weeks, and was going to be court stipulated to Broward County Halfway House for one year. I was so pleased; elated actually, but with the knowledge of Jacob having been raped, I felt heaviness, too.

I was sitting outside, trying to figure out the best way to broach the Jacob dilemma, when I heard a bit of a commotion. The loud voices were behind me and getting closer. I turned and saw four Dade County police officers approaching the unit. *Someone else reported it?* I was hoping. I remained outside, fearful that they might question me because I was still unsure of how I would report this Jacob incident without revealing the source of the information.

"Good afternoon," one officer acknowledged me. I nodded, with a tight-lipped smile, barely making eye contact.

They buzzed at the entrance, and Dr. Jerry came to the locked unit's door and let them in.

My heart was racing with angst. About fifteen eternal minutes later, the officers walked out. We exchanged polite nods as they walked off. Dr. Jerry, who was steps behind them, approached me and sat.

"What's going on?" I must have looked like the cat that ate the bird.

"You know Mike, the security guard, and his partner, Jerome?" I nodded, though I felt my eyes grow wide. "They're being arrested for raping Jacob."

Oh my gosh! Did Ralph say something? The other guards will find out that he ratted on one of their own. With only two weeks left here, he's not going to be safe.

"Good, those bastards!" Dr. Jerry shot me a look at my uncontained eruption.

"I know you knew about the rape." Now I looked like the cat who ate *two* birds.

So I explained that I had just learned about it through a patient that morning, and I was trying to figure out a way to expose Jerome and Mike without revealing the source.

"This patient has so much potential. I wanted to keep him safe until he got out of here." Then something occurred to me. "The police are arresting them already? The rape only happened last night. Isn't it, by law, still considered an "alleged" rape until the investigation is completed?"

Dr. Jerry went sullen. "Last night wasn't the first time it happened. When I met with Jacob in his cell after a severe beating a couple weeks ago, I noticed traces of blood on his underwear near his anus and on his mattress. I had an immediate medical exam ordered. After the report found torn anal tissue and semen, I pressed Jacob for more information. That boy was scared to death. The guards said that if he ever reported them, the next time they raped him, they'd use a baseball bat."

I gasped at the thought. Poor Jacob! He wasn't even a bad kid. He had just been caught doing something on a dare and got in front of a judge who was having a crappy day. He should never

have been admitted to this hellhole. Well, at least I know that
Ralph is safe, that he wasn't the one who told. *Wait...*

"Dr. Jerry, how did you know I already knew about the
rape?"

"Ralph came to me this morning shortly after meeting
with you. He explained that he discussed this with you, but after
he left you, it was weighing heavily on his mind. He felt bad for
Jacob. He couldn't let those guards do that to him again. He had
no idea that it hadn't been the first time. I explained that I already
knew about it and things were being taken care of. I couldn't tell
him that the police were coming today to speak to every inmate
who resided in cells around Jacob's."

As it turned out, Dr. Jerry had been in contact with the
police and Child Protective Services for about two weeks.
Finally, they had enough physical evidence and the arrests were
made. As for Ralph, he was secretively interviewed only
moments before when the Dade County officers walked past me
into the building. Ralph told the police everything. It was his
recollections of the previous night's events that removed any
doubt and led to the eventual arrests. As for Jacob, he was being
transferred to a psychiatric hospital for evaluation and treatment
for this horrific turn of events.

Then I realized, Ralph put himself on the line anyway,
putting his safety and future aside for the safety of another. My
eyes filled, tears hovering at the brink of my lower eyes.

At our next session the following week, Madison relieved
me of all my professional responsibilities. She brought me coffee
again. I pretend to take a sip, but didn't swallow it. I really
disliked sugar in my coffee. She sat down, looked me straight in
the eye and explained that she was moving back to Russia. I was
shocked; she despised her family.

"Really, Madison, how did this come about?" I was filled
with curiosity. She explained that Brad discovered the truth; or,
more accurately, Madison was forced to tell him because he was
relentless about seeing an ultrasound of their growing fetus. Of
course, Madison didn't have one. He then adamantly requested
that they go together to her doctor; he also wanted a paternity

test. As manipulative and clever as Madison was, she couldn't negotiate her way out of this. Feeling overwhelmingly defeated, she finally told Brad the truth.

He threatened to press charges and he knew the law. Madison was terrified that if he pressed charges and a thorough investigation was done, he would find out that she was a mail-order bride and, more currently, an escort. She also was still legally married and didn't have citizenship. She would be arrested, her husband would find her, and she would likely be deported. She was broken. At almost 32 years old, Madison had absolutely no stability, no support, and basically living on the run. She decided that if she went back to her country, she would have a better chance of making changes that could enhance the quality of her life.

There was no time to have any valuable termination process; she was booked on a flight in three days. This session would be her last. Paradoxically, during this final session, Madison related authentically and had more access to her emotions. This is not uncommon for some patients; it is easier to expose themselves during termination, because they know they don't have to come back and really process and work through painful affect states. I noticed this with Madison and interpreted what was happening. She nodded at my remarks; she appeared to be really listening. I recommended that she continue treatment in Russia and suggested areas she needed to work on.

She stood up to leave at the end of the session, thanked me, and shook my hand. She squeezed my hand so tight, it actually ached after. I felt sad when she walked out. But I also felt alleviated of the burden I was carrying while working with her. I hated that I felt relief, but I did. I still think about Madison and hope that she has found inner peace and gained some stability in her life. I wasn't so sure that she would ever be capable of maintaining internal or external stability, but I try to be hopeful when thoughts of her cross my mind.

And again, my thoughts drifted back to Ralph. Unlike Madison's abrupt termination, Ralph's truly was full of hope when he left the detention center, just two weeks after he put his safety on the line to protect Jacob. We all missed him on the unit,

I especially. But we felt satisfaction knowing he had better opportunities where he was going.

About six months after his departure, Dr. Jerry and I took a trip north to Broward County Halfway House to visit Ralph. He had been in touch by phone and asked that we visit. He seemed to be doing quite well, based on our conversations. When we went in, we were directed toward the library. That was where Ralph was at the time we got there. He actually hugged both Dr. Jerry and me. I was so happy to see him; I felt warm inside.

Ralph had started the library, and was enrolled in GED courses. He was also doing a lot of writing on his own, and shared that he was planning to go to college to study English literature. I was so filled with joy. Ralph looked happy, too, and he seemed to be remarkably less guarded. It was a priceless moment; he looked at home.

I thought about Ralph's journal and how loss pervaded his existence. I imagined with hope, that his current and future journals would thematically grasp the experience of resiliency. When I looked Ralph straight in his eyes immediately before we left, that's what a saw: a young man who overcame obstacles that many others would have been unable to, and a remarkable resiliency that saved him.

That was the last time I saw Ralph. Once he left the halfway house, he was set up in supportive housing and was preparing to go to college. I wonder about him all the time. I keep thinking that eventually I will see a book in Barnes & Noble under "New Bestsellers" with his name on it.

My eyes welled up as I thought back on my relationship with Ralph. I began to think about the therapeutic encounter in general, and all of the patients that I have had the pleasure to know and work with. People pass through our lives, relationships begin, and sometimes they end. Each one leaves us with something; many change us or our perspective.

Each termination of the therapeutic relationship is difficult, as we need to leave the shared encounter behind us, learn from it, be changed by it and move on. There is an odd lack of authenticity to it. It ends because the therapeutic journey is over, not because we no longer care for the person. And most times, we as clinicians never know how our former patients' lives evolve. We hope that what each individual learned through the encounter stays with them as they continue to grow and evolve.

My thoughts shifted and I was thinking about the human tragedy in my own life — losing my mom. As the years pass, it gets easier, but it is always there — *always* — and there are times that the magnitude of the loss overwhelms me. I amaze myself sometimes, as I wonder about my resiliency and how despite the fact that I am sad about my loss, I have found the strength to live and maintain hope for my own journey. Although each person is unique, being resilient is a human potentiality; and one that if accessed, can bring one strength, hope, meaning, vigor and create the ability to overcome challenges. My melancholy moved to joy as I thought about the many successes my patients experienced as I helped them to foster and overcome many profoundly difficult challenges.

I was immediately reminded of the rock I tripped over earlier this day during a run on a trail. I fell as my toe caught the edge of the rock, and next thing I know, I am practically kissing the ground. I got up, didn't even brush myself off, and just kept running. My dirt-covered knees made me feel tough.

The path is never without bumps; some people encounter more than others. The goal is to process the bumps in the road, learn from them, garner inner strengths, and make a choice to overcome them. Ralph was an excellent example of this process. I knew Tess was capable of this same human process. Tess was able to overcome many external bumps on her trail. Tess's largest and most resistant obstacle was herself. And this created for a bumpy road.

And it's the bumps that make this job so interesting — and often surprising. Sometimes, as much as you know about patients, occasionally even more than a family may know about them, you may still be surprised by their actions. Take Madison. All that she revealed to me, and yet it wasn't until later that I discovered her real name was Natasha. And it was not until the end that she surprised me with news that someone could be "sorta pregnant." I chuckle when I think about that now, but at the time, I found the action irredeemable.

A few weeks after Madison returned to Russia, Tess showed up for one of her sessions. The way she carried herself filled me with dread. She had been making marked progress recently. I felt relieved when she had begun writing again. And, honestly, I was filled with excitement, as my book was about a week away from going to print. I already had my first book signing scheduled.

So when Tess came to session, her beautiful blue eyes seeming even more prominent than usual, but with a vacant look to them, I was alarmed. My immediate association was to the vacancy I saw in my sister's eyes after being in the ambulance with my mother when her heart finally stopped. My sister was in complete shock and traumatized. *Oh, no, now what happened with Tess?*

It was only four months since Marc died. Tess flopped down on the patient chair and flatly stated, "Helena died." I was truly shocked and also deeply concerned. Helena had become a consistent and supportive person in Tess's life; Tess had been able to depend on her, and Helena's presence provided companionship.

"What happened?" I was completely beside myself with empathetic distress. Tess flatly explained that Helena, only fifty-one, died suddenly; her husband found her dead on the bed the previous evening. Tess suspected it was a heart attack, but she didn't know all the details. Helena would be buried in South America, her country of origin, so Tess would not even be able to say good-bye.

"I'm so sorry to hear this, Tess."

"See, Jacquie. You're all I have. Coming to see you is the highlight of my week." I was deeply moved by this statement. And though I experienced such sadness for Tess, I also felt a bit anxious. It is difficult to work with patients who don't have a support network outside of therapy.

She again brought up her will and her plan to make me the primary beneficiary. "There really isn't anyone else I feel as close to. And besides, you'll fit into my clothes." Again, I saw flashes of me sorting through Tess's belongings. I tried relentlessly throughout our treatment to help Tess establish some supportive relationships with the people in her life, but she was always so resistant.

"Why have you been so opposed to building relationships with your remaining family members? What about your cousin's daughter?"

"I have been so hurt and disappointed by people, and I won't put myself in a position to be hurt again." She then shifted back to the loss of Helena. She was quite defended against feeling the depth of her loss, so she expressed her feelings by stating practically that she needed to find a new healthcare worker. Within a week she did; this time, a woman in her 20s named Ruby.

Tess quickly developed a comfortable relationship with Ruby, and again seemed to be doing better; she was writing again. When *In the Therapist's Chair* was released, Tess was practically the first to buy a copy. After reading it, Tess brought it into session, laid it on my desk and stated, "You are a brilliant writer, Jacquie!"

I probed her for thoughts and feelings surrounding her experience of reading my book. *I did reveal some quite personal details; I wonder how this has affected her.* And as though she were reading my mind, she commented, "I'm so sorry to hear about your mother, Jacquie. I had no idea. How painful it must have been for you to go through my battle with cancer so close to your mother's death. And you were always so strong for me."

I felt touched by her empathy, but remained neutral. I didn't want to burden her with my own losses and struggles. I wanted her to feel that I could still manage to contain her despite my own life circumstances.

As it turns out, despite the comparisons she always made between us and the protective advice she provided about makeup and finding boyfriends and marriage, the most difficult relational process that occurred within our dyad fundamentally ended up being her comparison of my style of writing to her own. She was and continues to be so impressed with my writing, but also envious. This remains a primary focus of our therapy to date, particularly since I am writing a new book — this book — and she is in it. Her primary area of difficulty has to do with my youth and my credentials, as I stated earlier. It has been trying for Tess to define her own value and worth because she is continually comparing herself to me. We are working hard to change that, and despite Tess's inability to write for a few months following reading my first book, she has been motivated to write relatively consistently.

The richness of our work together continues to be moving and challenging. At our last session, Tess unknowingly provided me with the most fitting closure to her story. She came in and settled into the patient chair.

"Jacquie, I know you run outside every day, but it's been a cold, dark winter and you're still so pale." She then placed something on my desk. "I got you something."

I looked down. It was a brand-new container of blush with a big brush to go with it. I smiled somewhat wryly. *Thanks, Tess. Just what I needed.*

Conclusion:
Reflection from the Therapist's Chair

As the session door closes on *Bare*, I feel myself accountable to conclude these stories with further reflections from the therapist's chair. Using basic tenets, I will describe how I have developed my own style of working with my patients. I experience the therapeutic encounter as an art. Although psychology is traditionally considered a science, when done well, a psychotherapist can create a truly engaging and moving encounter — one that leads a patient toward living a more authentic and fulfilling life — that can seem as much an art as a methodical discipline. It involves creativity, flexible thinking, openness, curiosity, personal attunement, and intuition. Also vital to the process is the ability to step outside the box, take risks, be bold and courageous, and accept and be oneself.

Though I provide a sort of template to understand how I think and work, these views become complicated and convoluted in practice. Therapy is not an open-book test with principles laid before you to refer to once the session comes to life. It's something you access within you in the moment. Since *Bare* has allowed a private look into the world created between my patients and myself, I hope I have given you the extraordinary opportunity to really feel and experience how the following abstract ideas translate into real discourse within the context of the therapeutic relationship.

Through my intense training, I have been exposed to many different theoretical orientations, both through formal academic training, literature, and supervision. These experiences have afforded me the luxury of integrating ideas and techniques to develop my own way of being with and treating patients. I do not espouse a single way of working, but rather adapt and incorporate different methods based on the individual needs of my patients.

I take clinical risks with my patients by adapting and informing my interventions to meet the needs of each individual patient. Rather than applying abstract theory to a unique human being, I respond through intuitive listening; I stay with the patient's experience in the moment, and apply different techniques based on what the patient needs.

Using the hermeneutical method, I interpret from the patient's lived experience in the moment, and then borrow concepts and ideologies from phenomenology, existentialism, and depth psychologies. I work actively with my patients, and my trend of relating is primarily informed through the understanding of underlying psychodynamics.

The therapeutic relationship is a co-created dyad — a relationship where through the interaction between my patient and myself, I learn a lot about how the patient relates with themselves, their world, and others. The dyad is the relationship between me and each individual patient. The distinction of the dyad as co-created essentially means that the relationship evolves uniquely based on the two individuals in the relationship. So, it expresses that each relationship with every patient will be unique. It also implies that every patient will feel, express himself/herself, and respond differently with different therapists. The "trial period" — the beginning sessions where patient and therapist evaluate how they feel the therapeutic fit is — is important for this reason. Both patient and therapist should feel that they can work together.

The stories in *Bare* have shown how I respond uniquely to each patient and the many different evolving dyads. My relationship with Tess is an excellent example. Tess has profound difficulty connecting with people; it is one of her primary therapeutic dilemmas. She feels alone. And thus, she created a solitary existence. After her "Fall from Glory," she no longer feels comfortable reaching out to others, which ultimately leaves her lonely as she ages. Since her self-worth relies on her physical beauty, once she thinks she has lost this, she is deeply distressed and feels worthless.

We, or at least I, had a difficult time establishing rapport with her in the beginning stages of our relationship, as she focused on my external appearance instead of her own feelings of being a broken and deformed woman. Even after this impasse was processed and there was awareness on Tess's part, her guardedness and lack of true connectedness remained throughout our relationship. There was closeness, an attachment, but it lacked the intensity I had with some of my other patients in *Bare*. This was our co-created dyad. Since Tess had profound difficult expressing the core of her vulnerabilities, there was a bit of distance in our relationship. And because I sensed this with Tess, but not with my other patients, it told me a lot about why she was aging alone.

Hearing and listening are two totally different ways of being with a person. We clinicians must, through empathic listening, "hear" our patients. This is one of the qualities that truly distinguishes the experience of sharing with one's therapist versus talking with a friend. I consider this the cornerstone of any successful therapeutic encounter.

I listen to my patient's narrative, his/her story as they share and experience it. I suspend my own subjective experience and assume nothing, until through further exploration of my patient's internal world, I come to understand it as they experience it. That is, I can never presume that a patient's emotional experience is like mine; I hold in abeyance my own emotions and "hear" what is happening for each individual patient as they each experience it, in the moment, and through his/her own unique process.

Through this suspension of my own preconceived internal thoughts and feelings, I leave the space in the room open for genuine empathic listening. Then, by the use of this distinctive listening process, I become a receptacle for my patient's lived experience. I hear and sense what they are really feeling. The stories in *Bare* provided the opportunity to experience this process as it happens in the room. It may seem simple, but it actually can be quite complex, as I have shown through my exchanges with my patients. When I learn, via this process, of my patient's internal experience, I then open up the therapeutic space and create curiosity, help my patients put words to their emotions, and generate a greater intimacy between each patient and myself. This is not only an effective and invaluable technique, as you have seen in *Bare*, it varies within each dyad.

My position as therapist is a collaborative one. I do not like any of the traditional psychoanalytic concepts that imply a hierarchical therapeutic relationship. Rather, I experience the relationship as reciprocal, and actively work and share with my patients as they work and share with me. I have found that this creates a safe environment for my patients, which ultimately leads to a secure place for them to share difficult thoughts and feelings.

In working collaboratively, there are times where I will use self-disclosure. I have learned through my clinical work that if timed correctly, self-disclosure can really help patients feel more comfortable and safe to share intimate details of his/her inner experience. I can intuit when a patient is stuck in a moment of shame or discomfort surrounding something they want to share. By offering my own experience of a similar emotion state, it provides a sense of comfort that the room is a judgment-free place and that I, too, am human and therefore, also have struggled.

Intra-psychic dynamics evolve through a long process of internalizing one's experience of others. Simply stated, one self-develops through the ongoing process of taking in relationships with others. The relationship with the other eventually becomes one's own, and through this development, *one's sense of self* can be understood as a composite of the many relationships and experiences one has — particularly early in one's life. Again, this is a complex process, and a didactic description diminishes the totality of this lived experience. Through the first-person narration in *Bare*, this intricate process comes alive as it occurs and reveals itself in the therapeutic encounter.

Tony's story perfectly illustrates this process. As I piece together his history, it becomes clear to me how his unsettling relationship with himself, his sexual self, and others have evolved. We see Tony's struggles, or lack thereof, as a direct result of his internalization of the abusive and boundary-free relationship with his mother.

A consistent theme throughout my own personal and professional development, as well as my work with each of my patients, includes the establishment and embracing of one's own uniqueness. In *Bare*, I show how I guide my patients toward a recovery of their true selves. I listen carefully and thoroughly to my patients' stories and work to discover their inner being: the self that has been lost. I want to know each and every one of my patients totally, authentically, and unconditionally. I listen. I hear. I sit. I am open. I am immersed in his/her world. I focus on each patient's individual strengths and guide them through a process of discovery; a journey that allows them to embrace his/her authentic self and the concomitant development of self-worth and self-acceptance.

As I have come to accept my own inner being authentically and bared my own struggles throughout these stories, while writing this conclusion, I had the following dream.

I find myself on the track, running 800-meter repeats, feeling super-strong and holding a 6:30 minute-per-mile pace. I feel the sense of freedom I always experience while running. As I stop to take some fluid, I reach for the bottom of my shirt to wipe the sweat from my face. I notice that I am wearing my flowing mint green dress. Concerned that I might trip over the bottom of the dress, I lift it, tuck it in my running shorts, and continue my workout.

I woke up laughing. My first thought, "Wow, what a closing for my book." And then, "Glad I had shorts on, or *Bare* would have been more than a metaphor."

Psychotherapy is the art of healing, discovery, and reviving the authentic unique self. And just as I continued my track workout in my dream, I will continue my own life journey alone — alongside each and every one of my patients.

Index

Other Books by University Professors

The Polarized Mind: Why It's Killing Us and What We Can Do About It
By Kirk J. Schneider, PhD
Paperback: $19.95
ebook: $18.95

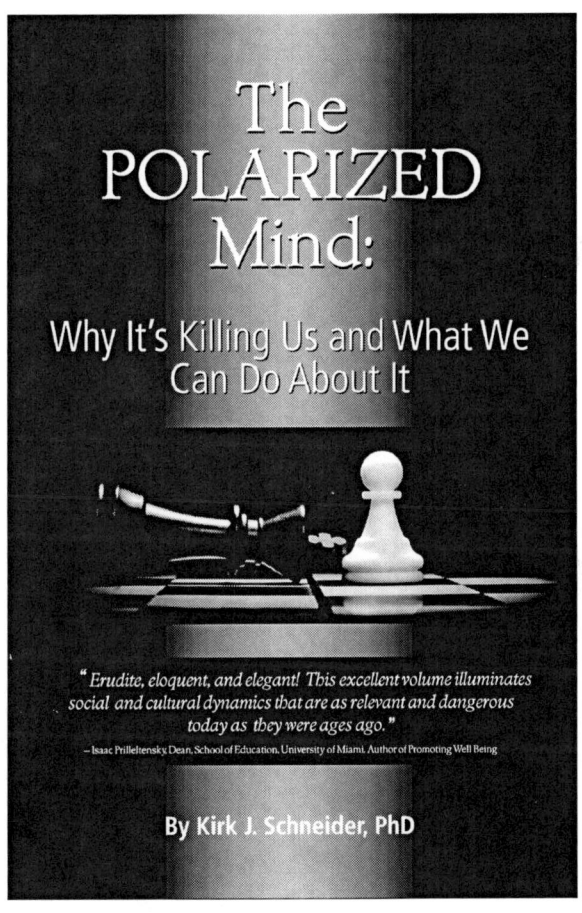

CPSIA information can be obtained at www.ICGtesting.com
Printed in the USA
BVOW07s1049300714

361048BV00002B/11/P